CULTURE AND THE THOMIST TRADITION

Thomism's influence upon the development of Catholicism is difficult to over-estimate – but how secure is its grip on the challenges that face contemporary society? *Culture and the Thomist Tradition* examines the crisis of Thomism today as thrown into relief by Vatican II, the twenty-first ecumenical council of the Roman Catholic Church. Following the Church's declarations on culture in the document *Gaudium et spes* – the Pastoral Constitution on the Church in the Modern World – it was widely presumed that a mandate had been given for transposing ecclesiastical culture into the idioms of modernity. But, says Tracey Rowland, such an understanding is not only based on a facile reading of the Conciliar documents, but was made possible by Thomism's own failure to demonstrate a workable theology of culture that might guide the Church through such transpositions.

A Thomism that fails to specify the precise rôle of culture in moral forma-tion is problematic in a multicultural age in which Christians are exposed to a complex matrix of institutions and traditions, both theistic and secular. The ambivalence of the Thomist tradition to modernity, and modern concep-tions of reality, also impedes its development. Must a genuinely progressive Thomism learn to accommodate modernity? In opposition to such a stance, and in support of those who have resisted the trend in post-Conciliar liturgy to mimic the modernist forms of mass culture, *Culture and the Thomist Tradition* musters a synthesis of the theological critiques of modernity to be found in the works of Alasdair MacIntyre, scholars of the international 'Communio' project and the Radical Orthodoxy circle. This synthesis, intended as a post-modern Augustinian Thomism, provides an account of the rôle of culture, memory and narrative tradition in the formation of intellectual and moral character. Re-evaluating the outcome of Vatican II, and forming the basis of a much-needed Thomist theology of culture, the book argues that the anti-beauty orientation of mass culture acts as a barrier to the theological virtue of hope, and ultimately fosters despair and atheism.

Tracey Rowland is Dean of the John Paul II Institute in Melbourne, Australia, and part of the international 'Communio' school of post-Conciliar Catholic theologians.

RADICAL ORTHODOXY SERIES
Edited by John Milbank, Catherine Pickstock
and Graham Ward

Radical Orthodoxy combines a sophisticated understanding of contemporary thought, modern and postmodern, with a theological perspective that looks back to the origins of the Church. It is the most talked-about development in contemporary theology.

CULTURE AND THE THOMIST TRADITION

After Vatican II

Tracey Rowland

[Handwritten inscription:]

Fr. Meleki,

Here it is: "postmodern Augustinian Thomism". Now that we have our marching orders, let's get to work! I hope you enjoy this half as much as I did!

Sincerely,
Adam
2008

Routledge
Taylor & Francis Group

LONDON AND NEW YORK

First published 2003
by Routledge
2 Park Square, Milton Park, Abingdon, Oxon OX14 4RN

Simultaneously published in the USA and Canada
by Routledge
270 Madison Avenue, New York, NY 10016

Routledge is an imprint of the Taylor & Francis Group

© 2003 Tracey Rowland

Reprinted 2004, 2005 (twice)

Typeset in Baskerville by
Prepress Projects Ltd, Perth, Scotland
Printed and bound in Great Britain by
MPG Books Ltd, Bodmin

British Library Cataloguing in Publication Data
A catalogue record for this book is available from the British Library

Library of Congress Cataloging in Publication Data
Rowland, Tracey, 1963–
Culture and the Thomist tradition : after Vatican II/Tracey Rowland.
p. cm. (Radical orthodoxy series)
Includes bibliographical references and index.
1. Christianity and culture. 2. Catholic Church – Doctrines. 3.
Thomas, Aquinas, Saint, 1225?–1274. I. Title. II. Series.
BX1795.C85 R68 2003
261'.088'22–dc21   2002027546

ISBN 0-415-30526-8 (hbk)
ISBN 0-415-30527-6 (pbk)

For Stuart Adair Rowland
and James V. Schall SJ

The Forms of the Tradition have lost the background against which they could be understood and now give the impression of something in a museum, guarded by antiquarians and unthinkingly photographed by tourists.

Hans Urs von Balthasar

CONTENTS

ACKNOWLEDGEMENTS

I am indebted to Anthony Fisher OP for the generous gift of his time and attention to detail, and in particular for his organisation of an afternoon of academic discussion on the central themes in this book with Dr Hayden Ramsay.
I am also indebted to Dr Janet Martin Soskice and Prof. Denys Turner of the
Divinity School in Cambridge and Aidan Nichols OP and Fergus Kerr OP
for their comments on an earlier draft of this work and to Fr. Aidan for his
contribution of the Foreword.

I also wish to thank the editors of the *Radical Orthodoxy* series for their
interest in my work, particularly Dr Catherine Pickstock. The 'Radical
Orthodoxy' circle includes both Anglican and Catholic scholars who seek to
provide a coherent critique of the secular and to re-envisage the realms of
culture from a theological perspective. In this sense their work can be seen as
a continuation of de Lubac's project which partially informed the theology of
the Second Vatican Council. Far from being enthralled with 'secularity', they
observe that what secularity has most ruined and actually denied are the very
things it apparently celebrated: embodied life, self-expression, sexuality,
aesthetic experience and human political community. My work shares these
orientations and seeks to contribute to this general project by a development of themes found in the work of Alasdair MacIntyre and members of the
Communio circle of scholars, particularly David L. Schindler and Kenneth L.
Schmitz of the John Paul II Institute in Washington DC.

A special thanks to Adam Russell of the *Lycée Henri IV*; the Revd Peter
Knowles OP and Dr Isabell Naumann ISSM for their help with translations;
and to the monks of St. Michael's Abbey, Farnborough, for permission to
use their artwork for the cover of the book and for their prayerful support
throughout the enterprise.

Fiona Lourey deserves a medal for her usual calm in the midst of chaos
and practical common sense. My thanks are also due to Dr Darcy McCormack
for his advice on the structure of the book, to the Revd Dr Peter Joseph for
proof-reading the penultimate draft with his characteristic thoroughness,
and to Barbara Shea, Dean of Mannix College, for her understanding of the
notion of a Christian *ethos*.

ACKNOWLEDGEMENTS

An earlier version of Chapter 3 has been published in the *International Catholic Review: Communio* (Winter 2001) and is reprinted here with the editor's permission.

Among my friends I particularly wish to thank Anna and Anthony Krohn, Patrick Quirk and Clara Geoghegan for their sharing of theological insights over a couple of decades, Michael Lynch who is in the process of writing his own work on the theology of culture for his numerous tips on good references, and Thomas Bradley for some formative discussions on the political philosophy of the culture of modernity.

My thanks are also due to my colleagues and students at the John Paul II Institute in Melbourne for all manner of practical assistance, especially my research assistants, Joshua Martin and Sarjit Alexander Sidhu; to Maria Srodon, Sophie Levagne and Amanda and Emile Perreau-Saussine for their companionship at Fisher House, and to James and Joanna Bogle for some splendid memories of London, Eton and Somerset.

Finally, I owe a considerable debt of thanks to the Sisters of Mercy in Rockhampton whose convent was my childhood home, particularly to Sr. Patrice Kennedy and the late Sr. Mary Clotilde, and to my mother Pauline for seeing to it that I had a Christian education. Above all, I honour the memory of my Anglican grandmother, Dorothy Davies, who taught me the Apostles' Creed before I started primary school, and most other things of value I know. This work could not have been written but for them and for the patience, courage and numerous insights of my husband, Stuart Rowland.

FOREWORD

First and foremost, this book is an analysis of differing approaches to the philosophy and theology of culture in the 'academy' of our day. It is also, however, an indictment, and at times a searing one. It would be a pity if the formal restraint of its language deflected the reader's attention from the passion that underlies it. It seems well to begin this foreword here.

The *gravamen* from which the book sets out is chiefly of interest to Catholic Christians in its readership – but owing to the global influence of their religion this can hardly be a parochial beginning. Tracey Rowland brings an accusation of superficiality – of damagingly facile optimism – against the Catholic Church of the 1960s and 1970s. Naively, at the Second Vatican Council (1962–5), in the course of preparing a 'pastoral constitution' on the rôle of the Church in the 'modern world', hierarchs and theologians offered a vote of confidence to the Western-derived culture of modernity, without due consideration of that culture's rooted inconveniences and flawed presuppositions. A religion with a substantial intellectual patrimony of its own, and a claim, in divine revelation, to a fulcrum independent of the world's fashions, managed to pass up the chance of offering a theological critique of the 'down' side to that Liberal–humanist wave, which then as now was inexorably spreading. The reason, as Rowland hints, is surely to be found in a fear of 'integralism'.

Integralism is the notion that the Church, though her own vocation be exclusively supernatural, nonetheless has the right, when majoritarian, to dictate to natural society's shapers the form their work should take. But, in the anti-integralist counter-claim that the cultural realm is a law unto itself, the principal theological error of integralism – the separation into two separate realms of nature and grace – continued to live and thrive unnoticed. A framework of thought that would sever the arts and sciences from theology in the name of the autonomy of the secular actually condemns nature to separation from grace. Furthermore, to cite a theological master, Romano Guardini, whom Church authorities might have consulted but did not, culture is never, in point of fact, self-created from its own essence. Agents with their own philosophies, thinkers with their own agenda, lie behind its various developments, and the more diffuse their influence the more potentially pervasive. But just how healthful *were* the influences thus tacitly invoked to replace the strains of Christendom?

More recently, through the magisterial teaching of a subsequent pope, John Paul II, and the growing corpus of reflection on culture produced by theologians associated with the multilingual journal *Communio*, some hope has emerged that the difficulties created by such thoughtless strategies can be made good. And here Rowland's spadework helps considerably to fill with solid earth the ditch that has opened up between, on the one hand, the Catholic doctrinal, liturgical and spiritual tradition and, on the other, a cultural formation largely incapable of acting as its vehicle. Positively, Rowland seeks a proliferation of cultures where (in the technical but by no means inaccessible vocabulary she introduces) 'any given *ethos* is governed by the Christian virtues, the process of self-formation or *Bildung* is guided by the precepts of the Decalogue and the revealed moral law of the New Testament and the *logos* or form is provided by the "identities in relation" logic of the Trinitarian processions'. A Catholic culture, unlike a Protestant, never mind a secular, version of the same, will always be, in the historian Christopher Dawson's favoured word, 'erotic': unified in its various domains by a passionate urge for spiritual perfection.

It may at once be surmised that the overall thrust and tone of this book, despite severity of strictures, is in dogmatic terms enormously constructive, but how, by that very token, is it not also sectarian? This brings me to the second of Rowland's *gravamina*, which concerns the deficiencies of the secular culture now predominant, deficiencies for which a theologically forged statement of the proper structure of culture may act as a helpful foil.

The Liberal tradition of secular humanism, which by fits and starts has come gradually to dominate Western civilization since the seventeenth century, carries with it an anthropology and, behind that, a metaphysic (or anti-metaphysic) of its own. Its individualism – 'self-centricity' – is inseparable from its increasingly subjective view of beauty, goodness and truth – its rejection, in other words, of these qualities as the 'transcendental properties of being' for which classical Christian thought took them. The subjectively valued individual in an objectively valueless world resembles the smile on the face of the Cheshire cat. Hardly surprisingly, then, that by the late nineteenth century the philosophical frailties of the Liberal tradition were becoming apparent. An alternative arose, with the philosopher and cultural critic Friedrich Nietzsche as its fountain-head, which capitalised on the philosophical frailties of Liberalism, at once radicalising its individualism and unmasking its illusion that in a heartless cosmos respect for human hearts still makes sense. The Liberal emphasis on personal autonomy now becomes the Nietzschean imperative to self-assertion in a world where the only beauty is exultation in self-created power. Postmodernism, inasmuch as it is the victory of Nietzsche over the Liberals, takes force as the key to meaning in culture. It is only by violence that one arbitrary meaning is assigned where another, equally groundless, would do.

Rowland believes that classical Christian thought – which she takes to be a synthesis of patristic and medieval thinking at their best, and represented with peculiar acuity in the Thomist tradition – will, when confronted with these Liberal and Nietzschean strands in modern sensibility, remain paralysed or even impotent – 'in crisis' – until it undertakes a strenuous criticism of the new. Without this enquiry, it will resemble a surgeon who, not knowing where to cut, cannot heal.

The scope of the investigation is as wide as the cultural domain itself. Nothing can be exempted, from the market place to the bedroom, the artist's studio to the shopfloor. In the analysis of what a variety of modern institutional ways of behaving do to us she is greatly indebted to the neo-Aristotelianism of the ethicist Alasdair MacIntyre, who emphasises the need for institutions to require virtue and also engender it. (But she goes beyond him in asking that they be quasi-sacramental: a hospital must be hospitable, and so have Eucharistic undertones, if it is to suit sickly humanity under the regime of grace.)

In considering the vagaries of souls immersed in mass culture, she appeals to the dogmatic theologian Hans Urs von Balthasar for whom the test of culture is whether it mediates an experience of the transcendentals congruent with the grace of the Incarnation, without which participation in wider culture will be impoverishing, not enriching. Here, over against modernity's cultivation of deliberate forgetting, she stresses the importance of memory. Through memory, those features of the human past that can add to sapiential experience may be corporately celebrated, as in historic Christianity's cycle of feasts and the sequence, determined not only by human biology but also by the significance of the life of Christ, of its sacramental rites of passage.

From two American thinkers, William Norris Clarke and David Schindler, she takes the idea – appropriate to the image of the Trinity in man – of an underlying form in all human activity that combines 'substantiality' with 'relationality'. We are only ourselves in relation to others, yet in relation to others we are truly ourselves. We must be abroad for the sake of others if we are to be at home with ourselves. It is chimerical to suppose that such refined metaphysics is superfluous for cultural activity, irrelevant to the management of political parties or the devising of a popular song. Every practice will always turn out to have some kind of an 'onto-logic', and so a spirituality or anti-spirituality that animates it. If it is not Trinitarian – which is as much as to say, if it does not bear the form of love – then it will, in the modern era, almost certainly be mechanistic and controlling, for the underlying logic of the Enlightenment traditions is that 'self-centric' variety which most naturally expresses itself in reliance on technique, privileges go-getting activity not contemplative receiving, and treats efficacy as assertion rather than creative generosity.

Over against Thomists of another ilk, Rowland considers herself a 'postmodern Augustinian Thomist'. By these words she not only declares some of her fellow-disciples of Thomas imperceptive (too ready to make an accommodated peace with Liberal modernity), she also summarises in a phrase her own programme for the re-energising of Christendom. She will retain the universalism of Thomas, as expressed in natural law thinking, the validity of moral absolutes, and the ubiquitous relevance, under grace, of the virtues. But she will embody that universalism in a cultural form that, like the Augustine of the *Confessions* and the *City of God*, values narratives. To shape an ethical identity adequately fitted to the state of the world requires exposure to the cumulative story of grace's supervening in, through and beyond, the fabric of the temporal. In a society seared by sin, egregious in errors, 'plain persons' can best find the principles of the homespun natural philosophy they need through pondering the experience of beauty, goodness and truth which memory contains. This is true above all of the memory of how the transcendentals broke upon humankind in the unique peace of the Kingdom, in the world of the Resurrection revealed by anticipation in the crucified and exalted God-man, Jesus Christ. And how, finally, is this 'postmodern'? Chiefly by an unflinching rejection of the characteristic languages of modernity, even at their most seductive (such as the language of human rights).

Here the present writer, for whom such 'rights' are simply the dependent reflection, in human subjects, of the objective order of the world, cannot follow her, and yet he is brought back gratefully to her thought at last. In his view, what is objectionable about the 'rights industry' is the tone in which, in advanced Liberal societies like the United States, such rights can be asserted. A braying, litigious tone used in one's own regard betrays not only an absence of the undertow of thanks which should always be present for the gift of existence but also a practical unawareness of the true *scandalum magnum* of the public world, the plight of its poor. If Tracey Rowland's book does not touch closely on either of these themes – the metaphysics of being and the 'preferential option for the poor', it is still highly relevant to the re-awakening, in the circle of the virtues unknown to modernity, of that quality of modesty which instinctively thanks God and restrains self. In this way, her study can serve tacitly these further dimensions as well as the many realms the author consciously touches and illuminates. I wish her book a wide and fair hearing.

Aidan Nichols OP

INTRODUCTION

In the first half of the twentieth century, Thomist scholars sought to defend St Thomas from the charge of having neglected the theme of culture. Augustinus Fischer-Colbrie and Robert Brennan both argued that, although Aquinas wrote no treatise on the subject of culture, 'he knew all the principles that form the groundwork of a philosophy of culture', and, further, that the belief in the 'modern' discovery of culture merely illustrates the ignorance of Rousseau and other Romantic and post-Enlightenment philosophers of the richness of the Thomistic framework.[1] The underdeveloped account of culture from the perspective of the Thomist tradition has, however, continued to be the subject of criticism. For example, Fergus Kerr has observed that 'traditional theology overlooks the way that human beings are rational creatures immersed in history', whereas Nikolaus Lobkowicz has stated that 'Aquinas did not develop anything like a theory of history and therefore was not very interested in culture either'.[2] One way of reconciling the two perspectives is to conclude that, while St Thomas did foreshadow aspects of contemporary accounts of the philosophical and theological significance of culture, his intellectual projects were not focused on the rôle that culture plays in the formation of the soul because he wrote during a period in history when Christendom was at its zenith. Although, he noted that Gothic tribesmen did not regard stealing as morally wrong until after they had been Christianised, he did not develop this observation into a full theory of how persons are influenced in their moral development by the culture of the community into which they have been born. If thirteenth-century Paris had been occupied by Islamic and Gothic tribesmen as well as by Dominican and Franciscan friars and lay Christians, and if the city were surrounded by pagan temples and mosques as well as by Benedictine abbeys, then the effect of such a social framework upon moral formation may have required analysis. However, Aquinas wrote at a time when all the arts, the working week, the holidays, the kings and the laws were overtly Christian.[3] For Aquinas, Christendom was the presumed context for his audiences.[4] The Church was the teacher of the truth, the dispenser of the mysteries, the barque of fellow travellers. In effect, Aquinas shifted to the Church much of the rôle of the

1

polity in Aristotle. In this classical Thomistic model, Christians immerse themselves in the culture of the Church, and the Church, through her sacraments, liturgies, scholarship, religious and laity, Christens the world.

Since Aquinas could assume Christendom as a 'given', the rôle of culture in moral formation was not a problematic requiring his attention. The development of a 'postmodern' Thomism in which the concepts of culture and tradition are central has only become necessary at this juncture in history when Christendom is but a historical memory for a significant proportion of the population, and the Christian soul is forged within a complex matrix of institutions founded upon a mixture of theistic, quasi-theistic and anti-theistic traditions.

The apparent endorsement of this complex matrix by the fathers of the Second Vatican Council in the Pastoral Constitution *Gaudium et spes* has, however, complicated the response of the Thomist tradition to this need for an explicitly theological understanding of the realm of culture.[5] The Thomist tradition now finds itself in a position where it is intellectually engaged on two fronts: there is the continuing engagement with the Liberal tradition, which is now into its third century, and there is the engagement with the late Romantic Genealogical tradition. Both the Liberal tradition and the Genealogical tradition are themselves engaged in a confrontation in which the key issue is the culture of modernity and its Enlightenment-derived conceptions of rationality. This means that if the proponents of the Thomist tradition seek to engage the ideas of these rival traditions they need to know where they stand on the definitive issues of the culture of modernity and its conception of rationality.

This work is therefore addressed most generally to the problematic of the Thomist tradition's need for an understanding of the theological significance of culture, and, second, to the specific issue of the value to be given to the culture of modernity. Whereas some scholars believe that the culture of modernity is neutral in relation to the flourishing of Christian practices, or even a second *praeparatio evangelii* in the manner of classical culture, other scholars who identify with the tradition regard the culture of modernity as the very solvent of Christian practices. In particular, there presently exists a quite dramatic disjunction between the apparently positive treatment of modern culture in *Gaudium et spes* and contemporary critiques of modern culture or select aspects thereof as a 'culture of death' (John Paul II), a 'polity of death' (Catherine Pickstock), a culture with the form of a machine which is resistant to grace (David Schindler) and a culture which is toxic to the flourishing of virtue and the precepts of the natural law (Alasdair MacIntyre). The issue of the culture of modernity can therefore be described as a 'crisis point' for the tradition, that is a problematic which will test the tradition's success or failure in making rational progress towards some further stage of development.

In his analysis of epistemological crises within traditions, Alasdair MacIntyre argues that any resolution of such crises will embody three necessary elements:

> First, this in some ways radically new and conceptually enriched scheme must furnish a solution to the problems which had previously proved intractable in a systematic and coherent way. Second, it must also provide an explanation of just what it was which rendered the tradition, before it had acquired these new resources, sterile or incoherent or both. And third, these first two tasks must be carried out in a way which exhibits some fundamental continuity of the new conceptual and theoretical structures with the shared beliefs in terms of which the tradition of inquiry has been defined up to this point.[6]

Part I of this work is therefore devoted to an examination of the elements of the 'crisis' created by the tradition's undeveloped account of the rôle of culture in moral formation, and in particular the treatment of culture in *Gaudium et spes* and in post-Conciliar magisterial thought. From this examination three conclusions are reached:

1   that the Thomist tradition requires a theological hermeneutic of culture;
2   that the ambivalence of the tradition in relation to the culture of modernity continues to impede the tradition's development; and
3   that the tradition requires an account of the influence of culture on moral formation in such a way that it does not lead to relativist conclusions or otherwise undermine the universality of the natural law doctrine.

Part II focuses on the first and second of these unresolved issues. It will be argued that the culture of modernity's dominant Liberalism may be construed as an example of what John Paul II calls 'a philosophical system, an ideology, a programme for action and for the shaping of human behaviour' which is hostile to the integrity of the self and hence to the ideals and practices of the Thomist tradition. The argument is developed by subdividing the concept of culture into the categories used by the German *Kulturgeschichte* school: *Geist*, *Bildung* and *Kultur*. These categories are related to the Greek concepts: *ethos*, *nomos* and *logos*. Chapter 3 therefore focuses on an account of the *Geist* or *ethos* of modern institutional practices, Chapter 4 on rival accounts of *Bildung* or self-formation, and Chapter 5 on the *logos* of the *Kultur* or civilisation of modernity. Each of these chapters also relates back to a particular aspect of the problematic treatment of the concept of culture in *Gaudium et spes*. Chapter 3 juxtaposes Thomist critiques of modern institutional practices with the Conciliar deference to the knowledge of 'experts', Chapter 4 questions the apparent Conciliar endorsement of 'mass culture' and relates the problem of mass culture to the Conciliar recognition of a 'right to culture' and Chapter 5 seeks to qualify the Conciliar endorsement of *Gaudium et spes* paragraph 59 – the 'autonomy of culture' principle – by examining contemporary developments of de Lubac's argument that 'no culture is really neutral' and hence autonomous.[7] In doing so, Part II provides both a recommendation for a radically new and conceptually enriched scheme, in response to MacIntyre's first necessary element of a resolution to an epistemological crisis, and an explanation of just what rendered the tradition, before it had acquired these new resources, sterile and incoherent, in accord with MacIntyre's second necessary element of a resolution.

A sub-issue within the broader 'crisis' is that of the preferred methodology of the Thomist tradition. As a generalisation, it can be said that contemporary Thomist scholarship is characterised by a division between two influential schools: the proponents of the so-called Nouvelle Théologie, with their emphasis upon historical scholarship, a retrieval of Patristic thought and critiques of neo-scholasticism; and the projects of Anglo-American scholars who adopt the methodology of twentieth-century British analytical philosophers and apply this methodology to a study of Thomist concepts – a methodology which includes as a central element the need to exclude historical from philosophical argument. This division is the subject of numerous articles in contemporary journals and is described as a quarrel between Anglo-American 'analytical Thomists' and Continental Balthasarians.[8] Alasdair MacIntyre, whose early academic training was in analytical philosophy, has suggested that the analytical school's strengths and weaknesses derive from its exclusive focus on a rigorous treatment of detail – one that results in a piecemeal approach to philosophy, isolable problem by isolable problem. He suggests that its literary genres are the professional journal article and the short monograph.[9] From the Continental perspective, the analytical Thomist's approach looks suspiciously Cartesian and its anti-historical character runs counter to the argument that concepts do not in fact operate within historical and cultural vacuums. A shorthand description of the Balthasarian methodology may be found in the following statement by David Schindler:

> The 'analytic' precision sought with respect to the object (other), in short, is first that sought by the lover (integrative clarity in the service first of 'aesthesis'), rather than by the technologist (fragmented clarity for purposes primarily of control).[10]

In Kantian terms, this means that 'synthetic thought', which requires what von Balthasar calls 'seeing the form', is as important as 'analytical thought' and should precede the piecemeal rigorous treatment of detail. Although Balthasarians acknowledge that philosophers across a range of disciplines might endorse the same concepts, the Balthasarian idea of the 'symphonic' quality of truth means that von Balthasar's disciples are more interested in how the concepts are related to other elements of the tradition, and the history of their formulation, development, and cultural embodiment, than they are in demonstrating, for example, that a particular concept to be found in Aquinas may also be found in Kant, or has resonances in Heidegger or is presumed by Wittgenstein.[11] The Balthasarians aim to demonstrate the splendour of the truth by sewing together a rich tapestry of biography, poetry, history, Trinitarian analogies, logical analysis and the truths of Revelation. This is also consistent with the Radical Orthodoxy approach, which seeks to 'unite exegesis, cultural reflection and philosophy in a complex but coherently executed collage'.[12] In effect, this means that they 'smudge' the boundaries of philosophy, theology and literature, and are generally indifferent to the claims of those who would enforce the interdisciplinary boundaries drawn by philosophers of the Enlightenment(s) in the seventeenth and eighteenth centuries.

The three chapters in Part II therefore follow the methodological approach typical of scholars associated with the Radical Orthodoxy and Balthasarian circles of alternating between sociological, philosophical and theological arguments and drawing upon a symphony of authorities, the most significant in this instance being Alasdair MacIntyre. The contribution of MacIntyre is undoubtedly seminal for the development of a 'postmodern' Thomism that takes into account the importance of culture in moral formation, for MacIntyre has highlighted more effectively than anyone else within the Thomist tradition the nature of the relationships between moral inquiry and social practices. This work does not seek to offer a comprehensive analysis of MacIntyre's critique of the culture of modernity, but rather focuses upon select aspects of that critique which relate to:

1   the problems created by the treatment of culture in *Gaudium et spes* as identified in Chapter 1;
2   the need for a theological hermeneutic of culture; and
3   the appropriate place of the concept of culture within the Thomist tradition's account of moral and intellectual formation.

Although MacIntyre has been described variously as a 'Communitarian', a 'Virtue-Ethicist', a 'Revolutionary Aristotelian', a 'Romantic Thomist' and a 'postmodern Thomist', it is suggested that the most appropriate categorisation of MacIntyre's position, from the publication of *Three Rival Versions of Moral Enquiry* onwards, is that of a 'postmodern Augustinian Thomism' – an example of what Gratian and medieval canonists described as a *concordantia discordantium canonum* – a synthetic reconciliation of apparently rival principles.[13] MacIntyre's position may be classified as 'postmodern': first, it is constructed from a perspective that views the primary problem as the culture of modernity and its need of transcendence; second, although he has a place

for metaphysics within his intellectual framework, this place is not founda-
tional in an epistemological sense – rather the starting point is that of the
soul caught within the contradictions of the culture of modernity; and, third,
he incorporates critiques of the Liberal tradition from the Genealogical and
Marxist traditions and focuses the attention of the Thomist tradition upon
the issue of the rôle of culture and a narrative tradition in moral and intellectual formation. This interest in the relationship between 'culture' and the
formation of the soul, is a quintessential postmodern theme.

On its own however, the term postmodern carries the negative connota-
tion of a mere *bricolage* – an assemblage of haphazard or incongruent elements – and thus the added Augustinian adjective has at least two advan-
tages. First, it helps to associate MacIntyre's philosophical enterprise with
the Augustinian theology of grace associated with the Nouvelle Théologie
scholars, whose insights it will be argued are necessary for the theological
grounding of MacIntyre's otherwise sociological and philosophical critique of
modernity. Second, the qualifier 'Augustinian' helps to convey the idea that
central to the synthesis is an interest in the typically Augustinian themes of
the relationship between the secular and the sacral orders, the rôle of memory in the formation of the soul and the importance of a narrative tradition for
intellectual and spiritual development. Indeed, given the significance of the
Augustinian element, one can argue that MacIntyre's project exhibits some
of the characteristics of what Romanus Cessario calls the 'custom of reading
Aquinas as if he were Bonaventure'.[14]

MacIntyre's work alone does not however provide a comprehensive postmodern Augustinian Thomist critique of the culture of modernity and understanding of the rôle of culture in moral formation. For this it is necessary to
venture beyond the boundaries of philosophy to the realm of theology. This
is because the culture of modernity and its practices have been formed not
only by the severance of the orders of faith and reason, but also, more fundamentally, by those of nature and grace. To this end, it will be argued that explicitly theological arguments, such as those of David Schindler and Kenneth
Schmitz, need to be linked to the more sociological and philosophical analysis
of MacIntyre in order to develop the tradition in a manner that gives it the
theoretical capacity to critique the culture of modernity (the engagement
with the 'moderns') and simultaneously to engage the arguments of the postmodern Genealogists. Whereas MacIntyre's work examines the relationship
between culture and virtue, and offers a critique of the culture of modernity
as a complex inter-relationship of norms and institutions that are hostile
to the flourishing of virtue, Schindler and Schmitz supplement this with a
critique of the culture of modernity from the perspective of its resistance to
grace, including, of course, infused or supernatural virtue.

Schindler and Schmitz may also be classified as postmodern Augustinian
Thomists. Although they are not generally known by any particular label,
they are both members of the Thomist tradition in the broad MacIntyrean

sense: they both belong to the Communio school of theology, which derives its lineage from von Balthasar, de Lubac and the *Ressourcement* movement with its interest in retrieving the treasury of Patristic thought, and they are both interested in developing a postmodern metaphysics of the person.[15] This particular metaphysical outlook draws an analogy between the rôle of relationality in an account of the Trinitarian processions and the rôle of relationality in an account of human identity. They both agree with Jacques Derrida's rejection of the principle of simple identity, and thus are united with the postmoderns against the presuppositions of Cartesian rationality. Like MacIntyre, they agree with the postmodern Genealogists that conceptions of reason are not theologically neutral, and, again like MacIntyre, they argue that this does not necessarily lead to nihilism.

The major concern within the tradition regarding any acknowledgment of the significance of culture for moral formation is that it will subvert the centrality of the doctrine of the universally objective natural law in Thomist ethics. Romanus Cessario alludes to this concern in the following paragraph:

> The term 'human experience' has been made to carry considerable theological weight in recent decades. Theologians influenced by Marxist thought find the category fruitful for theological analysis and critique, as did authors involved in the Modernist crisis at the turn of the century. It would be unfortunate if reaction to these schools of thought resulted in a wholesale rejection of such an important element in Christian moral theology.[16]

In Part III the focus is therefore on the third unresolved issue – that of the need for an account of the rôle of culture in moral formation which does not undermine other elements of the tradition. This is necessary both to:

1 meet arguments from within the tradition against historicism and ethical relativism; and
2 satisfy the third of MacIntyre's criteria for overcoming an epistemological crisis within a tradition.

In Chapter 6 it will be argued that, far from fostering ethical relativism, MacIntyre's concept of a narrative tradition can serve as a bridge between the realms of faith and reason, and, further, is necessary to keep the tradition from falling into a one-sided emphasis on either faith or reason, such as is characteristic of Kantian rationalism and Barthian fideism. Moreover, without the experience of the practices of a narrative tradition and reflection upon them, persons are less likely to perceive the principles of Aristotelian–Thomist practical rationality and the goods of human flourishing as self-evident.

The final chapter seeks to demonstrate that this emphasis given to the rôle of culture and a narrative tradition within a postmodern Augustinian Thomism need not displace the natural law doctrine of Thomist ethics. However, it will be acknowledged that there are differences between the account of natural law found in the works of MacIntyre and Schindler and the presentation of this doctrine by 'New Natural Law' theorists. In particular, MacIntyre explicitly rejects the project of transposing the natural law doctrine into the language of natural rights; and, although Schindler and Schmitz have not gone as far as an outright rejection of this project of transposition, they have acknowledged problems inherent within it. In the final section of this chapter, MacIntyre's arguments against the adoption of the natural rights discourse by Thomist jurists and moral philosophers are defended and related to ideas in previous chapters regarding the tacit interpretation of meaning and the expressivist account of language.

In the Conclusion, the elements of a postmodern Augustinian Thomism will be summarised and tested against Alasdair MacIntyre's three criteria for overcoming a crisis within a tradition.

Part I

CULTURE AS A THEOLOGICAL PROBLEM

1

THE TREATMENT OF CULTURE IN
GAUDIUM ET SPES

The 'crisis' within the Thomist tradition regarding its stance towards the Liberal tradition and the culture of modernity was not solely created by the treatment of culture in the Conciliar document *Gaudium et spes*. However, this document represents a pivotal point in the magisterial engagement with the culture of modernity, and, like the Second Vatican Council itself, its treatment created an 'explosive problematic'. This chapter seeks to provide an account of the elements of the problematic and the theological and philosophical ideas of those Conciliar *periti* who were influential in the drafting of the specific section of *Gaudium et spes* that deals with culture. In so doing, *Gaudium et spes* will be situated within the wider history of the magisterial effort to deal with the problem of modernity and the effort within the Thomist tradition to develop an understanding of the relationship between culture and theology, and, in particular, an account of the significance of culture in moral formation.

Modernism and modernity

The history of the stance of the Catholic magisterium in relation to the complex phenomenon of modernity may be traced through the Papal encyclicals of the nineteenth and early twentieth century. The popes of this era were concerned with modern*ism* as a constellation of ideas about the relationship between philosophy and theology, especially about the possibilities of a natural (philosophical) theology, and the relationship of subjective experience to faith and the authority of tradition. They were also concerned about the implications for the Church, and its conception of the common good, of the principles of modern political philosophies, both Liberal and Socialist. This is especially clear in the encyclical *Rerum Novarum* of Pope Leo XIII; but it is also manifest in various decrees throughout the late eighteenth and nineteenth centuries which were prompted by the persecution of Catholics in France and other countries undergoing modern political revolutions.[1] The import of these documents could be summarised as an opposition to the philosophical presupposition of the Enlightenment that faith is merely a matter of subjective experience; the Rousseauian–Marxist idea that institutions, not original sin and the vices (such as greed and avarice) which flow from this, are the cause of social injustice; and the Liberal idea of the primacy of the individual will. These decrees, while demonstrating an awareness of the major principles operative within 'modern theology' and 'modern political philosophy', nonetheless fell short of a systematic critique of 'modern culture' as has appeared in the twentieth century in the works of scholars from such diverse intellectual traditions as Thomism and Anglicanism, Hegelianism and the Marxism of the Frankfurt school, and the Genealogical tradition from Nietzsche. At the close of the twentieth century the definitive demarcation lines within scholarly circles are between the pre-modern, the modern and the postmodern, while within specifically theological circles the issue is not so much whether one is a self-described Protestant or Catholic, but that of where one stands in relation to the *cultural formation* described as 'modernity'. Alasdair MacIntyre hints at this as early as 1969 in his observation:

> It has become increasingly plain that whether a man calls himself a Christian, a Marxist, or a Liberal, may be less important than what kind of Christian, Marxist, or Liberal he is.[2]

Similarly, Aidan Nichols has more recently observed that when it comes to the judgement of modern culture, 'Catholics – as well as Orthodox, Lutherans, Anglicans and others – may find themselves divided *across*, rather than *along*, confessional lines'.[3]

Modernity as a specific cultural formation

The importance of focusing on modernity as a *specific cultural formation* has been repeatedly emphasised by Charles Taylor. Taylor (1995) defines a culture as a specific understanding of 'personhood, social relations, states of mind, and virtues and vices' or 'a constellation of understandings of person, nature, society and the good'; and he further distinguishes the 'acultural' from the 'cultural' theory of modernity. Whereas the acultural theorists acknowledge that social transformations may be facilitated by our having certain values and understandings, just as they are hampered by the dominance of others, they argue that the transformations are not *defined* as the espousal of some such constellation. On the contrary, in his account of the transformation from the culture of Christendom to the culture of modernity, Taylor concludes:

> It is not that we have sloughed off a whole lot of unjustified beliefs, leaving an implicit self-understanding that had always been there, to operate at last untrammelled. Rather one constellation of implicit understand-

ings of our relation to God, the cosmos, other humans, and time, was replaced by another in a multifaceted mutation.[4]

Such a construction of the issue means that the concept of 'modernity' cannot simply be equated with 'what is contemporary'. It is rather, as Taylor argues, a 'constellation of implicit understandings' about the relationship of the human person to 'God, the cosmos and other humans'. As these understandings become embodied within social practices they form a culture.

The comparatively narrow focus on *particular aspects* of the culture of modernity within the papal encyclicals of the late nineteenth and early twentieth century is not surprising since at the time of their formulation this culture was still undergoing construction. The processes that Charles Taylor calls 'mutation', Alasdair MacIntyre 'severance', John Milbank and Catherine Pickstock a 'heretical reconstruction' and William T. Cavanaugh 'secular parodies' of the classical Christian synthesis were well under way but had not yet reached their apotheosis.[5] However the absence of a *theological* examination of this cultural phenomenon called 'modernity' or the 'modern world' by the Conciliar fathers in the years 1962–5 is perhaps one of the most striking features of the documents of the Second Vatican Council. In this context, Kenneth Schmitz recently reflected:

> Had we been more perceptive we might have guessed that the foundations of modernity were beginning to crack under an increasingly incisive attack. But we had no such cultural concept as 'Modernity'; all we had instead was the historical category: modern philosophy.[6]

John O'Malley in *Tradition and Transition: Historical Perspectives on Vatican II* has also alluded to this lacuna:

> At the time of the Council we did not think to ask from it any consistent theoretical foundation for *aggiornamento*, because most of us were not aware of the importance of having one.[7]

O'Malley concludes that 'the Council's fundamental injunction to remain faithful to the authentic past while adjusting to contemporary needs was transformed from a practical norm for reform into an explosive problematic'.[8] There was no consideration, at least not at a philosophical and/or theological level, of the question of what is, in essence, the *culture* of modernity, and how such a culture affects the spiritual and intellectual formation of persons and their opportunities for evangelisation. The subsequent calls for a 'relevant' approach to pastoral issues thus offered a concept that was empty of content and which appears to have been influenced by Martin Heidegger's call for an 'authentic' response to the situation of the 'self' which finds itself 'thrown' (*geworfen*) within the culture of modernity.[9] The difficulties associated with the opacity of Heidegger's concept were subsequently multiplied when given a Christian gloss and popularised in Catholic communities throughout the world. Parishioners, clergy and the religious were called upon to be 'relevant' by adopting an 'authentic' response to the 'modern world', in circumstances where all three concepts – 'relevance', 'authenticity' and 'the modern world' or 'modernity' – were, of themselves, in O'Malley's words 'an explosive problematic'.[10]

Thus, although much attention was paid by the Church's magisterium to 'Modernism' throughout the latter half of the nineteenth century and the early decades of the twentieth century, the notion of 'modernity' as a 'cultural formation' had not yet arrived within the theological frameworks of the Conciliar fathers in 1962. In this context, Hervé Carrier has observed that 'prior to the Council, the capacity for cultural analysis was almost wholly ignored in the theological formation provided at the time' – the word 'culture' did not even appear as an entry in the *Dictionnaire de Théologie Catholique*.[11]

The Conciliar openness to modernity

In his opening address to the Council, John XXIII set the tone for what became the post-Conciliar enthusiasm for the culture of modernity:

> In the present order of things, Divine Providence is leading us to a new order of human relations which, by men's own efforts and even beyond their very expectations, are directed toward the fulfilment of God's superior and inscrutable designs. And everything, even human differences, leads to the good of the Church.[12]

This belief in the latently Christian orientation of the social trends of the 1950s may also be found in John XXIII's encyclical *Pacem in Terris*, wherein he described the 'mutual acknowledgement of rights and duties in society' as a 'kind of *preparatio evangelii*' since it brings human beings to an awareness of a world of values such as 'truth, justice, charity and freedom', and brings them to a 'better knowledge of the true God, who is personal and transcendent'.[13] There is, however, no analysis within *Pacem in Terris*, theological, sociological or otherwise, to support the judgement that the mutual acknowledgment of rights and duties leads to a greater appreciation of 'truth, justice, charity and freedom' and ultimately the personal, transcendent God. One can, for example, believe in the importance of a mutual acknowledgment of rights and duties on purely Hobbesian grounds without being remotely interested in truth, justice, charity and freedom as understood in a Christian sense, let alone in a personal transcendent God. Indeed, it may be argued that the very linking together of these values as if they have some natural relationship to one another carries within it intrinsically Christian theological presuppositions.

A utilitarian, for example, may very well believe in rights and duties while regarding charity as completely irrelevant to questions of jurisprudence and political philosophy. In other words, what is missing from *Pacem in Terris* and John XXIII's optimistic judgements about the directions of social values in the 1950s is precisely what Taylor calls a *cultural* analysis – an understanding that clusters of values fit together into constellations that become embodied in the practices and beliefs of individuals and the institutions in which they work, and, further, and most significantly, that one can have, for example, a culture which embodies a belief in rights and duties without having any interest at all in a notion of justice that is linked to a transcendent truth, including the theological virtues of faith, hope and charity.

Consistent with the theme of 'openness' to the world and a general optimism about the degree of common ground between Christians and non-Christians, G. Turbanti argues that the attitude of Paul VI was not so much one of caution, critique or condemnation, as one of welcome to what were construed to be 'universal values in modern culture'.[14] Again, as with John XXIII, it appears that Paul VI had little understanding of the fact that the concept of 'universal values' is itself highly problematic. It can be understood in at least two senses: first, that there are a range of goods or values that are universally required for human flourishing regardless of the peculiar social circumstances of individuals. However, 'universal' can also mean transcending all divisions among traditions or 'common' to all traditions. In the first sense, the expression is but a synonym for the idea of natural law; in particular, what are now commonly called 'the goods of human flourishing'. However, in the second sense, it is a postulation of a belief that there are some values or goods which are common to all traditions, or that different traditions, regardless of their theological pedigree, will reach the same or similar conclusions about the goods of human flourishing. It is this second sense that is problematic in the context of the engagement of the Thomist tradition with the culture of modernity and its dominant Liberal tradition. If it is true that conceptions of justice, rationality and virtue are tradition dependent, as Alasdair MacIntyre and various proponents of the Genealogical tradition argue, then giving content to these supposed 'universal values' becomes a highly difficult intellectual exercise. Although those who belong to one of the 'Abrahamic religions' may find that they share interpretations of the goods of human flourishing in common, the notion of 'universal values' implies not merely inter-Abrahamic faith agreements about the most basic precepts of the 'natural moral law', but also the possibility that there exists an area of common ground between the theistic traditions and the Liberal tradition in relation to the goods of human flourishing. Moreover, for the optimism of the 1950s to be vindicated there would need to be a large area of common ground not only between the theistic traditions and the Liberal tradition(s), but also between the theistic traditions and the Genealogical.

The belief that it is possible to effect a synthesis of the Liberal and Thomist traditions is described by George Weigel, one of its contemporary proponents, as the project of 'Whig Thomism'.[15] It can be traced to the works of nineteenth-century 'Liberal Catholics' such as Lord Acton in England and the comte de Montalembert in France.[16] It continues in Jacques Maritain's efforts to reconcile Thomistic natural law with the Liberal natural right doctrine and his endorsement of the natural rights doctrine in the United Nations' *Declaration on Human Rights* in 1948. This strategy of reconciling natural law with natural right was prefigured in Leo XIII's *Rerum Novarum*, and has been followed in the encyclicals of John XXIII, Paul VI and John Paul II. However, in the work of John Paul II it is clear that the Pope is taking *only the rhetoric* of the Liberal tradition, not its philosophical substance, while, in relation to Leo XIII's adoption of the rights rhetoric, Ernest Fortin argues that this was *not* part of a project to synthesise the Thomist and Liberal traditions, but merely the expedient adoption of a weapon to use against socialism at a time when the Thomist tradition lacked the conceptual tools to deal with that particular ideology.[17] Fortin further argues that Leo XIII failed to appreciate the 'radical heterogeneity of the positions whose amalgamation was being sought'. Nonetheless, the 'Whig Thomist' project was further developed in John Courtney Murray's defence of the American polity, of which Weigel's contemporary defence of the 'culture of America' is a logical extension. To some degree, elements of 'Whig Thomism' are also to be found in the New Natural Law theory of John Finnis, Germain Grisez and Robert George.[18]

This adoption of pieces of the conceptual apparatus of the Liberal tradition, and, in some cases, its substantive content, occurred at a time during which the persuasive authority of the Liberal tradition had begun to wane. The watershed year of 1968 is now commonly held to mark the beginning of the period of postmodernity and a growing recognition of the internal contradictions within the Liberal tradition and the tradition's tendency to compensate for its lack of any explicit connection to a theological framework by creating its own alternative soteriology. In terms of the intellectual *avant-garde*, 1968 represents the point at which the theorists of the Liberal 'Enlightenments' were replaced by Marx, Heidegger, Freud and Nietzsche, and 1989 represents the year when Marx dropped out of this quartet. Notwithstanding Francis Fukuyama's declaration of the end of history in 1989, theological issues continue to dominate both domestic and international politics. Postmodern scholars argue that this is not surprising as all political and philosophical positions are dependent upon a framework of theological presuppositions. Works such as John Milbank's *Beyond Secular Reason* and Alasdair MacIntyre's *Three Rival Versions of Moral Enquiry* challenge the claim of the Liberal tradition and its 'value-free' sociology to theological neutrality.

The idea that the Thomist tradition should either be synthesised with elements of the Liberal tradition (the Whig Thomist project) or at least adopt the conceptual apparatus of the Liberal tradition (the New Natural Law project) therefore reached its peak of magisterial legitimacy after the intellectual elites of Western societies began to be disenchanted with the Liberal tradition. In other words, at the same time as the hegemony of the Liberal tradition, and in particular its claim to theological neutrality, began to be challenged by those who preferred Nietzsche and Heidegger to Locke and Kant, or by those, such as Milbank and MacIntyre, who prefer Augustinian 'narrative traditions' to Kantian 'pure reason', the project of synthesising Aquinas with Kant and various other members of the Liberal tradition became fashionable among Thomists and members of the hierarchy. Against such an intellectual history, Augustine Di Noia has observed that:

> The post-Conciliar interpretation of John XXIII's vision of *aggiornamento* as updating theology is, from the perspective of post-modern eyes, a project which has never really caught up; while conceived more grandly as modernisation, it is already far behind.[19]

The conclusion of a number of contemporary scholars is that the response demanded but not met by the Modernist crisis, which included the question of the stance of the magisterium towards the Liberal tradition, but was much more complex and broader in its ambit than this, was the elaboration of a theology of culture.[20]

'Culture' in *Gaudium et spes*

Although the Conciliar fathers generally lacked an understanding of modernity as a specific cultural formation, the popular interpretation of *Gaudium et spes* is that this particular document should be construed as programmatic for the Church's response to the phenomenon of modernity.[21] As John Langan observed:

> *Gaudium et spes* is neither the earliest nor the deepest nor the ultimate expression of those forces of modernity and faith which shape the post-Conciliar Church, but it occupies a significant place because of the moment in history in which it was issued and because of its status as an expression of the mind of the universal Church.[22]

As a preliminary point, it should be noted that all commentators agree that *Gaudium et spes* was a compromise document – that it is the outcome of quite intense debates about the relationship between nature and grace and in particular the tension between the incarnational and eschatological dimensions of Catholic theology.[23] Walter Kasper expresses the problem in concrete form when he says that there remains within the text a 'certain lack of clarity with respect to the relationship between man's character as God's image according to Genesis 1:26 and that of Jesus Christ according to

Colossians 1:15'.[24] In his account of the history of the document's drafting, Charles Moeller stated that in the last two stages of the drafting process a decision was taken that a 'balance must be struck between the opposing tendencies', and as a consequence the document acquired a 'dialectical character with multiple contrasts'.[25] In effect, this means that *Gaudium et spes* cannot be read without an overarching theological framework in which the contrasts can be reconciled. However, no such framework was offered by the Conciliar fathers and as a consequence the document became the subject of a riot of interpretations, especially by those plain persons who lacked a training in theology and philosophy, as well as many clergy and religious in positions of authority within the Church's institutions. Roberto Tucci observed that Chapter II of *Gaudium et spes*, in which the concept of culture is treated, did not have any prehistory during the preparatory phase of the Council, and Henri de Lubac said of several chapters of Part II that 'a number of Fathers would have preferred that they be treated in an encyclical, or relegated to an appendix, with annexed documents'.[26]

Not only was the substance of the document the result of theological compromise, but its form has been described as, *inter alia,* an 'innovation in genre' (Aidan Nichols), 'a novelty whose structure is unprecedented in the history of the councils' (Walter Kasper) and 'an approach which treats Christ more as *Omega* than as *Alpha*' (Edouard Hamel).[27] Notwithstanding the common vernacular translation of its title as 'The Pastoral Constitution on the Church in the Modern World', the document lacked the form of a constitution. It was not drafted in a legal manner with emphasis given to the definition of key terms. In particular, there was no theological examination of concepts such as 'modern man' and 'modern world' despite the repeated reference to them. Just as Francis George has observed that the concept of 'Church' in Conciliar documents is characterised by a certain 'terminological looseness', so too are the concepts of 'modern man' and the 'modern world'.[28] Moreover, this 'terminological looseness', evident in the Latin text of the document, is compounded in various vernacular translations. For example, *huius temporis* becomes in English 'modern world' rather than the more literal 'of this time'. Such a loose translation can completely change the nuance of a phrase and, in turn, the interpretation of a document: the word 'modern' is not simply a synonym for contemporary, but is a theologically and philosophically loaded term.[29]

The form of the document also bears evidence of a series of compromises. The form alternates between sociological observations and theological propositions, between an emphasis on the common hopes of Catholics and non-Catholics and an emphasis on the inadequacy of all non-Christocentric perspectives, and between a conversational tone and a more dogmatic tone. Walter Kasper has noted that initially, in the first draft of the document, the idiom of the Church's natural law tradition was used, but this was later abandoned because by making reference to the natural law tradition 'the

Fathers would thereby have deprived themselves a priori of the chance to secure an ecumenical consensus'.[30] Indeed, Karl Rahner observed that the 'Council unreflectively used a mode of expression that has the character neither of a permanently valid dogmatic teaching nor of a canonical regulation, but must rather be understood as the expression of "pastoral instructions" or "appeals"'.[31] When taken together, the fact of compromise, the multiple contrasts, the unprecedented form, the absence of a clearly defined theological framework for its interpretation, the alternation between dogma and pastoral appeals and the terminological looseness all contributed to the complexity of the 'explosive problematic'.

In the immediate post-Conciliar era, the most commonly applied hermeneutical key to the interpretation of this document was the 'opening the windows' metaphor taken from a comment made by John XXIII to an ambassador.[32] This one metaphor, which was not even used in an official speech, became tied to the Conciliar slogan *aggiornamento*, and was thereby made to bear an enormous theological weight. In a series of questions put to Pope Paul VI and various of his advisors in 1966 by Karl Barth, Barth inquired, 'What does *aggiornamento* mean? Accommodation to what?[33]

Although *aggiornamento* does not literally mean 'accommodation', the notion of an 'updating to meet the requirements of some external standard' was implicit within it, raising the question: 'What is the external standard?'; or, as Barth asked: 'Accommodation to what?' Moreover, the popular interpretation of the concept was that of an 'accommodation'. For example, Hayles, in *Pope John and His Revolution,* wrote: 'The Church cannot live effectively in the world save by clothing herself in the garments of the living contemporary culture and that, again, is what *aggiornamento* means'.[34] Such an interpretation was also fostered by those sections of the *Decree on the Appropriate Renewal of Religious Life*, according to which the education of the religious should take place with reference to the 'prevailing manner of contemporary social life, and its characteristic ways of feeling and thinking'; and according to which the 'living, praying and working practices of religious should be adapted to the requirements of a given culture'. The words 'with reference to' and 'adapt to the requirements of' do not necessarily mean the same thing as 'accommodate', 'follow', 'mimic' or 'ape', but this was their popular interpretation. The idea that *aggiornamento* might mean an updating or development of theological resources to provide a coherent critique of the culture of modernity, rather than a simple accommodation to it – that is, an interpretation which coupled the concept of *aggiornamento* to the pre-Conciliar *Ressourcement* project which sought to effect a richer synthesis of the Patristic and Scholastic heritage – never succeeded in influencing the *Zeitgeist* of the Council, as the accommodationist interpretation did. This second interpretation has only come to the fore in the latter half of the papacy of John Paul II, following the 1985 Extraordinary Synod, which sought to reflect upon interpretations of the Second Vatican Council.[35]

The need for a theological hermeneutic of culture

The polyvalent character of the *aggiornamento* concept and its metaphor of 'fresh air' offered no guidance for a philosophical or theological interpretation of the 'spirits' of the 'modern world'. For example, the spirit of the 'modern world' *circa* 1964 could be represented by the Beatles and the burgeoning youth 'pop culture', or it could be represented by developments in medical theology, including the contraceptive pill; it could be interpreted by reference to political developments, including the election of a nominally Catholic President of the politically Liberal United States at the height of the Cold War, by the arms and space races and by the recent defeat of fascism by a coalition of states, many of which were thereafter governed according to some version of Liberal theory. These cultural 'icons' do not, however, speak for themselves, but require interpretation within a theological framework. For example, the interpretation of World War II as a victory for Liberalism over totalitarianism overlooks the facts that the Soviet Union was a major contributor to, and beneficiary of, the allied victory in World War II, and that Hitler's published speeches indicate that he was primarily fighting a war not against Liberalism so much as against Judaism and Christianity, which Hitler construed to be merely devices to 'protect the weak from the strong'.[36]

Thus the spirit of the modern world *circa* 1964 could have been interpreted – from a more philosophical and theological perspective – as the military defeat of German neo-paganism by an alliance of Liberal, Judeo-Christian and Communist forces, signalling not an end but a continued engagement between these forces; the emergence of medical science as a pseudo-Divinity that would seek to control both the creation and destruction of human life; the triumph of emotivism and commercialism in art over a conception of beauty which is intrinsically connected to goodness and truth, requiring self-discipline, skill and study, and so on. These are but illustrations of a *theologically* grounded hermeneutics of culture, without which concepts such as the 'modern world' in ecclesial documents are ambiguous and open to a host of interpretations.

Although the authors of *Gaudium et spes* acknowledged that the concept of 'culture' is multifaceted, they nonetheless failed to identify precisely what *they* meant with each usage of the term. The definition that appears in the document is in paragraph 53, where it is stated that the word culture 'in the general sense refers to all those things which go to the refining and developing of man's diverse mental and physical endowments'. This includes the *Genesis* notion of dominion over creation through labour, the importance of custom, institutions, family and polity; the features of language and spirituality and the historical, sociological and ethnological aspects. This definition is extremely broad in coverage, but shallow in analysis, and not explicitly related to the grace–nature problematic as one would expect in a theological document. A more critical mode of analysis is to subdivide the concept into what T. S. Eliot identified as its three dominant senses – the culture of the individual, the culture of the group (or institution) and the culture of a society as a whole.[37] These subdivisions are recognised in the German language by three separate words: *Bildung, Geist* and *Kultur*.[38] These terms are used by the German *Kulturgeschichte* scholars to signify:

1   the *Geist* or *ethos* of a specific civilisation and its institutions;
2   a specific form of *Bildung* or self-development; and
3   a special type of *Kultur* or civilisation.

The relationship between these German terms may also be traced to the Greek terms: *ethos, nomos* and *logos*. 'Spirit', '*Geist*' and '*ethos*' are generally treated as synonymous, but *nomos* may be construed as the element that gives each conception of self-formation or *Bildung* its guiding principles or laws, whereas *logos* may be construed as that which gives a given civilisation or *Kultur* its overarching and particular form. Thus an Augustinian Thomist conception of culture can be defined as one in which any given *ethos* is governed by the Christian virtues, the process of self-formation or *Bildung* is guided by the precepts of the Decalogue and revealed moral laws of the New Testament, and the *logos* or form is provided by the 'identities-in-relation' logic of the Trinitarian processions.[39]

The neglect of important pre-Conciliar scholarship

No such Augustinian Thomist conception of culture, however, acted as a standard for the analysis of elements of the culture of modernity to which reference was made in *Gaudium et spes*, nor was any theological alternative clearly proposed. In particular, the question of the *logos* of the culture of modernity was never addressed, because, as Schmitz and others have observed, the Conciliar fathers generally lacked a notion of modernity as a *specific cultural formation*. This lacuna existed notwithstanding the fact that some attention had already been given to the issue in pre-Conciliar German Scholarship. Dating from at least the late eighteenth century, a perennial theme in German scholarship has been the contrasts or, in Erich Przywara's terminology, 'polarities', between Greek and Roman culture, French and German culture, and Protestant and Catholic culture. As early as 1853 the distinction between 'modernity' and 'previous times' had been made in Catholic scholarship by Joseph Kleutgen, Prefect of Studies at the Gregorian, and in 1886 Rudolf Eucken published a Thomistic analysis of the culture (understood as *Kultur*) of modernity.[40] In 1907 Albert Ehrhard published *Katholisches und moderne Kultur*, and in 1927 a collection of essays by different authors was published under the title of *Wiederbegegnung von Kirche und Kultur in Deutschland*. In his work, Ehrhard listed five groups of factors that made the culture of modernity problematic for the Church, including the re-birth of pagan–classical cultural ideals, the rejection of universalism in favour of the nation-state, and subjectivism and individualism. Each of these factors remains a problem for the Church almost a century later.

The theme of modern culture was also implicit in much of the inter-bellum scholarship of Erich Przywara, who was influenced by conceptions of *paideia* in the work of John Henry Newman; and in the works of Przywara's own student Hans Urs von Balthasar.[41] In 1926 Romano Guardini published the essay *Gedanken über das Verhaltnis von Christentum und Kultur.*[42] By 1950 this theme was developed in a series of lectures entitled *Das Ende der Neuzeit*, which was subsequently published in English in 1957 as *The End of the Modern World*. In this work Guardini concluded that to the extent that Europeans commonly believed that 'culture is self created out of norms intrinsic to its own essence' they were mistaken.[43] This is, prima facie, the exact antithesis of the statement to be found in *Gaudium et spes* paragraph 59 that the Church recognises the 'legitimate autonomy of the cultural realm'. At various times after the Council and before his death Guardini expressed his concerns about the theological directions of post-Conciliar thought in letters to Paul VI. In 1965 he wrote:

> At the time of my first theological studies something became clear to me that, since then, has determined my entire work: what can convince modern people is not a historical or a psychological or a continually ever modernising Christianity but only the unrestricted and uninterrupted message of Revelation.[44]

Neither Guardini nor Przywara nor von Balthasar had been chosen as Conciliar *periti*.[45] Nor was the work of the English historian Christopher Dawson or the German sociologist Max Weber on the sociological differences between Catholic and Protestant cultures of any apparent influence on those who drafted *Gaudium et spes*.[46] Rather, the section on culture seems to have been constructed without reference to any particular *theology* of culture but does bear witness to Maritain's general political project of *rapprochement* with the Liberal–humanist tradition. According to Cardinal Garrone, Jacques Maritain's 1937 work *Humanisme intégral*, which was a development of an earlier work *Religion et Culture*, was an important influence on the formulation of *Gaudium et spes*.[47] It was this work in particular which provided a philosophical framework for the project of synthesising the Liberal and Thomist traditions.

Specific examples of the problematic

Examples of the difficulties inherent in any account of the relationship between theology and culture may be found in the specific section on culture in *Gaudium et spes*. An understanding of culture as a specific *Kultur* can be found in the introduction to Chapter 2 of Part II. In this section, reference is made to 'preventing increased exchanges between cultures from disturbing the life of communities, overthrowing traditional wisdom and endangering the character proper to each people'.[48] Without further reference to principles to be found within the corpus of Catholic thought, this subsection sounds like an endorsement of the ideas first propounded by the German Romantic Johann Gottfried Herder, according to whom each national culture has its own unique characteristics which, when taken together, give rise to a specific and intrinsically valuable civilisation or *Kultur*.[49] If this section is taken literally it becomes another 'explosive problematic' for missionaries in countries where there remain elements of a pre-Christian and especially anti-Christian culture. If one adopts a Herderian interpretation of this section, the logical conclusion to be drawn is that missionaries should not introduce Christian ideas that will contradict the pantheistic or polytheistic 'traditional wisdom' of pre-Christian cultures as, for example, that of the Australian aboriginal people. These cultures were unique, and thus, by Herderian standards, of intrinsic merit. This is not to argue that the Conciliar fathers were consciously promoting a Herderian conception of *Kultur*, but rather that the language of the section is seemingly Herderian and thus requires further clarification.[50] In particular, there needs to be an examination of the relationship between a Christian conception of inculturation and the Herderian promotion of the preservation of *all* cultures that exhibit the Romantic qualities of individuality and originality.[51] The need for such a clarification has been identified by Albert Outler, a Methodist delegate at all four sessions of the Council. Outler interpreted the treatment of 'culture' in *Gaudium et spes* as an attempt to synthesise the 'ecclesiocentric traditions of *evangelization* of any and all cultures, and the sociocentric perspectives on *culture* and cultural diversity that ran from Vico through Herder to Tyler and on into contemporary sociology and anthropology'.[52] He concluded that the notions of 'culture' as what the *humanum* adds to nature, and 'evangelization' as what the *humanum* needs from God, are under review with no stabilization in sight as yet.[53]

The following subsection of *Gaudium et spes* entitled 'Some Principles for Proper Cultural Development' turns in the direction of an understanding of culture as *Bildung*, that is as a specific form of self-formation:

> when man works in the fields of philosophy, history, mathematics and science, and cultivates the arts, he can greatly contribute towards bringing the human race a higher understanding of truth, goodness and beauty, to points of view having universal value; thus man will be more clearly enlightened by that wondrous Wisdom, which was with God from all eternity, working beside Him like a master craftsman, rejoicing in his inhabited world and delighting in the sons of men.[54]

This statement is certainly capable of an interpretation which is consistent with themes found in the works of the Fathers, the Scholastics and, in twentieth century theological thought, in the work of Erich Przywara and Hans Urs von Balthasar, among others. However, if one ignores or is unaware of the implied Trinitarian framework that draws attention to the relationship between spiritual formation and intellectual formation, and gives a specific Christian content to the concepts of truth, beauty and goodness, then the section is more immediately evocative of the works of Wilhelm von Humboldt and Friedrich Schiller on the subject of self-development and the 'aesthetic education of man'.[55]

The danger inherent in this section of the document is therefore that of substituting for a specifically Christian form of *Bildung* a typically 'Aristocratic Liberal' conception, which equates virtue with education, and grace with intellectual ability.[56] This tendency to esteem intellectual ability and to treat education as an end in itself is the subterranean link between the Encyclopaedist and Genealogical traditions. Nietzsche merely makes explicit the 'Aristocratic Liberal' demotion of goodness from the category of a transcendental property of being, to a principle of the maximisation of individual freedom, by his observation that not all are equally intellectually endowed. The 'Aristocratic Liberal' or 'neo-classical' projects of cultivating a *schöne Seele* (beautiful soul) are thus closed to all but a 'natural' elite. Such a conception of self-formation is congenial to intellectual aesthetes, but any such appreciation of truth and beauty which conceives of goodness as something other than a transcendental property of being, or something which holds no relationship to truth and beauty, falls short of the Christian ideal. Indeed, John Saward, following St Bonaventure, suggests that Satan 'tries to sever the beauty of Christian art from the truth of the dogmatic creed and the goodness of the moral virtues' and concludes that 'all diabolical wickedness has at its root a perverted aesthetic'.[57]

This particular subsection of *Gaudium et spes* therefore highlights the need to develop an explicitly theological understanding of the relationship between truth, beauty and goodness – as the three transcendental properties of being – and culture in its various manifestations, without which no clear distinctions are made between a Christian understanding of truth, beauty and goodness, and neo-classical conceptions. In particular, it highlights the importance of the rôle of grace in self-formation. If this dimension is eclipsed the self is left to form itself with nothing but the materials of its own will and intellect, and becomes, as a consequence, a Pelagian self. This danger was recognised by Joseph Ratzinger as early as 1969, when, in his commentary on *Gaudium et spes*, he described sections of it as embodying *eine geradezu pelagianische Terminologie*, that is 'a downright Pelagian terminology'.[58]

Ratzinger gave as a specific example of the Pelagian spirit the treatment of the concept of freedom in paragraph 17. He argued that the treatment tends to focus on the modern Liberal philosophical interest in freedom of personal choice, rather than an ontological conception of freedom as 'living in the presence of God'. Whereas the alternative conception of freedom as 'personal choice' does have a place within a theological framework under the concept of free will, the Thomist tradition differs quite fundamentally from the Liberal in its treatment of free will. The Liberal idea that education by itself without the power of grace can direct the will towards good ends may be construed as a special species of Pelagianism.

A second treatment of the theme of freedom as personal choice appears in paragraph 41. It too is typical of the problem that Ratzinger has identified as the use of a Pelagian terminology. The first sentence of the section begins with the statement: 'Modern man is on the road to a more thorough development of his own personality, and to a growing discovery and vindication of his own rights'.[59] The term 'modern man' is not explained, nor is it clear how, from within the parameters of Christian doctrine, it can be deduced that personalities are now more highly developed by the culture of modernity. Since it is grace that is the major element for the development of Christian personalities, any judgement of 'modern man' from a Christian perspective must consider the question of how 'modern man' is more disposed to the reception of grace than 'pre-modern man'. Paragraph 41 however makes no reference to grace as such. It speaks of the work of God's spirit upon man, which is an inference of the significance of grace, but it does not develop this subject or the issue of the problems created when the work of God's spirit is rejected. It does however conclude with a warning against a 'kind of false autonomy' that would ground human dignity 'in an exemption from every requirement of divine law'.[60] The need for the personality to have a Christian form of development might therefore be implied, but the whole tone of the discourse remains suggestive of the Liberal–humanist tradition with its idea of self-perfection through education and exercise of will-power. A philosopher or theologian reading the section may be expected to know of Jacques Maritain's distinction between an anthropocentric humanism and a theocentric humanism; however, the plain person reading the same text is unlikely to make a distinction between the two. This is especially so given the bald statement in paragraph 54 that 'we are witnesses to the birth of a new humanism, one in which man is defined first of all by this major responsibility to his brothers and to history'.[61] On its own, the concept of a major anthropological change effected by the 'modern world' and of the human person owing a responsibility to history sounds more Hegelian than credal Christian.

In Christian doctrine there are only three definitive moments in human history. The first occurs at the Creation–Fall, with the loss of the preternatural gifts; the second occurs at the Incarnation–Passion–Resurrection when the Word is made flesh and a new order of grace is established; and the third will occur at the end of time with the resurrection of the dead, the general judgement and the renewal of the cosmos. Although it is true that 'the circumstances of the life of modern man have been so profoundly changed in their social and cultural aspects, that we can speak of a new age of human history' and, further, that certain processes such as industrialisation and urbanisation have created a 'mass-culture' (*Gaudium et spes* paragraph 54), it by no means follows that these developments are either advantageous for the development of a specifically Christian personality, or neutral in relation to such a development.

The general uncritical assessment of the rise of a 'mass-culture' among members of the theological establishment in the early 1960s is evident in the following statement of the Conciliar *peritus*, Albert Dondeyne:

> The democratization of culture has not merely encouraged a certain uniformity; it has also created new forms of culture, among them what modern literature calls 'mass culture'. Under the influence of the aristocratic cultural ideal of former times, this is very superficially dismissed as cultural decadence, whereas in reality it is a genuine contemporary cultural creation.[62]

Although in one sense it is true that 'mass culture' is a 'genuine contemporary cultural creation' in the *Kultur* sense of the concept, Dondeyne leaves unexplored the relationship between this specific *Kultur* and the possibilities for a specifically Christian form of self-development, that is *Bildung*, within it.

Finally, in the same subsection of *Gaudium et spes*, there is a shift from a concept of culture as *Bildung* to a concept of culture as *Geist* or *ethos*. This subsection speaks of the 'values of the culture of today' and identifies them as:

> Study of the sciences and exact fidelity to truth as scientific investigation, the necessity of teamwork in technology, the sense of international solidarity, a growing awareness of the experts' responsibility to help and defend his fellow man, and an eagerness to improve the standard of living of all men, especially those who are deprived of responsibility or suffer from cultural destitution.[63]

The final two words – 'cultural destitution' (or in the Abbott translation 'culturally poor') – hark back to the *Bildung* notion, but the subsection is otherwise focused on a presentation of the spirit or *ethos* of modern institutional practices. The reference here to the 'growing awareness of the experts' responsibility to help and defend his fellow man' (or in the Abbott translation, the 'responsibility of experts to aid men and even to protect them') is more powder for O'Malley's 'explosive problematic'. It immediately raises the question: What is the basis for the authority of these benevolent 'experts'? For example, in post-Conciliar history a major employer of 'benevolent experts' has been the United Nations. Its policies, however, are frequently at odds with the Church's teaching, as evidenced in the conclusions of the Cairo and Beijing Conferences. Further, the whole notion of 'government by experts' stands in tension with the tradition of Catholic social thought, which emphasises the importance of the principle of subsidiarity, and the tradition of governance in Catholic institutions, which has favoured what in Weberian terms would be classified as 'charismatic authority' over 'bureaucratic authority'. Indeed, Joseph Ratzinger has observed that even *within* the Church one now finds a 'tangle of authorities which almost inevitably triggers feelings of their "inscrutability" and "powerlessness" for those who are the subject of their deliberations', and Walter Kasper has stated that 'the Church's excessively bureaucratic form of organisation creates institutional pressures that stifle hope'.[64] The idea that persons with social science qualifications *ipso facto* have solutions to the problems of the 'culturally poor' is thus highly problematic.

The 'autonomy of culture'

Walter Kasper has suggested that a motivating force behind *Gaudium et spes* was the rejection of 'integralism', which he defines as the idea that it is possible for the church to 'provide the answers to secular questions directly from the faith', and he further construes *Gaudium et spes* as the Church's recognition of the 'autonomy of secular fields of activity'.[65] He asserts that 'the Council accepted the fundamental concept of the modern age', that 'secular matters are to be decided in a secular fashion, political matters in a political fashion, economic matters in an economic fashion' and, further, that none of these issues are to be decided 'magisterially theologically'.[66] Similarly, Cardinal Aloysius Ambrozic, in a recent address to the Pontifical Council for Culture, reflected that the more he thought of the Second Vatican Council, the more he was convinced that it was 'either mainly or at least significantly, an attempt to reconcile the Gospel and the Enlightenment', and, further, that this was especially true of *Gaudium et spes*.[67] Evidence for these conclusions of Kasper and Ambrozic may be found in the speeches of Cardinal Lercaro, whose interventions in the first Conciliar debate on the *Gaudium et spes* schema have been described as being of decisive importance.[68] Lercaro's desire to defer to the authority of secular scholarship is evident in the following excerpt:

> Above all, the Church must acknowledge itself to be culturally 'poor'; it must therefore wish to be more and more poor. I am not speaking here of material poverty but of a particular consequence of evangelical poverty precisely in the domain of ecclesiastical culture. In this field too, as in that of institutions and Church property, the Church preserves certain riches of a glorious but perhaps anachronistic past (scholastic system in philosophy and theology, educational and academic institutions, methods of university teaching and research). The Church must have the courage, if need be, to renounce these riches or at least not to presume on them too much, not to pride itself on them and to be more and more

cautious of trusting them. For in fact, they do not always put on the stand the lamp of the gospel message but often hide it under a bushel. They may prevent the Church from opening itself to the true values of modern culture or of ancient non-Christian culture; they may limit the universality of the Church's language, divide rather than unite, repel many more men than they attract and convince. ... Such renunciation of the cultural patrimony is not an end in itself but a way to acquire new riches, and, humanly speaking, greater intellectual acumen and a more rigorous critical sense.[69]

This speech, like *Gaudium et spes* itself, is characterised by a certain terminological looseness. It is far from clear in this passage what one is to make of the idea that the Church is 'culturally poor' and 'should wish to be poorer' or how one is to construe the notion of the 'true values of modern culture' or the 'renunciation of cultural patrimony'. Moreover, it is even less clear how the Cardinal's desire for a 'culturally poorer' Church can be reconciled with the principle in the final draft of *Gaudium et spes*, of the individual's 'right to culture', unless it is presumed that the individual will exercise this 'right' outside the Church. Also implied in this speech is a complete renunciation of the idea found in the works of such scholars as Christopher Dawson and Feliks Koneczny, that the Church is not merely the teacher of truth, dispenser of the mysteries and barque of fellow travellers, but the creator (mother and guardian) of culture. In all, it is an excellent example of the ambiguity that flourishes when the precise sense in which the concept of culture is being used is not made evident.

Further, it would appear that neither Dondeyne nor Lercaro regarded an experience of beauty as something significant for moral formation, let alone a good of human flourishing, nor had they considered the effect of the architecture, music, literature and norms of human relating that are typical of mass culture upon the opportunities for plain persons to experience beauty and self-transcendence. The indifference of *periti* and bishops to certain riches of Catholic culture suggests that at the time of the Council there existed a certain amount of confusion about the relationship between a specifically Christian conception of an aristocratic culture and various Aristocratic Liberal versions, and, further, that the Protestant rejection of beauty as a transcendental was finding its way into the Catholic mind. This was to have enormous secondary effects within the realms of ecclesiastical architecture, music, art and liturgical practice.[70]

What is required for the mitigation of the confusion is an understanding of how the Church perceives the relationship between the orders of grace and nature, and in particular how the transcendentals of truth, beauty and goodness are instantiated within the *ethos* of institutions, the self-formation of the person and the form of a given civilisation, including its arts. From the so-called Nouvelle Théologie perspective, any framework which severs the order of grace from that of nature, and severs the natural and social sciences and the arts from theology, is as defective a construction as that of integralism. In both cases the relationship between the two orders is characterised as 'extrinsicism'. In the case of integralism the orders are severed but the Church reserves to herself a prerogative to dictate terms to the so-called secular order, whereas the general spirit of the Lercaro interpretation, to which reference has been made above, suggests that the Church should divest herself of both juridical and intellectual authority and even reverse the order of the hierarchy of disciplines to give priority to the social and natural sciences. In effect, such a perspective invites the wholesale secularisation of culture. The logic of the Nouvelle Théologie alternative was to foster the idea that all realms of culture have a theological significance and this significance is related, at least in part, to the Christian virtues (in the context of institutional practices), the norms of the moral law, including their symbiotic relationship with the virtues (in the context of the formation of the self) and the Trinitarian, rather than mechanical or Cartesian, form (in the context of the *logos* of a civilisation). This means, in effect, that while there may be 'secular' fields of activity, to use Kasper's expression, in the sense of fields of activity which lie outside of the jurisdiction of the Church, there is, in another sense, no field that is ever truly 'secular' in the sense of being unrelated to, or autonomous of, theological presuppositions. For example, neither 'economics' nor 'politics' is a 'value-free' science. Rather, both are sub-branches of the discipline of ethics that is intrinsically related to theology.[71]

Bernard Lambert's affirmation of 'secularism'

The argument that the concepts of an 'autonomous culture' and 'secularisation' tend to foster one another is acknowledged by Bernard Lambert, a Conciliar *peritus* closely associated with the drafting of the final version of *Gaudium et spes*. Lambert states that the sociological phenomenon of secularisation 'carries through the logical development of creation'.[72] He defines secularisation as 'the process by which a society frees itself from religious notions, beliefs or institutions which used to order its existence' – 'society now is constituted as an autonomous society and finds in its own consistency, methods, structures and laws for its own organisation'.[73] *Gaudium et spes*, he asserts, had above all 'to make men of our time understand the dimensions of the autonomy of the secular'.[74] He further argues that the teaching of the Council draws on two fundamental points: 'the autonomy of the profane, of the order of culture – that is to say, all human development – and the ambivalence of all'.[75] Leaving aside the question of what Lambert meant about the 'ambivalence of all' of which he said nothing more than that it should be taken as an 'existential fact', the significant point in his argument is that he treats the 'order of culture' as synonymous with the 'order of the secular or profane' and holds that the autonomy of this order is rooted in the 'very ground of being'.[76] Prima facie, this is directly contrary to Guardini's assessment that the idea of culture as 'something self-created out of norms intrinsic to its own essence' is 'a mistake', and that 'the Christian judgement knows the falsehood of autonomous areas of human activity'.[77]

Moreover, in responding to the question of whether secularisation is an evil in itself, Lambert replies that according to the Second Vatican Council secularisation is not necessarily evil, and, further, that *Gaudium et spes* endorses a 'frank acceptance of secularity in its laws as well as in its tragic existential character'.[78] To defend this judgement, he makes reference to paragraph 36 of *Gaudium et spes*, which contains the statement that 'by the very circumstances of their having been created, all things are endowed with their own stability, truth, goodness, proper laws and order'.[79] Although this statement of principle is an uncontroversial Thomistic proposition, it is not clear how such a principle can be used to defend a positive judgement on the processes of secularisation. While all things do have their own proper laws and order, stability, truth and goodness (and one may add beauty or splendour and integrity), it by no means follows from this that the processes of secularisation will respect such laws and values. The alternative vision, as David Schindler argues, is that the Church is 'destined to form from within everything in the cosmos: every act, every relationship, every cultural or social or economic order', and, further, that this is the authentic meaning to be given to *Gaudium et spes* when it is read from the perspective of paragraph 22.[80] If by the expression 'the autonomy of culture' one simply means that it is not possible to deduce the laws of thermodynamics from the Scriptures, then it would perhaps have been prudent to have phrased this proposition more precisely, instead of using a multifaceted term like 'culture' to stand for the notion of the physical and chemical laws of the created order.

Lambert therefore appears to have based his entire analysis of *Gaudium et spes* on an extrinsicist account of the relationship between nature and grace, whereby the two orders are kept distinctively separate – an interpretation that has been fostered by the terminological looseness of the document – but one which is nonetheless inconsistent with the Christocentric orientation of other sections of the document (especially paragraph 22) and other documents of the Council (such as *Lumen Gentium* paragraph 54), and with the Catholic side of the Catholic–Lutheran debate over the two orders.

The affirmation of the secular in
Rahner and Maritain

Lambert's interpretation of *Gaudium et spes* as endorsing, or at least accepting, the processes of secularisation is not, however, idiosyncratic, since it falls within the general theological framework of Karl Rahner and the philosophical framework of Maritain's 'integral humanism'. In his 1954 paper on the 'Theological Position of Christians in the Modern World', Rahner argued that Christians must accept that Christendom is now over, that Christendom was never an ideal Christian cultural order, that Christians must accept that they are now a mere diaspora, and, further, and most significantly, that this last sociological fact should be construed theologically, as a 'pre-ordained "must be" in the history of salvation'.[81] Rahner recognised that the culture of modernity is hostile to Christianity, and that in such a culture the truths of Christianity will no longer appear to plain persons as 'self-evident'; but these facts notwithstanding, Rahner asserted that any kind of Christian counter-cultural offensive is futile, because the culture of modernity is a 'must be' in the sense that the Cross was a 'must be' and the perennial problem of poverty is a 'must be'.[82] Rahner did not, however, offer *any* criteria for discerning when a state of affairs should be judged, from a theological perspective, a 'must be', to be endured, rather than a challenge to be met. He merely suggested that the 'authenticity of a given aspect of the secularisation process' may be discerned by Christians through the exercise of a global moral 'instinct'.[83]

The notion of the 'autonomy of the secular order' is also found in the philosophical work of Jacques Maritain. In *Humanisme intégral,* Maritain presented an outline of 'a new Christian order no longer sacred but secular in its forms' and promoted the idea of the 'autonomy of the temporal order'.[84] In his account of the latter he observed that 'the secular order has in the course of the modern age built up for itself an autonomous relation with regard to the spiritual or consecrational order' and that this is an 'historical gain'.[85] However, he also stated that 'this does not mean that the primacy of the spiritual order will be disregarded'.[86] The difficulty here is that of understanding how one is to construe the meaning of an 'autonomous' state with 'secular forms' which nonetheless recognises the primacy of the spiritual order. It is one thing to say that practical judgements regarding the common good should be made by representative members of the laity – 'juridical autonomy from ecclesiastical governance' – but quite another to suggest that the realm of the political is unrelated to, or autonomous from, the theological. Maritain clearly wished to retain some kind of link between the spiritual and the political that will qualify the notion of 'autonomy'. However, his construction of the issue invites the question: What is the logic of a Christian order with secular forms and conversely an autonomous secular state subordinate to the spiritual order? If by this he means a state governed by Christian laity according to the norms of the natural law, a proponent of the Liberal tradition is entitled to ask: In what way is this different from a 'consecrational order', or different from what Aidan Nichols in *Christendom Awake* called 'a society where the historical Christian faith provides the cultural framework for social living, as well as the official religious form of the state'?[87] Conversely, a Thomist may well ask: How does a secular form differ from what von Balthasar called an *anima technica vacua*?

Just as MacIntyre and others have drawn attention to the problems created by the fact that the meaning of 'rationality' and 'justice' and 'virtue' differ from tradition to tradition, in this instance the problem appears (at least in part) to arise from the word 'secular' having at least two common and different meanings. The first, favoured by the Liberal tradition, is 'having nothing to do with religion' or 'autonomous of religion', and the second is 'not juridically related to the Church but still Catholic in *ethos*'. For example, a practising Catholic who holds a position in society as a medical doctor is described as having a 'secular' vocation. This does not however mean that the person's vocation is in no sense influenced by his or her faith. Similarly, a Catholic politician whose faith informs his or her voting behaviour has a 'secular' vocation but is not promoting 'secularism'. The burden of those Thomists who seek a political *rapprochement* with the Liberal tradition is that of explaining why a proponent of the Liberal tradition will ever accept a political philosophy which opposes the concept of a 'secular' order in the first 'liberal' sense of the term.

In his reflections on the Council, Maritain defended the openness of *Gaudium et spes* to the culture of the modern world on the ground that it overcame a certain 'Manichaean' attitude within the Tridentine Church, according to which the Church was all good and the world outside her institutions all bad. However, Maritain also acknowledged that post-Conciliar Catholicism exhibited a tendency towards the 'temporalization of Christianity' and a habit of 'kneeling before the world'.[88] He did not however link these tendencies to the concepts of the 'autonomy of the secular' or 'autonomy of culture'. One may, however, argue that any affirmation of the 'autonomy of the secular' or the 'autonomy of culture' is fraught with philosophical and theological complexity, and, in particular, that a 'plain meaning' interpretation carries within it an implicit extrinsicism in the interpretation of the nature and grace relationship, which has ultimately fostered the 'temporalization of Christianity'. The tendency to market Christianity by reference to its 'relevance' for the world, rather than explaining its rôle in the salvation of the soul, is ultimately counter-productive. The prophetic mission of the Church, which includes its responsibility for the evangelisation of whole societies, becomes increasingly marginalised. No public relations campaign driven by spin-doctors is able to substitute for the witness of saints.

Conclusion

Whereas O'Malley has blamed the lack of any consistent theoretical foundation for *aggiornamento* for the creation of the explosive problematic of Vatican II, an objective of this chapter has been to demonstrate that one major element in this problematic is the lack of precision regarding the use of the concepts of 'culture' and the 'modern world' and, further, that, at a more fundamental level, a theological framework was required which was sufficiently sophisticated to place the concept of culture within the context of the grace–nature relationship. This is essential if the Conciliar documents are to be interpreted in a manner consistent with the Church's own tradition, broadly construed, and to engage intellectually proponents of the Genealogical and Encyclopaedist traditions. The necessity for the first of these objectives was acknowledged by Henri de Lubac as early as 1968:

> A council need not speak of everything. Even what it does speak about need not be based on theological theories worked out beforehand and tested for rational coherence ... The *Pastoral Constitution on the Church in the Modern World* is no exception to this general rule.[89]

One does not have to agree with de Lubac that theological theories need not be tested for rational coherence before being applied by Councils of the Church to conclude that such a statement from so eminent a scholar and Conciliar *peritus* is evidence of the need for a theological hermeneutic of culture for interpreting documents such as *Gaudium et spes* and the culture of the modern world in general. Barth's question needs to be answered: 'Accommodation to what?'

A similar admission that the fathers of the Second Vatican Council lacked an adequate theological hermeneutic of culture was made by Karl Rahner at a conference in Cambridge in 1979. After drawing an analogy between the decisive break in the transition from Jewish to Gentile Christianity at the Council of Jerusalem in 49 AD, and the decisive break in the transition from pre-Conciliar to post-Conciliar Catholicism after the Second Vatican Council, Rahner commented:

> Today, as a matter of fact, perhaps even in contrast to patristic and medieval theology, we do not have a clear, reflective theology of this break, this new beginning of Christianity with Paul as its inaugurator ... And yet I would venture the thesis that today we are experiencing a break such as occurred only once before, that is, in the transition from Jewish to Gentile Christianity ... such transitions happen for the most part and in the final analysis, unreflectively; they are not first planned out theologically and then put into effect.[90]

Although one may agree with Rahner that the Second Vatican Council effected a radical caesura with the culture of pre-Conciliar Catholicism of such proportions as to justify an analogy with the Council of Jerusalem, the question of the prudence of such a transition arises, given that, as Rahner acknowledged, there existed no developed theological framework in which to examine the various 'pastoral strategies' adopted. Rahner concluded his reflections with the comment that the Conciliar fathers acted unreflectively, according to the 'hidden instinct of the Spirit and of grace that remains mysterious'.[91] However, this is a type of blind trust in the prudential judgements of pastors that has never been demanded by Catholic doctrine. One may take the position that elements of the pre-Conciliar framework, including cultural practices, were in need of reform, without passively subjecting oneself to pastoral strategies formulated in theological vacuums according to 'a grace that remains mysterious'. As Aquinas argued, the virtue of prudence demands foresight, caution, circumspection, memory, reason and understanding, among other dispositions, all of which require deep reflection. In this context, the exercise of such reason and understanding and other actions of the intellect would at least require as a framework for analysis some basic outline of a theology of culture. Both Rahner and de Lubac acknowledge that this was completely missing, or at least something undeveloped to be considered after the Council. Moreover, the position of the Church vis-à-vis Judaism is a very different issue from that of the stance of the Church in relation to modernity. For the analogy with the Council of Jerusalem to hold, there needs to have been a decisive event analogous to the Incarnation. Arguably, the cultural revolution of the post-war period, though socially traumatic, was no such decisive event. In the absence of any express theological analysis of the culture of modernity, the endorsement of it as a historical 'given', whose existence must simply be accepted as a 'must be' to which the Church must accommodate her pastoral practices and even, according to some interpretations, her ecclesiology, remains a problematic within theological thought and practice that cannot be defended by high-sounding references to the 'spirit of the Council'. The following chapter therefore examines the manner in which post-Conciliar magisterial thought has begun to engage with this problematic by a belated recognition of the *theological* significance of culture.

2

'CULTURE' WITHIN POST-CONCILIAR MAGISTERIAL THOUGHT

Introduction

A recognition of the theological significance of culture has become a dominant theme in post-Conciliar magisterial thought, beginning with Paul VI's Apostolic Exhortation *Evangelii Nuntiandi* (1975) and running through John Paul II's encyclicals, homilies and public addresses. Although there has been very little qualification of the principle of the 'autonomy of culture', there has been a recognition of the significance of culture for moral formation, and, in particular, the problem of the secularisation of culture for the flourishing of Christian practices. This is reflected in the statement of Bishop Rino Fisichella of the Lateran University that the relationship between the gospel and cultures is no less than the 'oceanic problem' of the day.[1] The purpose of this chapter is therefore to examine the treatment of culture in post-Conciliar magisterial thought, especially in relation to the issue of the culture of modernity.

The split between the gospel and culture

Within 2 years of the conclusion of the Council, Maritain wrote of the tendency of Catholic scholars to 'kneel before the world', and the problem of secularism within the Church was acknowledged prior to the conclusion of the Council by Paul VI.[2] In the encyclical *Ecclesiam Suam*, Paul VI criticised those who 'think that the reform of the Church should consist principally in adapting its way of thinking and acting to the customs and temper of the modern secular world'; and observed that this 'craving for uniformity' – between the thinking of scholars within the Church and the ideas of those outside the Church – is observable even in the realm of philosophy and especially in ethics.[3] He reiterated the Gospel counsel to be 'in the world but not of it'.

A decade later, in 1975, in his Apostolic Exhortation *Evangelii Nuntiandi*, Paul VI acknowledged that the modern world seems to be 'for ever immersed in what a modern author has termed 'the drama of atheistic humanism'.[4] This is a reference to de Lubac's 1944 work, *Le Drame de l'humanisme athée*.

However, in the same paragraph he also affirmed *Gaudium et spes* paragraph 59 (the 'autonomy of culture'), defining it as a 'legitimate secularism' according to which one discovers 'in creation, in each thing or each happening in the universe, the laws which regulate them with a certain autonomy, but with the inner conviction that the Creator has placed these laws there'. This 'affirmation', which appears to be having it both ways – that is, an endorsement of *both* de Lubac and Rahner – raises the question: 'What kind of autonomy is it that is regulated by divinely ordained laws?' Further, it leaves unanswered the question of whether the divinely ordained laws remain beyond further acts of Providence. And what, if any, effect did the Incarnation have on such laws? The most that one may conclude from this treatment is that Paul VI understood that the relationship of theology to culture, and thus of grace to nature, is the central issue, but he did not adjudicate between the positions offered by de Lubac and Rahner. His *modus operandi* seems to have been to try to avoid taking sides in the dispute and to make positive comments about both positions. This means that there is no magisterial resolution of the 'crisis' created within the tradition by the existence of different and apparently mutually contradictory accounts of the relationship between nature and grace. Speaking of the passages in *Gaudium et spes* referring to the autonomy of culture and of 'earthly affairs', and juxtaposing this notion, however construed, with the Christocentric hermeneutic of paragraph 22, Walter Nicgorski has observed:

> The critical eye wants to know what kind of independence this is that is so thoroughly and deeply dependent; and as for the autonomy of culture of the sciences and disciplines, what kind of autonomy is it that if taken seriously produces unintelligibility? The critical eye begins to suspect that faith embraces the modern world at the price of speaking out of both sides of the mouth and that a deep tension, if not contradiction, is involved here.[5]

The corollary of Barth's question 'Accommodation to what?' is 'Autonomy from what?'

Side-stepping such questions and without passing judgement on the conceptual tools one might use in a theological study of culture, Paul VI nonetheless concluded that:

> The split between the Gospel and culture is undoubtedly the tragedy of our time ... I have maintained that a faith that does not affect a person's culture is a faith not fully embraced, not entirely thought out, not faithfully lived.[6]

This 'split between the Gospel and culture' becomes, in the papacy of John Paul II, the dichotomy between the 'civilisation of love' and the 'culture of death'.[7] The latter is characterised by a rejection of truth, beauty and goodness as transcendental properties of being, and a concomitant failure to recognise the sanctity of human life and human relations in favour of the 'Nietzschean values' of personal autonomy, self-assertion and the consequent instrumentalisation of social relations. Alternatively, the 'civilisation of love' requires as its cornerstone the recognition that 'Jesus Christ, the Redeemer of Man, is the centre and purpose of human history', and therefore the humanity in which he shares is worthy of reverence, not domination and exploitation. This principle was enunciated in the very first sentence of *Redemptor Hominis* and is widely regarded as John Paul II's shot across the bows of the Marxists for whom the first sentence in Marx's *Communist Manifesto* asserts that the dynamic of world history is class struggle. Such a Christocentric theological sociology is required because of the Pope's judgement that secular humanism cannot prevent the descent to nihilism. On this point John Paul II is in agreement with Nietzsche.[8]

The Christocentrism of John Paul II

The intensely Christocentric orientation of John Paul II's publications includes frequent references to paragraph 22 of *Gaudium et spes*, which begins with the following statement:

> The truth is that only in the mystery of the incarnate Word does the mystery of man take on light. For Adam, the first man, was a figure of Him who was to come, namely Christ the Lord. Christ, the final Adam, by the revelation of the mystery of the Father, and His Love, fully reveals man to man himself and makes his supreme calling clear. It is not surprising, then, that in Him all the aforementioned truths find their root and attain their crown.[9]

This is the most Christocentric paragraph in the entire document, and it stands out against the 'teminologically loose' and 'terminologically Pelagian' paragraphs that were mentioned in Chapter 1 of this book. Indeed, David Schindler, among others, has suggested that this paragraph should be treated as the hermeneutical key to the rest of the document.[10] Its explicit Christocentrism 'changes the meaning of *aggiornamento* and indeed of modern political and economic achievements'.[11] Far from fostering some version of extrinsicism, the adoption of the Christocentric theme of paragraph 22 as the hermeneutical key to the document has the effect of distinguishing between 'autonomy' in an ontological sense and 'autonomy' in a juridical sense. In effect, it means that, while the natural and social sciences and the arts may be 'autonomous' in the sense that they are not the subject of ecclesiastical governance, they are not 'autonomous' in the sense of having their own frames of reference external to the theology of the Incarnation. Thus

Schindler argues that the root meaning of the *iusta* or *legitima autonomia* of *Gaudium et spes* finds its proper meaning in an analogy of being based on the descent of God into the world, that is on the relationship between the Trinity and the creature established in Jesus Christ.[12] Support for such a reading of these otherwise opaque or apparently contradictory paragraphs of *Gaudium et spes* can be found in paragraph 50 of John Paul II's encyclical *Dominum et Vivificantem:*

> The Incarnation of God the Son signifies the taking up into the unity with God not only of human nature, but in this human nature, in a sense, of everything that is 'flesh': the whole of humanity, the entire visible and material world. The Incarnation then, also has a cosmic significance, a cosmic dimension. The 'first-born of all creation', becoming incarnate in the individual humanity of Christ, unites himself in some way with the entire reality of man, which is 'flesh' – and in this reality with all 'flesh', with the whole of creation.[13]

Although the Word made Flesh is, to use von Balthasar's terminology, 'the concrete universal', this 'concrete universal' needs to be made visible within the world. There needs, therefore, to be a communication of this Word to the world, and this communication is the mission of the Church. The Church is thus 'the Universal Sacrament of Salvation'. Cultures, understood in the *Kultur* sense, are the subject of this mediation and have the potential in turn to become epiphanies of God's glory. The *logoi* which give form to some *Kulturen*, however, make them inept or even hostile to the instantiation of the glory of the Incarnation, that is hostile to any attempt of the Church to mediate the grace of the Incarnation to the world. Hence the International Theological Commission under the leadership of Cardinal Ratzinger has drawn together the Christocentric anthropology of paragraph 22 of *Gaudium et spes*, and the seminal rôle of the Holy Spirit in revealing the truths of the Incarnation as per *Dominum et Vivificantem* in the following statement of principle:

> In the 'last times' inaugurated at Pentecost, the risen Christ, Alpha and Omega, enters into the history of peoples: from that moment, the sense of history and thus of culture is unsealed and the Holy Spirit reveals it by actualizing and communicating it to all. The Church is the sacrament of this revelation and its communication. It recenters every culture into which Christ is received, placing it in the axis of the 'world which is coming' and restores the union broken by the 'prince of this world'. Culture is thus eschatologically situated; it tends toward its completion in Christ, but it cannot be saved except by associating itself with the repudiation of evil.[14]

Such a perspective stands in dramatic juxtaposition to the Lercaro interpretation of the Church's 'cultural poverty'. Since 'culture tends towards its completion in Christ', the Church, as the Spouse of Christ (Ephesians 5:22) and the Universal Sacrament of Salvation (*Lumen Gentium* paragraph 48), is the mediator of Christ to the world, and hence of Christ to culture and through culture. Without such mediation, cultures will be formed according to different 'logics': they may become, to use the terminology of Albert Dondeyne, 'democratised', or they may be elite in some neo-pagan sense, such as the various twentieth-century totalitarianisms.

The culture of death and the Liberal tradition

In the 1999 Report of the Pontifical Council for Culture entitled 'Towards a Pastoral Approach to Culture', the authors of the document, under the leadership of Cardinal Paul Poupard, continued to tie the Christocentric theme to the issue of culture, but they indicated that aspects of the modern world are resistant to being given such an eschatological orientation.[15] To some degree, the 'axis' remains 'broken by the prince of this world'. On this occasion the authors made reference to John Paul II's vision of a 'Christian cultural project', the objective of which is to open the 'vast fields of culture' to Christ, the 'Redeemer of Man, and Centre and Purpose of Human History'.[16] However, in contradistinction to the values of this project, they summarised the values of what they called the 'cultural situation which prevails in different parts of the world today' as a subjectivist account of truth, the questioning of the positivist presuppositions about the progress of science and technology, an anthropocentric pragmatic atheism and blatant religious indifference.[17] Those who live within this cultural situation not only contend with values that are hostile to theism, but, in addition, if they live in the outer suburbs of densely populated and sprawling cities, have a tendency to be 'socially rootless, politically powerless, economically marginalised, culturally isolated, and easy prey for dehumanising business practices'.[18] Theistic values, to the extent that they still survive, are confined to the private sphere, and the culture so described is a 'culture of death'. As John Paul II stated in a speech to the scholars of Lublin University:

> The reduction inherent in the Enlightenment view of man, of 'man in the world', to the dimensions of an absolute immanence of man in relation to the world, ushers in not only Nietzsche's issue of the death of God, but the prospect of the death of man who in such a materialistic vision of reality does not in the final eschatological sense have any possibilities other than those objects of the visible order.[19]

Significantly, the authors of the Pontifical Council for Culture document make reference to John Paul II's statement in *Veritatis Splendor* paragraph 88 that 'believers themselves often employ criteria in decision-making which are extraneous or even contrary to those of the Gospel'.[20] This statement not only reiterates the observation of Paul VI that the tragedy of our time is the split between the Gospel and culture, but adds to this a knowledge of the fact that this split exists even within the lives of Christians and, by extension, ostensibly Christian institutions. Unfortunately, neither Paul VI nor John Paul II addresses the question of the historical cause of this split, and in particular the possibility that the treatment of 'culture' in *Gaudium et spes* may itself have contributed to the secularisation of Catholic culture (*Kultur*), the ethos (*Geist*) of the Church's pastoral institutions and the kind of self-formation (*Bildung*) fostered by the same pastoral institutions.

In one brief section of the Pontifical Council for Culture document, reference is made to Liberalism as the 'rival ideology' to collectivist atheist Marxism–Leninism, and to its 'struggling' to 'bring about happiness for the human race and to ensure responsible dignity for each person'.[21] There is however no consideration of the issue of to what extent this rival ideology is itself responsible for the values associated with the 'culture of death'. In other words, it is not clear from this document or the Pope's own statements whether he regards Liberalism as the ideology of individualist atheism, that is the obverse side to Marxism–Leninism's collectivist atheism, or whether he gives the ideology a more benign interpretation. Although John Paul II has been critical of all the major streams of Liberal ethical theory (utilitarianism, consequentialism and pragmatism) and aspects of Liberal economic and political philosophy ('economism' and the doctrine of the ethical neutrality of the state), an intellectual engagement with Liberalism *as a tradition* (understood in a MacIntyrean sense) remains a lacuna within the vast body of his publications.[22] Rather, when one pieces together all the various criticisms of individual elements of the Liberal tradition to be found within the works of John Paul II, which are quite extensive, what remains is a deference to the rhetoric of Liberal democracy, particularly the use of the natural rights discourse, coupled with a tendency to attempt to impregnate the democratic ideals and 'rights' with a Christian substance.[23] It is as if what is being presented is, in substance, 'Christian Democracy', but marketed by recourse to the rhetoric of the Liberal tradition. Thus, in rhetorical form 'Liberal' but in substance 'Christian'.

When Liberalism is examined as a tradition, it is not possible to escape the observation that its development is in part related to the theology of the Protestant reformers, particularly to their constructions of the relationship between the sacred and the secular. In his doctoral work on the concepts of culture and church in the teaching of John Paul II, Francis George observes that what seems to be missing in the discussions and homilies of the Pope on his visits to Germany and Britain is 'the recognition that people who are Catholic in faith might also in some sense be Protestant in culture'.[24] Implicit within this observation is the idea that there is a specifically Catholic form or forms of culture and a Protestant form or forms of culture. It is precisely a recognition of the existence of such a dichotomy that dominated the scholarship of Max Weber and Christopher Dawson, although each gave a different value to the two cultures so described.[25] It is also a position that may be found in the thought of lesser-known scholars, including the pre-War Polish sociologist Feliks Koneczny, and the Austrian sociologist Werner Stark.[26] In defining the essential properties of Protestant and Catholic cultures, Dawson adopted Werner Sombart's categories of the 'bourgeois' and the 'erotic'.[27] According to Sombart, the 'erotic' type par excellence was the 'man of desire', such as Francis of Assisi or Augustine of Hippo. In Dawson's thought, 'erotic' cultures are characterised by a passionate quest for the achievement of spiritual perfection, whereas 'bourgeois' cultures are characterised by an instrumental rationality and the priority of economic concerns.[28] Given such a choice of types, Dawson concluded that the Gospel is 'essentially hostile to the spirit of calculation, the spirit of worldly prudence and above all the spirit of self-seeking and self-satisfaction', and, indeed, that the Pharisee is the archetypical 'spiritual bourgeois'.[29]

John Paul II's call for a 'civilisation of love' based upon a Christocentric anthropology and thus a conception of culture that is 'eschatologically situated' can be transposed into Dawson's terminology as a call for a re-eroticisation of *Kultur*, or in Weber's terminology a 're-enchantment' of *Kultur*. The issue to which the comments of Francis George draw attention is that Protestant cultures are by this sociological definition non-erotic. They were founded upon the reformers' severance of reality into the categories of the secular and sacred and the consequent tendency of the 'secular' to be perceived to be 'autonomous' of theology, that is unhinged from the grace of the Incarnation. The whole tradition of Liberalism is built upon these divisions, and this is one of the reasons that, as MacIntyre argues, there needs to be an engagement between the Thomist and Liberal traditions on the plain of the cultural embodiment of their principles, rather than a mere comparison of the content of select concepts or theses.

Francis George concludes his survey of John Paul II's thought on the subject of culture in Germany and Britain with the observation that the 'possibility that Protestant cultures might model one way of linking the Gospel to modernity' which is different from Catholic cultural models is unexplored.[30] This in turn highlights one of the central issues of this work: can the culture of modernity be a *praeparatio evangelii* or *praeambula fidei* in the manner that Clement of Alexandria regarded Greek philosophy and classical culture, or is there something about its very form which makes it hostile to the instantiation of Catholic tradition? In concrete terms the question becomes: is it possible to synthesise aspects of the Liberal tradition to Thomism without fostering an *ethos* and/or *Kultur* within which Catholics become 'Catholic in faith, Protestant in culture'?

There is however evidence to suggest that, although John Paul II has not offered what Charles Taylor might classify as a 'cultural critique of modernity', which would necessarily include a genealogy of the Liberal tradition, his juxtaposition of the concepts 'culture of death' and 'civilisation of love' would certainly indicate that his thought is tending in this direction. Early in his pontificate, in *Dominum et Vivificantem* paragraph 56, John Paul II stated:

> Unfortunately, the resistance to the Holy Spirit which Saint Paul emphasizes in the *interior and subjective dimension* as tension, struggle and rebellion taking place in the human heart finds in every period of history and especially in the modern era its *external dimension*, which takes concrete form as the content of culture and civilization, as a *philosophical system*, an ideology, *a programme* for action and for the shaping of human behaviour.

Dominum et Vivificantem was published in 1986, before the implosion of European Communism, at a time in John Paul II's papacy when maximum effort was being given to the task of critiquing and destroying the philosophical system(s) of Marxism, its programmes for action and external dimensions. John Paul II clearly indicates in the above passage that Communism is more than a political philosophy – that it is an entire philosophical system or ideology which had taken a concrete form as the content of a particular culture, understood as *Kultur*, or civilization. The question that thus arises is whether one can also construe this statement as encompassing a critique of Liberalism as the 'content of culture and civilization' of the Western world – the world which John Paul II now regards as tending towards a 'culture of death'? It is this question that is at the centre of the dispute between the 'Whig Thomists' and the scholars whose postmodern Augustinian Thomist critiques of the culture of modernity will be examined in Part II.

More recently, in *Evangelium Vitae* paragraph 86, John Paul II employed the concept of 'modernity', but in terms that make it unclear whether he understands the concept as a 'cultural formation' or merely as an intellectual movement, whereas in *Tertio Millennio Adveniente* he made reference to the 'challenge of secularism', 'religious indifference' and the 'widespread loss of the transcendent sense of human life'.[31] In the context of this widespread loss, John Paul II further stated that the sons and daughters of the Church need to examine themselves to see to what extent they have been formed by the 'climate of secularism and ethical relativism'.[32] Again however there is no explicit analysis of the relationship between the tradition of Liberalism and the rise of religious indifference and the climate of secularism and ethical relativism, although it could be argued that a direct relationship between the two is implied, or is so obvious that John Paul II has not thought it necessary to emphasise the link.

One statement which would seem to imply a recognition that Liberalism is a culturally embodied tradition such as that criticised in *Dominum et Vivificantem* paragraph 56 is found in *Veritatis Splendor* paragraph 106:

> Today's widespread tendencies towards subjectivism, utilitarianism and relativism appear not merely as pragmatic attitudes or patterns of be-

haviour, but rather as approaches having a basis in theory and claiming full cultural and social legitimacy.[33]

In this statement the 'theory' or 'theories' in which subjectivism, utilitarianism and relativism have their foundation would seem obviously to be components of the Liberal tradition.

Nonetheless, in relation to the 'challenge of secularism', John Paul II states that it must be countered by a civilisation of love, 'founded on the universal values of peace, solidarity, justice and liberty, which find their full attainment in Christ'.[34] The concept of 'universal values' thus reappears and is given a Christocentric orientation without treating the question of whether those who lack a Christocentric orientation would give the same content to those four values as that given them by John Paul II. For example, the concept of *solidarity* finds its closest analogue within the Liberal tradition in the concept of fraternity, but here fraternity is based upon a common citizenship of a given polity, whereas solidarity in the thought of John Paul II is based upon a common theological anthropology derived from the book of Genesis. Similarly, Alasdair MacIntyre has written an entire work on the difference between Thomist and Liberal conceptions of *justice*; the concept of *liberty* differs markedly between those who believe in a natural moral law and those who do not, and Nietzscheans and Aristocratic Liberals disagree with the proposition that *peace* is a universal value, preferring *pathos* instead. As Walter Kasper has acknowledged, 'the systematic clasp holding together anthropology and Christology is the concept of the "image of God"'.[35] Take away the mutual belief in the human person as a creature made in the image of God, and the clasp is unlocked and the universalism falls away. Thus, although these values are in the natural law sense, 'universal', meaning that they are equally applicable to all persons, they are not universal in the sense that their definition or appeal is the same across a range of traditions. This does not undermine their validity in the natural law sense, but it does raise questions about the receptivity of the rival traditions to the definitional content that John Paul II seeks to give them, and the 'self-evidentness' of John Paul II's definitions for those who have been influenced by the values of the rival traditions. In particular, it raises the issue of whether the relationship between the Thomist tradition and the Liberal tradition is, in the terminology of Matthew Lamb, complementary, genetic or dialectical.[36] If the relationship is *complementary* then the traditions are not fundamentally antagonistic, but simply focus on different issues, treatments of which can later be synthesised. A *genetic* relationship is one in which one tradition is further developed or matured than another, and thus there is the possibility that the less developed tradition will 'catch up' with the more mature (in this context the more 'Christian' tradition), whereas a *dialectical* relationship is one of fundamental antagonism.[37] Whereas Whig Thomists see the relationship as in some ways genetic and in others complementary, the proponents of a postmodern Augustinian Thomism see it as dialectical.

In the context of other issues which divide Catholic scholars loyal to the magisterium of John Paul II, Daniel Finn has observed that it is frequently difficult to determine precisely where John Paul II stands, since his style of engagement with controversial questions is to make strong affirmations about goods on both sides of an argument, as well as denunciations about the dangers attendant on each.[38] Finn calls this the habit of using 'antithetical affirmations' and suggests that its merit is that it leaves the issues open for further debate while suggesting areas which require further consideration. However, Marciano Vidal has also observed that the negative aspect of this approach is that it 'renders ordinary interpretative procedures problematic' and 'leaves sharp tensions unresolved'.[39] The following reference to 'modernity' in a 1994 homily provides an example of what Finn calls an 'antithetical affirmation' and illustrates Vidal's argument that this approach leaves the sharp tensions unresolved:

> If by modernity we mean a convergence of conditions that permit a human being to express better his or her own maturity, spiritual, moral and cultural, then the Church of the Council saw itself as the 'soul' of modernity.[40]

The difficulty here is that such a definition of modernity is *sui generis*. If one leaves aside the definition and simply states that John Paul II believes that the Church of the Council saw itself as the 'soul of modernity', then one would be suggesting to almost all persons who had not read the entire sentence that John Paul II is in favour of modernity as it is generally understood in sociological parlance, that is as a mutation, severance or heretical reconstruction of the classical Christian synthesis, or, alternatively, if one follows Blumenberg's reading, a completely original set of socially embodied values to replace those left by the collapse of the classical Christian framework. Such statements not only 'leave the sharp tensions unresolved' and are antithetical affirmations in the sense that one takes a concept and 'affirms' it by giving it a definition antithetical to that normally accorded it, but one also renders such statements vulnerable to being selectively quoted for a polemical purpose.

However, it is clear that John Paul II rejects the Rahnerian idea that the rampant secularism in contemporary Western culture is a 'must be' in the sense that the cross was a 'must be' and Bernard Lambert's judgement that 'secularisation carries through the logical development of creation'. Such positions cannot be upheld against the theological sociology of *Redemptor Hominis,* which is based on the principle that 'Jesus Christ, the Redeemer of Man, is the Centre and Purpose of Human History', or against the numerous references to the 'challenge of secularism' scattered throughout his encyclicals and public speeches. For John Paul II 'secularism' is clearly fostered by the 'prince of this world' and is in some measure related to Liberalism.

Moreover, it can be argued that his expression 'the culture of death' is but a synonym for the cultural embodiment of the principles of the Liberal tradition combined with those of the Genealogical, and that there is nothing to be found in the corpus of John Paul II's publications which could be construed as recommending a synthesis of the *substance* of the Liberal and Thomist traditions.

The Greco-Latin heritage

In a recent encyclical of John Paul II, *Fides et ratio*, he again touches on questions that relate to the issue of the culture of modernity but without directly relating them to this problematic. In paragraph 72 he counsels against the strategy of jettisoning the Church's classical cultural heritage, that is her 'pre-modern' heritage:

> In engaging great cultures for the first time the Church cannot abandon what she has gained from her inculturation in the world of Greco-Latin thought. To reject this heritage would be to deny the providential plan of God who guides His Church down the paths of time and history.[41]

Unfortunately, John Paul II did not develop this idea beyond the above paragraph, by, for example, providing an account of what he believes are the indispensable elements for the Church in Greco-Latin thought and culture. Nonetheless, it is clear that he does not accept Cardinal Lercaro's idea of throwing the heritage overboard.

The contrary idea of abandoning 'what the Church gained from her inculturation in the world of Greco-Latin thought' represents, in summary, the position advocated in the immediate post-Conciliar era by Bernard Lonergan and John Courtney Murray, among others. Lonergan and John Courtney Murray were critical of the Thomist tradition's alleged 'classicism', according to which 'culture is encapsulated in the universal, the normative, the ideal, and the immutable', at the alleged expense of 'historical consciousness' understood as 'consciousness of the diversity, development and decay of cultures'.[42] According to Lonergan, classicism's idea of culture is normative, whereas the approach of 'historical consciousness' is empirical.

Leaving aside the issue of the merit of this dichotomy, including, of course, the question of why an account of culture cannot be both normative and empirical, the more immediately significant issue underlying the criticism of 'classicism' is the problem raised by the 'culture of America'. The 'American experiment', defined as a polity founded upon an alleged severance of the relationships between Church and State, theology and political philosophy, and the consequent marginalisation of religious questions to the 'private domain', created a theological problematic which was not envisaged within the classical theistic traditions. The proponents of the idea that the 'culture of America' and the Catholic tradition are compatible tend to prefer what Lonergan called the 'approach of historical consciousness' to the normativity of the classical traditions. This opens up the possibility that superior cultural orders may arise in the future – for example, the 'culture of America' – that were not foreshadowed in the classical traditions.

More generally, the 'anti-classicist' position is based upon a version of the following three propositions:

1   the classical era is over and the Church must accommodate herself to the culture of modernity;
2   classical Greco-Latin culture is Eurocentric and its imposition upon non-Europeans is a form of cultural imperialism; and
3   *Gaudium et spes* is authority for the idea that the ideal of a universal Christian culture has been abandoned and as a consequence each national group should have its own unique indigenous culture.

The third proposition embodies both the first and the second.

A recognition of the influence of the first proposition – though not an endorsement – may be found in recent statements of Cardinal Ambrozic, a member of the Pontifical Council for Culture. Underpinning the proposition is a latent Hegelianism. Ambrozic characterises the practical consequences of this mentality as 'an ungodly rush to christianise prevalent trends, revealing both a kind of inferiority complex on the part of Christians' and the 'humiliating act of subjecting Christian claims to the criteria of Kant's man come of age'.[43] Ambrozic concludes that the proponents of credal Christianity have been fighting a rearguard action for three centuries, and questions the prudence of a strategy that relies on the ability of Catholic intellectuals to defend the faith at the bar of modernity. Although Ambrozic does not explicitly say so, he implies that a better strategy may lie in a rejection of modernity's jurisdiction. In other words, why must we accept an account of rationality, and a culture built upon it, that expressly excludes Revelation?

In relation to the second proposition, that of the alleged Eurocentrism of Greco-Latin culture, the logic of John Paul II's statement in *Fides et ratio* is that, notwithstanding the geographical provenance of this culture, it retains a value for people of all societies, since one of its fundamental properties was its universalism. This is because Greco-Latin culture can in part be defined by its quest for the achievement of a universal culture that transcends social particularities in its recognition of a common humanity, but simultaneously respects that which is unique and good in different communities. In this manner, Ratzinger argues that Christian missionaries from Sts Cyril, Methodius and Boniface onwards have introduced peoples 'not to Greek culture as such, but rather to its capacity for self-transcendence'.[44] Such a position differs from that of Rousseau and Herder and other Romantics in that it includes as a premise the principle that cultural artefacts and practices can be judged to be worthy of promotion, or alternatively in need of rejection, according to the degree to which they embody the transcendental properties of the true, the good and the beautiful. This means that the Greco-Latin account of culture is normative, but it is also empirical in the sense that individual cultures can be empirically studied by reference to such transcultural standards or norms. There may therefore be a plurality of 'good cultures' operating within the architectonic norms of Greco-Latin culture. Moreover, John Paul II endorses the argument which was formerly emphasised by von Balthasar, that it was part of the plan of Providence that the Church be inculturated into Greco-Latin culture, for elements of that culture were a necessary *praeparatio evangelii*, whereas the whole cultural order of the Jews, including their rites, their laws and their monotheism, was a necessary *praeambula fidei*.[45]

The third proposition however is by far the strongest, as *Gaudium et spes* clearly uses the language of what Outler called 'the sociocentric perspectives on culture and cultural diversity that ran from Vico through Herder to Tyler and on into contemporary sociology and anthropology'. Again this highlights the fact that the authors of *Gaudium et spes* required a theological hermeneutic of culture so as to mediate between the normative 'classicist' model of culture and ideas to be found within the body of contemporary empirical sociological and anthropological scholarship. The fact that John Paul II has found the need to reaffirm the indispensability of the Church's 'Greco-Latin' heritage, and that Ratzinger has sought to emphasise that it was not a mere historical accident which determined that Christendom was in part built upon Greco-Latin foundations, but rather that the Church found classical culture's capacity for self-transcendence to be congenial to her own ideals, may be taken as an indication that this particular problematic thrown up by the treatment of culture in *Gaudium et spes* has been recognised at the magisterial level. It remains however to be considered in greater depth what the 'indispensable elements' of Greco-Latin thought and culture are.

In any such investigation, one important issue will be that of the rôle of Latin as the *lingua franca* of the Church. In his Apostolic Constitution *Veterum Sapientia* of 1962, John XXIII endorsed the use of Latin not merely as a passport to a proper understanding of the Christian writers of antiquity, or from a desire for bureaucratic uniformity, but as an element of the Church's tradition which is valuable for '*religious* reasons'. Following Pius XI, who held his own investigation into this issue, John XXIII argued that the Church, precisely because she embraces all nations and is destined to endure until the end of time, of her very nature requires a language which is *universal*, *immutable* and *non-vernacular*.[46] The use of a 'dead language' privileges no particular national group but unites all in a common linguistic tradition. Moreover, John XXIII argued that it is altogether fitting that the language of the Church should be noble and majestic and non-vernacular since the Church has a dignity far surpassing that of every merely human society.[47] Just as some vessels are put aside and consecrated for use in a liturgical context, so too, the argument runs, are certain forms of expression.

Within 6 years of the promulgation of *Veterum Sapientia*, Paul VI had reached the conclusion that this particular element of the Greco-Latin heritage could be thrown overboard, as it were, because although he acknowledged that the use of the vernacular means 'parting with the speech of Christian centuries' and 'becoming like profane intruders in the literary precincts of sacred utterance', nonetheless he was persuaded that 'modern people are fond of plain language which is easily understood and converted into everyday speech'.[48] The primary reason for the U-turn on this issue was thus not a rejection of any of the arguments given by Pius XI or John XXIII, but rather a judgement that these 'goods' were not as necessary as the deference to the modern preference for 'plain language'. Pastoral pragmatism had demanded that 'modern man's' preferences for the plain and profane be indulged.

Since the late 1960s, however, there has been a growing body of scholarship that is critical of the use of contemporary 'plain language' in a liturgical context. For example, Joseph Ratzinger has argued that the trend towards 'bringing God down to the level of the people' fosters self-centricity and the worship of the community as an end in itself, and that this practice is analogous to the Hebrew's worship of the golden calf, which was nothing less than apostasy.[49] Aidan Nichols describes the phenomenon as the 'de-railing of the theocentric act of worship onto the sidelines of social edification and group psychological therapy'.[50] H. J. Burbach has developed the argument that 'Sacro-pop' liturgical music and language, while posing as *avant-garde*, is the product of a '*dirigiste* mass culture' that reproduces the cheap taste of the low-brow consumer public and thus alienates those who seek an experience of transcendence in the liturgy.[51] Catherine Pickstock has argued that if the liturgical 'experts' wish to be relevant to the needs of those who live within the culture of modernity they would do well to 'overthrow our anti-ritual modernity, or, that being impossible, devise a liturgy that *refused* to be enculturated in our modern habits of thought and speech'.[52] Glenn W. Olsen has observed that 'to accept that the language of the liturgy should be taken from profane life is already to accept the notion that our lives are normally profane by nature', and that 'even more mischievous is the notion that the only good liturgy is a "rational" liturgy, that is, one in which symbolization is reduced in favour of explicit unambiguous meaning'.[53] The flaw in the latter mentality is that it undermines the proper orientation of liturgy towards mystery, that is the things which surpass rationalization. David Torevell concludes that the liturgical reforms were partly influenced by the prevalent cultural and social assumptions of modernity which first privilege the mind over the body and then locate all meaning in the mind of the subject, and partly from a lack of a sociological understanding of the nature of ritual which includes, as an essential element, the use of words and actions which are different from the ordinary or 'every day'.[54]

Implicit within these arguments is a critique of a number of different elements of the culture of modernity, including the tendency towards lowest common denominator cultural standards, the instrumentalist account of language, the project of a thoroughly rationalistic 'Christianity', the disjunction of form and substance and hence symbol and meaning, the severance of the relationships between memory, tradition and transcendence, the lop-sided emphasis on the immanence of God at the expense of His transcendence and the destruction of the *perichoresis* of the transcendentals. If liturgical norms are not formulated within a framework of a theology of culture which includes the notion that liturgy and 'high culture' go together because we offer only our best to God, then the liturgical life of the Church is wide open to what Gabriel Motzkin, a Jewish scholar of modernity, describes as 'emotional primitivism'.[55] In other words, 'emotional primitivism' is the logical consequence of an implicitly Rousseauian account of culture, including liturgical culture, which privileges the ordinary, everyday, mundane and uneducated. This is ultimately not even pastorally pragmatic since it has no appeal to the educated members of the Church and is just 'more of the same' for those described by the Pontifical Council for Culture as 'socially rootless, politically powerless, economically marginalised and culturally isolated'.

Although these criticisms of the demise of Latin in the life of the Church, particularly her liturgical life, are by no means exhaustive of the list which could be compiled, they at least indicate that the principles of *Veterum Sapientia* may ultimately find themselves vindicated at the bar of history. At a 2002 conference called to mark the fortieth anniversary of the promulgation of *Veterum Sapientia*, John Paul II referred to a knowledge of Latin as the 'indispensable condition for a proper relationship between modernity and antiquity, for dialogue among cultures, and for reaffirming the identity of the Catholic priesthood'.[56] Given this statement it would seem reasonable to conclude that John Paul II regards the Latin language as at least one of the 'indispensable elements' of Greco-Latin thought and culture.

Conclusion

The most important issue remains whether it is part of the plan of Providence that the Church accommodate her practices to the culture of modernity through an assimilation or synthesis of elements of the Liberal tradition with Thomism. Since the publication of *Gaudium et spes*, the Popes and the magisterium as a whole have not committed themselves to addressing this specific question. Nonetheless, John Paul II's publications lend weight to the argument that Liberalism, like Marxism, may be construed as a 'philosophical system, an ideology, a program for action and for the shaping of human behaviour' which is hostile to theism in general, and the Thomist tradition in particular. Indeed, one way of construing his pontificate is to suggest that the first decade was focused on the problem of Marxism, whereas the second decade was focused on the problem of Liberalism, especially the moral and theological versions thereof. However, it also clear that John Paul II is not opposed to the idea of borrowing elements of the conceptual apparatus of these two rival traditions, and in this sense he appears to be adopting a strategy which might be described as the 'Blumenberg legitimacy thesis' *in reverse*. Whereas Hans Blumenberg argued that the culture of modernity has legitimacy because it is not, as MacIntyre, Milbank, Pickstock, Cavanaugh, Taylor and others have argued, the result of mutations, severances, heretical reconstructions and secular parodies of the classical theistic concepts, but is rather the re-occupation of defunct classical theistic concepts by thoroughly original modern ideas; John Paul II's strategy seems to be one of evacuating popular concepts such as 'liberation' and 'rights' of their modern content (whether construed as thoroughly original *à la* Blumenberg, or severed, mutated and heretical *à la* MacIntyre, Taylor, Cavanaugh, Milbank and Pickstock) and then refilling them with a Christian content. If this reading of the strategy is accurate, then John Paul II's project is not that of Whig Thomism, or even a genetic reading of the relationship between Liberalism and Thomism, but is a project which seeks to transform one tradition (Liberalism) from its roots, as it were, by transfusing a new Christocentric anthropology and eschatology into the constituent conceptual elements of the tradition. The merit of this strategy depends upon how one understands the transmission of knowledge and meaning, particularly the rôle of a narrative tradition, and other issues in linguistic philosophy. These issues will be taken up in Part III.

By reference to the work of scholars whose insights, it will be argued, constitute a postmodern Augustinian Thomism, Part II seeks to defend the proposition that Liberalism is a 'philosophical system, ideology and programme for action' hostile to Thomism, through an analysis of the Liberal tradition's embodiment within the culture of modernity. Each chapter of Part II therefore deals with one of the three subdivisions of the cultural embodiment of principles identified in Chapter 1 as *Geist*, *Bildung* and *Kultur*, and the 'explosive problematic' created by their treatment in *Gaudium et spes*. In particular, Chapter 5 provides a reading of the form of the culture of modernity that is heavily reliant upon de Lubac's argument that 'no culture is really neutral'. In it, there is an implicit denial of the popular construction of the 'autonomy of culture' concept; instead, it fosters the interpretation that while the Church acknowledges that there are 'laws of nature', she also holds they have been affected not merely efficiently and finally but also formally by Christ.

Part II

MODERNITY AND THE THOMIST TRADITION

3

THE EPISTEMIC AUTHORITY OF 'EXPERTS' AND THE *ETHOS* OF MODERN INSTITUTIONS

Since the specific issue of whether the culture of modernity is or can be another *praeparatio evangelii* continues to be a subject of controversy within the Thomist tradition, and thus represents an example of what MacIntyre calls an 'epistemological crisis' – an issue that retards the development of the tradition until it is resolved – each chapter in Part II presents arguments in favour of the case that the culture of modernity is in fact hostile to the instantiation of the principles of the Thomist tradition. Whereas those Thomists who favour a more positive reading of modernity and who seek to synthesise elements of the Liberal tradition to Thomism are marshalling their arguments behind the banner of Whig Thomism, those who take the view that the relationship between the Liberal tradition and Thomism is dialectical rather than complementary or genetic have not organised themselves into a particular school. Nor are their arguments against the culture of modernity organised in a systematic manner. Each chapter in Part II therefore represents an attempt to marshal the various critiques into a more systematic synthesis. The synthesis is labelled a postmodern Augustinian Thomism for reasons which have been given in the introduction, and it is submitted that, in the absence of any self-labelling by its proponents, this expression encapsulates the substance of the arguments that have been advanced by individual scholars against the presuppositions of Whig Thomism. Further, in each chapter of Part II, the particular aspect of the culture of modernity that is the subject of discussion will be related back to aspects of the problematic created by the treatment of culture in *Gaudium et spes*.

Thus, whereas the sociological phenomenon of the rise of the expert is treated in *Gaudium et spes* as some of the data to be taken into account by the Church in her approach to the modern world, there is no analysis in that document of the source of the epistemic authority of 'experts' who work within a diverse array of commercial, educational, legal and political institutions in modern society. Nor is there any analysis of the effect of specifically modern bureaucratic practices upon the moral formation of persons engaged in such practices, or reliance upon them for the provision of various services. The entire field of modern institutional practices, including that of the deference to the authority of 'experts', and the tendency to legitimise practices by reference to bureaucratic criteria, has, however, been a dominant theme in the work of Alasdair MacIntyre. Central to MacIntyre's critique of the culture of modernity is the argument that there are types of institutional structures which prevent or impoverish the ability of persons involved in those institutions to understand themselves or to develop as moral agents, and his conclusions have been supported by other scholars within the Thomist tradition. The purpose of this chapter is therefore to explore the claim that the *ethos* of modern institutions, including the deference to the authority of 'experts' and to bureaucratic criteria, act as a barrier to the flourishing of virtuous and, in particular, Christian practices. In relation to the specific issue of labour practices, it will be argued that there is a convergence of arguments to be found in the social justice encyclicals of Paul VI and John Paul II and the 'Aristotelian–Marxist–Thomist' critique of Alasdair MacIntyre.

The bureaucratised self

Two concepts that reappear throughout MacIntyre's publications are those of 'emotivism' and 'practices'. He defines emotivism as the 'doctrine that all evaluative judgements and more specifically all moral judgements are nothing but expressions of preference, expressions of attitude or feeling, in so far as they are moral or evaluative in character', and, further, that 'there are and can be no valid rational justification for any claims that objective and impersonal moral standards exist and hence that there are no such standards'.[1]

The concept of a 'practice' is defined as 'a typical undertaking in which the goods to be possessed depend for their acquisition on the inner development of the capabilities and character traits of the person engaged in the enterprise'.[2] The essential attribute of a practice is therefore its intransitive quality. It does not only produce something external to the participant but has an internal effect upon personal development. MacIntyre gives as examples of practices the productive activities of farmers, fishermen, painters, house builders, musicians, furniture builders and teachers, and games such as chess and football.[3] The particular character traits that are required for and enhanced by particular practices will differ from practice to practice, but all human behaviour worthy of the name of a practice will have some form of virtue-requiring and virtue-engendering capacity.

MacIntyre's indictment of the culture of modernity is founded in part on his argument that emotivist theories and doctrines actually govern the practices of our political, legal, commercial and, in many instances, health and educational institutions, and, further, that the practices associated with these institutions lack any such virtue-requiring and virtue-engendering capacities. On the contrary, they are merely 'legitimated' by an emotivist ideology that has two characteristic elements: 'it works to conceal the features of particular conflicts, of particular contestable concepts and situations, of particular unpredictabilities, and it does this by working to conceal conflict, contestability and unpredictability as such'.[4] It hides from vision the 'gap between the meaning of moral expressions and the use to which they are put'.[5]

Specifically, MacIntyre argues that Max Weber's account of the legitimacy of bureaucratic practices 'embodies just those dichotomies which emotivism embodies, and obliterates just those distinctions to which emotivism has to be blind'.[6] For Weber, questions of ends are questions of values, and on values reason is silent. Conflict between values cannot be rationally settled. As a consequence, MacIntyre concludes that 'bureaucratic authority is nothing other than successful power', and contemporary moral experience as a consequence of the involvement of persons within institutions has a paradoxical character:

> Seeking to protect the autonomy that we have learned to prize, we aspire ourselves not to be manipulated by others; seeking to incarnate our own principles and stand-point in the world of practice, we find no way open to us to do so except by directing towards others those very manipulative modes of relationship which each of us aspires to resist in our own case.[7]

To this dichotomy between the manipulator and the manipulated is related what MacIntyre identifies as the bifurcation of the social world into a realm of the organisational, in which ends are taken to be given and are not available for rational scrutiny, and a realm of the personal, in which judgement and debate about values are central factors, but in which no rational social resolution of issues is available. This bifurcation finds its internalisation, its inner representation, in *characters* who all share the emotivist view of the distinction between rational and non-rational discourse, but who represent the embodiment of that distinction in very different social contexts'.[8] Such characters are the 'moral representatives of their culture' because of the way in which 'moral and metaphysical ideas and theories assume through them an embodied existence in the social world'.[9] In contemporary society MacIntyre identifies the representative characters of emotivism as the rich aesthete, the manager and the therapist:

> The manager treats ends as given, as outside his scope; his concern is with technique, with effectiveness in transforming raw materials into final products, unskilled labour into skilled labour, investment into profits. The therapist also treats ends as given, as outside his scope; his concern also is with technique, with effectiveness in transforming symptoms into directed energy, maladjusted individuals into well-adjusted ones.[10]

Not only does MacIntyre question the legitimacy of bureaucratic and 'therapeutic' authority, but he concludes that the modern corporation is 'dangerous' because it 'splinters morality into dissociated parts' and makes moral incoherence a norm, the outcome of which is the creation of more than one self. As a consequence, the employee of the modern corporation is forced to fabricate 'distinct characters' while the structure of executive reasoning reproduces the structure of classical utilitarianism by placing limits upon what questions may and may not be treated as relevant.[11] The corporation itself delimits the range of possibilities; what it takes to be the good provides a moral horizon, and these limitations take the form of a definition of responsibility.[12] Hence, in his capacity as corporate executive, 'the manager not only has no need to take account of, but *must* not take account of certain types of considerations which he might feel obliged to recognize were he acting as parent, as consumer or as citizen'.[13]

In his assessment of the relationship between bureaucratic practices and the splintering of the self into ideologically defined rôles, MacIntyre's arguments closely parallel those of Central European scholars who addressed the issue during the Communist period. In his celebrated essay 'Politics and Conscience', Václav Havel observed that the 'process of anonymisation and depersonalisation of power and its reduction to a mere technology of rule and manipulation is the essential trait of all modern civilization'.[14] He suggests that this leads to a crisis of personal identity – people behave as if they were playing for a number of different teams at once, each with different uniforms, as if they do not know to which team they ultimately belong. Vaclav Belohradsky further argued:

> bureaucratisation generates a progressive impoverishment of the inner life, since the individual must assign to his acts a meaning not grounded in his own convictions and personal involvement, but in the impersonal calculations of an administrative power [and as this attitude becomes prevalent], it produces 'the ideologisation of culture'.[15]

The problem of the 'impoverishment of the inner life' in turn gives rise to what MacIntyre has identified as the reaction of the self against being splintered and fragmented and having its actions judged according to bureaucratic criteria. MacIntyre identifies the behaviour of the Sartrean rebel as the attempt by the self to defend its integrity. Whereas bureaucratic practices have a tendency to divide the self into its rôle-governed functions, the Sartrean rebel seeks to partition it out between rôles.[16] Authenticity becomes a virtue in and of itself – 'virtue has nothing to do any more with the content of action, but only with its relationship to the self'.[17] Both positions, that of the rebel and that of the manager, exclude the possibility of there being virtuous practices related to particular enterprises. One lacks a concept of 'man as such' and the other 'leaves no room for the exercise of rational, impersonal criteria'.[18]

This revolt of the Sartrean rebel against the 'bad faith' of bourgeois morality may also be interpreted as a specifically modern form of stoicism. The theme of the relationship between stoicism and modernity has been treated in a number of essays by James V. Schall.[19] Following the work of Moses Hadas, Schall locates the origins of classical stoicism in the Alexandrine revolution, which stripped the individual of his identity as a member of a small city-state and forced him to come to terms with an enormously expanded polity.[20] Schall concludes that 'since the polity was no longer able to be the intimate home wherein each person could acquire and practice the habits of virtue', the vast impersonality of the Alexandrine and Roman worlds left the individual isolated.[21] As a consequence, there was no place for a 'properly political activity' and the vast bureaucracies of impersonal forces increased in direct proportion to the decline of virtue in the person of the emperor.[22] Under these conditions, the Stoic and Epicurean response was to practise a philosophy of withdrawal from involvement in public life. The re-emergence of stoicism has also been recognised by Charles Taylor in the modern conception of the disengaged self that is 'capable of objectifying not only the surrounding world, but also his own emotions and inclinations, fears and compulsions, and achieving thereby a kind of distance of self-possession which allows him to act "rationally"'.[23]

The predicament of the Sartrean rebel is therefore essentially the same as that of the classical Stoics and Epicureans. Within the culture of modernity there is again an eclipse of the political, the scope for civic virtue is severely diminished and public life is administered by a vast bureaucracy. Many are forced to choose between the tragic options of being the subject of bureaucratic manipulation and/or manipulating others, *or* adopting some form of stoic withdrawal from public life. Significantly, however, both options catch the self within an emotivist 'ethics' in so far as MacIntyre has been able to demonstrate, in the first place, that Weberian rationality is emotivist and, in the second place, that Sartrean authenticity is also essentially emotivist.[24]

The eclipse of prudential judgement

Instead of the authority of institutions resting upon ideologies of bureaucratic expertise and the Liberal concepts of contract and consent, MacIntyre argues that institutions should derive their authority from principles of the Aristotelian–Thomist tradition of practical reason, in particular the rôle played within those traditions by *phronesis* (Aristotle) and *prudentia* (Aquinas). He acknowledges that pre-modern societies had formal organisations, that is decision-making hierarchies, but he argues that those in authority always had to justify their decisions against appeals to the authority of the tradition upon which the organisation had originally been established, and had to exercise the virtue of prudence in their deliberations.[25] He further argues that it is precisely because of the breakdown of traditions that 'Weberian' bureaucratic modes of organisation arise, and that it is of the essence of bureaucratic ideology to conceal the features of contestable concepts and situations which arise as a consequence of this breakdown.[26]

The lack of a tradition and an *ethos* based on a common acceptance of the values of that tradition means that those in positions of authority within institutions governed according to bureaucratic criteria have very limited scope for the prudential operation of their faculties of judgement. Whereas the virtue of prudence and its development within practices is a central idea in any Thomist account of the exercise of decision-making authority, the bureaucratic notion of managerial authority involves no such self-forma-tion. The virtue of prudence is irrelevant to the application of bureaucratic regulations. It is for this reason that MacIntyre concludes that managerial experts, in particular those in corporations, must not take into account con-siderations which they would otherwise want taken into account were they acting as parents or citizens outside the corporation. Public or corporate administration, according to the principles of Weberian rationality, cannot therefore be described as a 'practice' in the MacIntyrean sense.

Where viable pre-modern traditions of practical reason and prudential judgement continue to exist they shape the *ethos* of the organisations that are founded upon them, and the extent to which an organisation is flourish-ing can be determined by reference to the degree to which it reaches the ends and objectives prescribed by the tradition. In contrast, in institutions where bureaucratic practices predominate, the efficiency of the application of bureaucratic regulations and the achievement of bureaucratically formu-lated 'outcomes' themselves become the standard by which the institutions are judged to be more or less flourishing. Thus, just as MacIntyre argues that there are rival traditions of justice and rationality, the logic of this position is that there are also rival traditions of health care and education, and indeed various other types of institutional practices. For example, the Christian virtue of *hospitalitas* is simply not part of the intellectual frame-work of either the Nietzschean or Liberal approach to health care, and the Thomist conception of faith as the highest act of the intellect is, similarly, not part of the Nietzschean or Liberal idea of education. More fundamentally, the theological anthropology of the Thomist tradition cannot permit the kind of instrumentalisation and fragmentation of the person typical of the Liberal tradition that legitimises the conception of students in schools and universities and patients in hospitals as 'consumers' to be sold a 'product' or 'through-puts to be aggregated and averaged'.[27]

In contradistinction to the Nietzschean and Liberal conceptions, the Australian Thomist Anthony Fisher has argued that the *ethos* of medical institutions based on Christian principles should be determined by the 'sac-ramental aspects of health care', which he marshals under the categories of *diakonia, martyria* and *leitourgia*. Such an idea, that health care should have a sacramental dimension defined in part by its prophetic utterance and symbolic action (*martyria*), the celebration of its worship (*leiturgia*) and its entire pattern of behaviour (*diakonia*) or, in MacIntyrean terms, its various practices, may find a place in institutions based on other theistic traditions, but it would be completely out of place in medical institutions run according to the principles of the Liberal and Nietzschean traditions. Fisher's call for a consideration of the sacramental aspects of health care is equally applicable to other types of Catholic institutions, for example the sacramental aspects of practices in schools, seminaries, homes for the elderly, universities and residential colleges.

Although it is difficult to prove empirically a direct relationship between the desacralisation of such institutions (Catholic schools, universities and hospitals) in the post-Conciliar era, and the reference to the authority of 'experts' in *Gaudium et spes*, it is certainly clear that many institutions under the patronage of the Church are adopting or have already adopted the same institutional practices as those operative within secular institutions, and that this phenomenon continues to be justified by references to 'professionalisation' and the Church's need to consult secular expertise. The concept of 'professionalisation' is not itself subjected to analysis but operates in an ideological fashion to paper over contending visions of education and health care. For example, in many hospitals the pastoral work once undertaken by nuns who held no certificates or diplomas in pastoral care is now the responsibility of professional psychologists and 'grief counsellors'. Such persons need not actually believe in God or be practising Catholics, they simply require the requisite academic qualifications, which may or may not include a sociological knowledge of Catholic beliefs. They are fulfilling a rôle or function but the rôle is not necessarily related to their person, as was the work of the religious. The presence of one religious who believes and practises the Catholic faith may be more consoling for a grieving person than a whole faculty of 'expert counsellors' who do not enter into the personal suffering of their brother or sister in Christ, but remain 'professionally detached'. Similarly, teachers in schools administered by 'Catholic Education' bureaucracies throughout the Western world are employed to teach the Catholic faith, regardless of whether they actually believe and practise this faith themselves, providing that they hold the requisite teaching diplomas. Moreover, the philosophical anthropologies underpinning the studies in psychology and educational theory, which are the foundation of the epistemic authority of the teachers and counsellors, rarely embody the kinds of anthropological principles found in *Gaudium et spes* paragraph 22 or *Redemptor Hominis*, or, more generally, the idea of the human person as a creature made in the image and likeness of God. Thus the Congregation for Catholic Education has recently lamented:

> The fragmentation of education, the generic character of the values frequently invoked and which obtain ample and easy consensus at the price of a dangerous obscuring of their content, tend to make the school

step back into a supposed neutrality, which enervates its educating potential and reflects negatively on the formation of the pupils. There is a tendency to forget that education always presupposes and involves a definite concept of man and life. To claim neutrality for schools signifies in practice, more times than not, banning all reference to religion from the cultural and educational field.[28]

It is perhaps because of such problems that John Paul II, in *Fides et ratio* stated:

> The invitation [of *Gaudium et spes*] to theologians to engage the human sciences and apply them properly in their enquiries should not be interpreted as an implicit authorisation to marginalise philosophy or to put something else in its place in pastoral formation and in the *praeparatio fidei*.[29]

The deference to the authority of the 'human sciences' is not itself intrinsically wrong-headed. However, many studies in the social sciences and in psychology are based upon a flawed anthropology which does not begin from the position of the *imago Dei*, and this is problematic. Given a plain-meaning interpretation of the 'autonomy of culture' principle, many of the Church's educators no longer relate religious knowledge to so-called secular knowledge. As a consequence, institutions that are funded by the Church, and which ought to manifest a Catholic *ethos*, frequently end up fostering practices which are not real 'practices' in any Aristotelian Thomist sense, but merely ideological behaviour designed to minimise the scope for prudential judgement and practices which are in any sense sacramental. Under these conditions, the sacramental life of the institution, to the extent that it exists at all, is compartmentalised, that is cut off from the general life of the institution. In the context of educational institutions, Russell Hittinger has observed that what is billed as the uniquely Catholic component of the institution usually turns out to be 'a weird little subculture, like the bar in *Star Wars*, that has little connection to any sociological reality beyond the gates of the campus'.[30] To Hittinger's observations may be added the fact that the kinds of persons who are attracted to marginalised subcultures are frequently people with psychological disorders. As a consequence, an interest in religion becomes associated with dysfunctionality and irrationality – the exact opposite of what the Conciliar fathers intended in their call for an engagement with the human sciences.

Plain persons and professional administrators

In his Agnes Cuming lectures, MacIntyre develops a Thomistic critique of the professionalisation of administration by relying upon an interpretation of Aquinas on the subject of authority. He asserts that Aquinas held that 'what the law is, on fundamentals at least, rests with plain persons and that the most important things that lawyers and administrators know about law, they know as plain persons and not as lawyers and administrators'.[31] This is consistent with the traditional principle 'subsidiarity', according to which decision-making authority should be decentralised to the lowest level at which the decision can competently be made. However, MacIntyre adds to this general principle the argument that plain persons are generally competent to regulate the internal affairs of the institutions of which they are members, and, further, he reiterates the argument of Aquinas that plain persons are generally aware of the fundamental precepts of the natural law and their authority as law.[32]

Although MacIntyre does not offer a systematic account of how plain persons acquire an understanding of the precepts of the natural law, he does offer clues about how a defence of the argument might be constructed. First, he endorses certain aspects of the natural law theory of John Finnis that pertain to what Finnis calls the 'goods of human flourishing':

> Finnis has made the most important contribution so far in arguing that human beings have direct underived knowledge of basic human goods and that it is in terms of this knowledge that our grasp of the precepts of the natural law is to be understood.[33]

In MacIntyre's analysis this means that the plain person's primary knowledge of basic human goods is a matter of reflection upon practice. This is not the same as an intuitionist perspective since it is through 'practical reflection, and not as a result of some distinct intuitive act, that we grasp what the basic goods are'.[34] To this argument of Finnis, MacIntyre adds that, since 'for Aquinas it is a necessary condition of any precept having the obligatoriness of law that it be a precept of reason directed towards a common good (ST I–II, 90.1 and 2)', it is perhaps 'not so much by reflection on our individual inclinations alone as by reflection on and in situations in which some common good is at stake that we, as plain persons, arrive at our basic judgements about both goods and precepts'.[35] Such situations in which some element of the common good is at stake most commonly arise within institutions that have been created for the achievement of some particular good of human flourishing, for example families, schools or hospitals. Since plain persons are members of these institutions, MacIntyre argues that they are 'generally and to a significant degree proto-Aristotelians', for they are engaged in a range of practice-based and practice-structured communities which raise for them the question: What is my good?[36]

There is implied in this treatment of the condition of plain persons the proposition, argued by MacIntyre's colleague at Manchester University, Michael Polanyi, that there exists a 'tacit knowledge' of the principles of a background culture.[37] The plain person acquires a belief in the efficacy or truth of certain principles, not by taking part in dialectical discussions about first principles and the conclusions which may be drawn from them, but, rather, by 'taking in' the principles that underlie contemporary conduct and belief while immersed in social institutions – and, MacIntyre would add, by reflecting upon them. These principles in turn form a framework within which future experiences are interpreted. In the words of Andrew Louth, 'we bring a kind of interpretative framework within which we seek to interpret our conceptions: and this framework is tacit, it is something we have learnt by experience and cannot make wholly explicit'.[38]

MacIntyre's argument is that if social institutions are well-integrated, that is they are not pursuing mutually incompatible ends, and if the practices operative within those institutions are not ideological, then plain persons will acquire a tacit understanding of the goods of human flourishing. However, if the social institutions or their practices are in some way dysfunctional and ideological, then plain persons are likely to acquire a tacit knowledge of principles that are not conducive to their flourishing and thus not in accord with the natural law. MacIntyre observes that what is extraordinary about this predicament of the plain person in the culture of modernity is the fact that most institutions are the site of a 'civil war' between at least three rival versions of morality – the Nietzschean, the Liberal and the Thomist. However, these rival versions will not appear packaged as such. Instead, the plain person is presented with an array of practices and attitudes that are based on fragments of these rival versions. The different elements in the various conceptual schemes which have made up the dominant cultures of the Western world have been torn apart, and each element has assumed a somewhat different character, since 'rules, conceived apart from virtues and goods, are not the same as rules conceived in dependence upon virtues and goods'; and the same goes for 'virtues taken in isolation from goods and rules', and 'goods taken in isolation from virtues and rules'.[39] When everyday practices and the rules, goods and virtues they enact are reconceived as isolatable from one another, the problem for the plain person is that of how to articulate a pre-existing but hidden relationship from a reflection upon the disparate parts of his or her moral scheme.[40]

Plain persons are thus in a paradoxical situation. In order to construct a relationship apparently not yet established between the disparate parts of their moral schemes, they have to discern that the practices of modernity are pathological and the moral traditions fragmented; but a knowledge of what is pathological presupposes a knowledge of what is normative and this is exactly what is difficult for the plain person to acquire in the culture of modernity. In MacIntyre's words, 'only in so far as we have already arrived at certain conclusions are we able to become the sort of person able to engage in such enquiry so as to reach sound conclusions'.[41]

This is not however to argue that the predicament of the plain person is completely hopeless. Plain persons can transcend the matrix of dysfunctional and ideological practices which are basal to the *ethos* of modern institutions, but to do so they need first to reach the insight that the institutions *are dysfunctional* and that the arguments offered in defence of dysfunctional practices are merely 'ideological'.[42] The process of arriving at such insights in turn requires within the plain person a healthy scepticism of the epistemic authority of 'experts': in MacIntyre's terms, it requires plain persons to be reflective 'proto-Aristotelians'.

The 'onto-logic' of economic practices

The idea that every action or practice contains its own 'logic', that is it is either directed towards some genuine good or is in the service of 'false goods' such as power or ideological obfuscation, is directly related to the distinction made in economic philosophy between the transitive and intransitive dimensions of labour practices. The distinctions between these two dimensions of human action were recognised in classical Thomism, and later became a dominant theme in Romantic scholarship, including the Romantic dimensions of classical Marxism. Although MacIntyre has subsequently described the political activism of his pre-Thomist Trotskyist period as 'misdirected and wrong headed energy', he remains indebted to Marx for insights into the relationship between forms of reasoning and social practices.[43]

In this context, in his paper on Marx's *Theses on Feuerbach*, MacIntyre offers an interpretation of Marx's theory of *praxis* as latently Aristotelian.[44] He observes that from the standpoint of civil society (a theoretical construct whose dominant interpretation comes from Adam Ferguson) the individual is to be distinguished from the set of social relationships into which she or he has chosen to enter, and this severance of the individual from her or his network of social relationships finds expression in Liberal jurisprudence, for which the central concepts are those of utility, contract and individual rights. With both Marxists and postmoderns, MacIntyre is in agreement that the rights rhetoric is ideological. Its objective is to secure a social consensus in circumstances where there is no commonly accepted moral tradition by construing all human relations in contractual terms. MacIntyre's argument is that, in order to transcend the contradictions of a society built upon these ideological foundations, it is useful to have recourse to the following insight from Marx's *Theses on Feuerbach*:

> The standpoint of civil society cannot be transcended, and its limitations adequately understood and criticised, by theory alone, that is, by theory divorced from practice, but only by a particular kind of practice, practice informed by a particular kind of theory rooted in that same practice.[45]

Such a practice is defined by Marx in the first thesis as an

> [o]bjective reality in which the end or aim of the activity is such that by making that end their own individuals are able to achieve something of universal worth embodied in some particular form of practice through co-operation with other such individuals.[46]

MacIntyre concludes that 'practices whose activity can be thus characterised stand in sharp contrast to the practical life of civil society', and are 'best expressed in Aristotelian rather than in Hegelian terms'.[47] The contrast is to be found in the fact that in 'activities governed by the norms of civil society there are no ends except those which are understood to be the goals of some particular individual or individuals', while the 'ends of any type of practice involving what Marx calls "objective reality" are able to be characterised antecedently to and independently of any characterisation of the desires of the particular individuals who happen to engage in it'.[48]

As was explained above, MacIntyre believes that individuals discover in the ends of any such (Aristotelian) practice goods internal to and specific to that particular type of practice, which they can make their own by allowing their participation in the activity to effect a transformation in the desires which they initially brought with them to the activity.[49] Practices therefore have both an 'objective' (transitive) and 'subjective' (intransitive) dimension. The objective dimension refers to the thing produced or service offered, whereas the subjective dimension refers to the internal change effected within the individual participant in the practice. MacIntyre argues that it is these two dimensions to which Marx is referring in his third thesis wherein he writes of a 'coincidence of the changing of circumstances and of human activity as self-changing'.[50] He acknowledges that such a conception of a type of practice 'teleologically ordered to the achievement of a or the common good' may appear to be more Thomistic or Aristotelian than Marxist; however, he asserts that such an Aristotelian reconstruction of Marx's eleven theses is the 'key distinction [from Feuerbach] which the argument of *The Theses on Feuerbach* needs'.[51] In effect, this means that MacIntyre believes that Marx was correct in his identification of the problems associated with the civil society of Liberal political philosophy, but failed in so far as he sought a Hegelian rather than neo-Aristotelian and, ultimately, Thomistic solution.

Although Aquinas was certainly aware of the existence of both a transitive and immanent dimension of human actions (the objective and subjective dimensions), the capitalist transformation of these two dimensions, by which the subjective dimension is commonly decoupled from the objective, was not envisaged in the work of Aquinas. The emphasis upon the subjective dimension of labour does not become a dominant theme until the explosion of Romantic scholarship. This development can be explained by the rise of capitalist practices, which had the effect of alienating the worker from both the product of his labour and his place in community life, thereby highlighting, in a negative way, the importance of the subjective dimension.

The suppression of the subjective dimension and the concomitant conception of the worker as a mere producer of commodities, and ultimately as a commodity in himself, violates MacIntyre's Aristotelian notion of labour as a special kind of 'practice', that is as a 'typical undertaking in which the goods to be possessed depend for their acquisition on the inner development of the capabilities and character traits of the person engaged in the enterprise'.[52] From this theoretical foundation it is logical for MacIntyre to conclude that the notion of the limitless accumulation of money is inherently irrational (since it can take place without any moral development of the person engaged in the enterprise), and, therefore, 'capitalist practice, in so far as it involves this limitless accumulation, is also inherently irrational'.[53] Moreover, MacIntyre argues that 'the dominance of the capitalist market and the bureaucratic structures of corporate organisations has the effect that the subjects of thought and calculation are the methods of economic and social expansion, rather than the practices internal to the goods'.[54] In reaching these conclusions, MacIntyre is following Karl Polanyi's critique of the economic philosophy of Adam Smith. Polanyi's key argument is that a 'natural order' is one in which the economy is embedded in social relations, rather than, as is typical of contemporary corporate capitalism, one in which social relations are embedded in the economic system, making society a mere adjunct to the market.[55] From this perspective, the problem is not that of a market economy per se, but the particular form which the contemporary market economy has taken and, in particular, the 'unnatural' subordination of social relations to the dynamics of corporate capitalism.

The junction of 'Aristotelian Marxism' with Thomism

Since MacIntyre is opposed to Marx's atheistic philosophical anthropology but sympathetic to select aspects of his critique of capitalism, his work may be construed as a late-twentieth-century example of an intellectual stream within Christian scholarship that is critical of *both* elements of capitalist practice and what Feliks Koneczny described as the 'bureaucratic elephantiasis' typical of socialism.[56] For example, MacIntyre's Aristotelian Marxist adage: 'from each according to his capacity, to each according to his contribution' – accords with the general anti-corporate capitalist and anti-bureaucratic *animus* of the works of, *inter alios*, Eric Gill, Hilaire Belloc, Gilbert Keith Chesterton, Dorothy Day, Bob Santamaria, Catherine Pickstock, John Milbank and Werner Stark. Indeed, although various terms have been used to describe these authors, including 'Socialist' (Pickstock and Milbank), 'Christian Socialist' (Gill), 'Distributist' (Belloc, Chesterton, Day and Santamaria) and, in the case of Werner Stark, 'a peculiar symbiosis of Marxist propositions and the Catholic *ethos*', it may be argued that MacIntyre's Aristotelian

Marxist concept is in fact the more linguistically and philosophically precise, since what unites each of these authors is an Aristotelian and Thomist conception of the nature of work as a 'good of human flourishing', coupled with a Marxian-style critique of the effects of certain kinds of capitalist practices on the welfare of workers – particularly upon the intransitive dimension of their labour.[57] Since the capitalist order in all of its complexity could not have been foreseen by Aquinas, it received its first most extensive philosophical analysis in the work of the German Romantics, Marx and the Slavophiles, whereas the significance of the intransitive/subjective dimension of labour was not acknowledged in the corpus of papal social teaching until the encyclicals of John Paul II.[58]

In *Laborem Exercens*, John Paul II argued that the sources of the dignity of work are to be sought primarily in the subjective dimension, not in the objective one; and that it is precisely the reversal of this order (giving priority to the thing produced, rather than to the self-development of the worker) which characterises capitalism.[59] Moreover, John Paul II does not limit the problem of alienation to the traditional working class but offers a general warning against 'excessive bureaucratic centralisation, which makes the worker feel as though he is just a cog in a huge machine moved from above'.[60] Instead of increased centralisation, he promotes the principle of subsidiarity.[61] In direct opposition to a competitive ethics typical of the Scottish Enlightenment tradition, he states that 'all too often freedom is confused with the instinct for individual or collective interest or with the instinct for combat and domination, whatever be the ideological colours with which they are covered'.[62] In a statement which affirms MacIntyre's criticisms of the *ethos* of civil society, John Paul II further asserts:

> Economic development must be constantly programmed and realised within a perspective of universal joint development of each individual and people as was convincingly argued by my predecessor Paul VI in *Populorum Progressio*. Otherwise, the category of 'economic progress' becomes in isolation a superior category subordinating the whole of human existence to its partial demands, suffocating man, breaking up society and ending by entailing itself in its own tensions and excesses.[63]

Significantly, in an early essay on 'The Constitution of Culture through Human *Praxis*', John Paul II treated human labour as an aspect of the formation of culture.[64] Consistent with both MacIntyre and Marx he argued that work has an intransitive character and thus that labour practices are character forming. However, like MacIntyre, he rejected the implicit utilitarian character of Marxist thought, and in the place of productivity as an end in itself he placed the good of a 'disinterested communion' with the transcendental properties of truth, beauty and goodness:

that which is transitive in our culturally creative activity and is expressed externally as an effect, objectification, product, or work can be said to be a result of the particular intensity of that which is intransitive and remains within our disinterested communion with truth, goodness and beauty. This communion, its intensity, degree and depth, is something completely internal; it is an immanent activity of the human soul, and it leaves its mark and brings forth fruit in this same dimension. It is from this communion that we mature and grow inwardly.[65]

John Paul II expresses this symbiotic relationship between work and the transcendental properties, with the statement that 'not only is culture constituted through *praxis*, but human *praxis* in its authentically human character is also constituted through culture'.[66] This is essentially the same insight as MacIntyre's notion of there existing a two-way relationship between virtuous or vicious practices and the *ethos* of institutions. However, he adds a further insight which appears to be more Platonic and Augustinian than Aristotelian – that 'beauty exists that we might be enticed to work'.[67] This idea has a radically anti-materialist orientation, and is closer to the thought of Morris, Belloc, Gill, Chesterton, Day, Santamaria and aspects of early German Romanticism than to any theories to be found within the Liberal tradition. Indeed, Denis Maugenest goes so far as to assert that *Laborem Exercens* should be construed as John Paul II's invitation to adopt a 'mystical view of work' set within a theory of human activity as a whole.[68] He observes that this broader theological vision of work is 'very Slav' (and, indeed, one could say 'Slavophile'), and that 'Cartesian thinking feels less comfortable with it'.[69] However, it is precisely such a theological framework for an analysis of human labour that is required by the Thomist tradition if it is not to succumb to the utilitarian and consequentialist orientation of the Scottish Enlightenment philosophers, for whom the spheres of faith and reason, nature and grace, had been severed. Indeed, Milbank argues that essential to the economic regimes of the Scottish Enlightenment philosophers is a 'new secular aesthetic' detached from its transcendental link with the true and the good which recognises 'beauty' in the inner consistency and harmony of the operations of utility.[70] Moreover, the fact that inherent within John Paul II's conception is the idea that there is a relationship between work and the transcendentals, means that it is possible to reconceive work as an opportunity to participate in the transcendentals and offer the fruits of this participation to others as a gift. This construction does not deny that in the post-lapsarian order the good of work may seem less desirable, than, for example, the good of play, but it does dignify human labour with a meaning beyond that of a penalty for original sin and/or the medium for social competition, and it prepares the theoretical foundations for a theological analysis of the sacramental dimensions of work-related practices, such as that prescribed by Anthony Fisher.

MacIntyre's contemporary position vis-à-vis Marxism is thus not a discordant element in his development of the Thomist tradition. Essentially it is the elements within Marx's works dealing with the relationship between work-related practices and 'self-formation', as well as the Marxist criticisms of the inherently ideological nature of Liberal economic and political philosophy, that attract MacIntyre's interest. It is precisely what MacIntyre has identified as the latently Aristotelian elements of the Marxist critique of capitalism that John Milbank argues 'need to be retained and re-elaborated since they assist a Christian critique of secular order by showing that the presuppositions of Liberal political theory and of political economy are culturally specific'.[71] Milbank further observes that Marx called into question 'the sundering of the sphere of "making" from the sphere of "values", and hence the separation of a technologically conceived economics and politics from ethics, aesthetics and religion'.[72] In doing so, he demonstrated that 'all historical makings are not just "technological", but governed by a "thoroughly religious logic"'.[73] On this point the Marxist and Thomist traditions are in agreement. The notion of every practice (labour or otherwise) having its own internal religious or anti-religious 'logic' is essentially the same idea as David Schindler's notion of an 'onto-logic', and may in part explain why MacIntyre, even while a Marxist, opposed the Protestant and Liberal belief in distinct secular and sacred realms.[74]

Thus, although in theory one need not rely upon the Marxist tradition in order to develop a mature Thomist critique of capitalist practices, since the significance of the intransitive or subjective dimension was implicit within the works of Aquinas, even if it was undeveloped, one should at least give credit to the German Romantic tradition for focusing attention on the issue, and at a deeper philosophical level there remains a number of junctions at which the Thomist and Marxist critiques converge. As MacIntyre himself acknowledges, 'even in its atheism Marxism has some things in common with Christianity which both of them find lacking in liberal rationalism'.[75] These are:

1   the notion of labour as a type of practice;
2   the consequent emphasis on the intransitive/subjective dimension of human labour and the problem of alienation;
3   the critique of liberal economic theory as an ideology legitimating the subordination of social life to the laws of the market;
4   the insistence on the unity of theory and practice; and
5   the inevitability of a nexus between economics and politics and ethics, aesthetics and religion, and, indeed, one's understanding of the transcendental properties of being.

MacIntyre may be viewed as having travelled along the Marxist 'Romantic line' (in contrast to the 'Enlightenment line') and crossed to the Thomist at these various junctions.

Conclusion

In an article on the 'Social and Political Sources of *Akrasia*', Amélie Oskenberg Rorty observed that institutions are sources of constraint on the motivations of individuals. They 'define flow charts of duties and virtues, rights and obligations whose infractions carry severe costs and sanctions'; they 'set norms for the tenor of broader social interactions, finely tuned for status and power, formality and intimacy, emphatically tactful or aggressively confrontational'. They 'form the patterns and habits exercised in resolving ordinary conflicts'. And they 'define the terms of utility and fairness'.[76] Rorty's theme of the 'social constraint' that institutions place on the behaviour of their members may serve as an umbrella concept for the diverse array of observations and criticisms to be found in MacIntyre's work on modern institutional practices. However, where Rorty finds that *akrasia* is often the result of philosophies which give definition to the flow chart of duties, virtues, rights and obligations, MacIntyre's position is that the *ethos* created by modern institutional practices is so pathological that many persons are no longer capable even of *akrasia* – since *akratic* behaviour assumes a knowledge of right action on the part of the agent. Indeed, the emotivist self could be defined as a 'self incapable of *akrasia*' since the self's conceptions of what is right and wrong change to fit its emotions and social contexts.[77]

Moreover, of those who are not completely emotivist selves, there are many who are not even conscious of the nature of their 'moral culture', who cannot articulate the principles of their moral tradition, or who operate by reference to a *mélange* of principles tacitly cobbled together from rival traditions. Although such persons are not self-consciously emotivists, they are not persons who from the perspective of the Thomist tradition could be regarded as flourishing. MacIntyre's epitaph for the self entangled within the bureaucratic and emotivist ideology of modern institutions, is that:

> What for the kind of ancient and medieval inquiry and practice which Thomism embodied was the exceptional condition of the deprived and isolated individual, has become, for modernity, the conditions of the human being as such.[78]

To return to the point of departure – that of the value of 'experts' and the basis of their authority – an examination of MacIntyre's critique of modern institutional practices suggests that the only 'experts' whose authority may be legitimate are those who see through the ideological quality of such practices, and who continue to base their judgements upon a pre-modern tradition of practical reason, including the virtue of prudence. Other persons who attempt to adjust their behaviour to the *ethos* of modern institutional practices end up behaving in 'one sphere as quasi-Kantians, in another as imitation utilitarians, in yet another as neo-Aristotelians, and in a fourth as pragmatically distanced from all philosophical claims'.[79] Such an adoption of alternating sources of moral principles is not conducive to the flourishing of either the self, its institutions or the general culture.[80] Further, the conclusion to be drawn from the MacIntyrean critique of modern institutional practices, and its supplementation with the ideas of other Thomist scholars, is that these practices retard the development of the soul and the freedom of its moral agency to such a degree that those more noble souls who are aware of the problem have a tendency to seek refuge in some form of stoic withdrawal from public life. Others – the more Machiavellian – have a tendency to tack to and fro with changes in institutional wind patterns.[81] This destroys their integrity and undermines the good of friendship. The kind of loyalty and honesty demanded of true friendship is replaced by a utilitarian model of human relationships according to which there are no true 'friends' in an Aristotelian Thomist sense, merely a network of 'socially useful contacts', the less morally flexible of whom can be thrown overboard when the institutional wind currents change direction. Although such behaviour has not suddenly arisen in the twentieth and twenty-first centuries, the MacIntyrean argument is that modern institutional practices have a tendency to render this kind of opportunism 'normal' and even 'virtuous' and 'socially necessary'.

In the context of the general theme of *Gaudium et spes* – the engagement of the Church with the modern world – the most important conclusion is that the Church should not replicate these bureaucratic practices within her own institutions, but on the contrary should foster institutions with a sacramental *ethos*. Within such institutions, both plain persons and 'experts' may be formed according to Thomist principles of practical reason, and may participate in the practices of the institution without fragmentation, without exploiting others, without themselves being exploited or manipulated, and without having to feign the existence of a consensus of values by reference to an ideological rhetoric. In terms of the intellectual component of such an enterprise, a consideration of the sacramental dimensions of various institutional practices is required, such as that which Anthony Fisher has undertaken in the context of health care institutions. This is because a Thomist institutional *ethos* requires not merely the fostering of virtue-requiring and virtue-engendering practices in the Aristotelian sense, but also practices that are sacramental. At present, however, MacIntyre would argue that modern institutional practices could not even pass by Aristotelian standards, let alone the higher standards of a culture built upon the Christocentric theological anthropology to be found in the Conciliar documents and post-Conciliar papal encyclicals, such as *Gaudium et spes* paragraph 22 and *Redemptor Hominis*.

Finally, in the context of the issue of the merit of capitalist labour practices, it is submitted that criticisms found in *Populorum Progressio* of Paul VI, and the attention to the subjective dimension of labour practices in the thought of John Paul II, concur with the criticisms found in MacIntyre's construction of an Aristotelian Marxist Thomism that relate to the inadequacies of the Liberal tradition to address the issue of the 'onto-logic' of labour practices. This is not to argue that the Thomist tradition is, for example, totally opposed to a market economy, or in favour of some particular version of socialism; rather, it is to say that the understanding of the 'onto-logic' of labour practices offered by the magisterium, and elaborated by scholars such as MacIntyre, transcends the polemics of these two alternatives and offers its own theology of work, which includes a critique of both. Moreover, central to this critique is the philosophical presupposition that no sphere of life is completely autonomous of any other, and thus that economics is not autonomous of theology and, in particular, is not autonomous of the spiritual lives of workers. For these reasons the Church should ensure that her own institutions are governed by a thoroughly religious logic and sacramental *ethos*, rather than aping the mechanical logic and atheistic *ethos* of the corporate world which is predicated on the severance of the self into ideologically defined compartments.

4

'MASS CULTURE' AND THE 'RIGHT TO CULTURE'

In *Gaudium et spes* paragraph 60 the Conciliar fathers stated that 'everything must be done to make everyone conscious of the right to culture and the duty one has of developing oneself culturally'. The substance of this 'right to culture' is, however, never defined. This particular aspect of the 'explosive problematic' thereby raises questions about what it means to 'develop oneself culturally' and how such a project fits within the Thomist tradition. It also raises the question of the relationship between 'mass culture' and the 'exercise of the right to culture'. In this chapter it will be argued, first, that the inherent ambiguity in this concept can be clarified by a consideration of three rival versions of what it means to 'develop oneself culturally'. These correspond to Alasdair MacIntyre's three rival versions of moral enquiry: the Classical (Thomist), Enlightenment (Liberal) and Romantic (Nietzschean). Associated with each of these rival versions of moral enquiry is a rival version of culture – understood in the second sense to which reference was made in Chapter 1 – *Bildung*, self-formation or self-cultivation.

Second, it will be argued that, contrary to Albert Dondeyne's positive endorsement of the rise of 'mass culture' and contrary to the implied rejection in *Gaudium et spes* of the 'aristocratic manner of looking at culture' to which Bernard Lambert made reference, and contrary to Bernard Lonergan's criticism of the normative and 'classicist' understandings of culture, a classical Christian conception of *Bildung* or self-formation is *necessarily aristocratic* in the sense of being normative, preferring that which is most excellent, and recognising grades of distinction in the achievement of the norm. It is, however, important to distinguish between a classical Christian account of an 'aristocratic' formation of the soul, and alternative Aristocratic Liberal and Nietzschean accounts.

Third, it will be argued that the essential attribute of 'mass culture' is its hostility to any kind of aristocratic account of self-formation. From this it will be concluded that the Thomist tradition at this juncture in its history needs to take a strong stance *against* any kind of strategy which seeks to accommodate its practices to the norms of 'mass culture'.

Finally, the positions of Alasdair MacIntyre and Charles Taylor on the issue of the possibility of a higher synthesis of the principles of self-cultivation associated with the three rival 'sources of the self' will be examined.

The Aristocratic and Bourgeois Liberal models

As was explained in Chapter 1, Aristocratic Liberalism is a term used to describe a branch of Liberal thought which sought to foster a high culture based on the freedom of artistic self-development. The aristocratic aspect was manifested in a distaste for mass culture, a contempt for mediocrity and the primacy of the ideal of individuality within the works of the authors so described.

In order to understand this ideal of 'individuality', it is important to distinguish between it and 'individualism'. According to Steven Lukes, the earliest-known use of the French word *individualisme* is to be found in a reported conversation of de Maistre in 1820. De Maistre spoke of 'this deep and frightening division of minds, this infinite fragmentation of all doctrines, political Protestantism carried to the most absolute individualism'.[1] Lukes observes that there is, however, quite distinct from this concept, another one whose characteristic reference is German – this is the Romantic idea *Individualität* – the notion of individual uniqueness and originality, which stands in contrast to the rational, universal, and uniform standards of the Enlightenment.

It is this Romantic notion of individuality that is directly relevant to the Aristocratic Liberal model of 'developing oneself culturally'. Associated with it are the ideals of *Bildung* or self-formation and its object, *die schöne Seele* – the 'beautiful soul'. Hans-Georg Gadamer construes the quest for *Bildung* as an evocation of the 'ancient mystical tradition according to which man causes in his soul the image of God, after whom he is fashioned, and which man must cultivate in himself'.[2] It is such a Christian version of this tradition to which *Gaudium et spes* paragraph 57 appeals, wherein the Conciliar fathers compare the relationship between the Holy Spirit and the individual with that of a master craftsman with an apprentice. The outcome of such a project will, however, depend upon what image of God the individual has. For example, the image of God can be that of the Old Testament, or the Trinitarian God of the New Testament or the gods of classical Greece, the Goths or the Norsemen, to name but a few. The quest for a beautiful soul can be found in many religious traditions. It is for this reason that Romanticism is often perceived as a half-way house for many potentialities, including Catholicism and nihilism.[3] In each case the key question is: who are the gods to be emulated? Further, if the model is classical Christian, then, of course, it is not just an issue of emulation but also participation.

A major influence on the Aristocratic Liberal conception of *Bildung* was Shaftesbury's work, the *Characteristics of Men, Manners, Opinions and Times* in which he promoted the Platonic idea that there exists an intrinsic relationship between the true, the beautiful and the good.[4] However, he rejected the Augustinian and Bonaventuran developments of this idea, and anticipated the eighteenth and nineteenth century German project of jettisoning the Christian elements of the classical Christian synthesis.[5] In the end, the criterion of the beautiful, and of the beautiful soul, became its originality.[6] This Shaftesburian idea was promoted by, *inter alios*, Christoph Wieland, Wilhelm von Humboldt, and Friedrich Schiller, and as a result, Shaftesbury's neo-pagan version of self-cultivation had a continuing impact on generations of German and British scholars.[7]

One of the central tenets of this account of self-formation was that the richest and strongest personalities are forged by an experience of the extremes of life. This idea can be traced to Kant's 'Idea for a Universal History' and 'Perpetual Peace', in which he argued that man's faculties and capacities could be developed historically only through antagonism.[8] Following Kant, von Humboldt (as well as Schiller, Marx, Hegel, Darwin, Huxley, and Nietzsche, among others), took the view that antagonism was necessary for human development and progress. According to von Humboldt, 'all those situations in which contrasting extremes are most closely and variously intermingled are the most interesting and most improving'.[9] Hence, 'war seems to be one of the most salutary phenomena for the culture of human nature'.[10] Such a position suggests a regression of an understanding of the elements of human flourishing from a Christian perspective to a pagan one. The contrast between the Christian notion of 'original peace' and the pagan conception of 'original and perpetual conflict', which reaches its apotheosis in the work of Nietzsche, is already present in von Humboldt.

A second distinction between a classical Christian account of 'developing oneself culturally' and an Aristocratic Liberal conception is the fact that the fundamental pre-condition for *Bildung* is personal liberty, unencumbered by community or tradition. This too is a part of the Kantian heritage of Aristocratic Liberalism to which Schiller ascribed the *regula vitae*: 'determine yourself through yourself'.[11] Again this tendency in Aristocratic Liberalism is further developed in Nietzsche, for whom true heroism slakes its agonal thirst within the soul.

One of the strongest and most influential examples of this focus on personal liberty and 'liberation' from the strictures of a tradition is to be found in J. S. Mill's version of Aristocratic Liberalism.[12] In his account of the cultivation of the individual self, Mill divided human potentiality into three categories: the intellectual, the aesthetic and the moral. This division corresponded to the traditional transcendentals of truth, beauty and goodness; however, Mill ascribed the moral and aesthetic categories to the faculties of feeling and imagination only.[13] Since Aristocratic Liberals do not think that there is a morality prior to harmonious self-development, the good and the beautiful are for them no longer transcendental properties of being. Rather, the Aristocratic Liberal notions of the good and the beautiful, for which the theories of von Humboldt and Mill stand as leading examples, are essentially emotivist, whereas the conception of the true continues to follow along an Enlightenment (primarily Kantian) trajectory, which seeks objectivity by a process of detachment from the claims of theology and tradition.

The difficulty associated with such a conception of self-development is that of explaining the relationship between a conception of truth as objective and a conception of beauty and goodness as subjective. Speaking of von Humboldt's project, W. H. Burrow concluded that 'the gap between passion and reason, Romantic experimentalism and Kantian inner moral freedom, remained unplugged except by the metaphors of aesthetics'.[14] R. E. Norton reached essentially the same conclusion:

> By emptying *Bildung* of its ethical significance and thus concentrating solely on what amounts to the predominately aesthetic act of modelling the materials of personality into pleasant, concinnous design, the original impetus behind the desire for acquiring a beautiful soul, could at its worst, degenerate into the effete and sterile pursuit of solipsistic self-gratification.[15]

It is precisely such a degeneration that characterises the transition from eighteenth- and nineteenth-century Aristocratic Liberalism to twentieth-century 'Bourgeois Liberalism'. Whereas the Aristocratic Liberals shared a tendency to reject conceptions of self-formation found within the Judaic and Christian traditions, to return to ideas found within classical culture and to synthesise these conceptions with a Kantian emphasis upon autonomy – the attempt to 'marry Helen of Troy to Faust and let them breed'[16] – the Bourgeois Liberal tradition discarded these 'aristocratic elements' and focused on the 'bourgeois' concern for wealth creation and socio-political equality. Although earlier Liberals still believed that the transcendentals were the necessary goals of self-development (according to a pre-Christian account of those transcendentals), later Liberals do not speak of truth, beauty and goodness as transcendentals at all. Their projects are not focused upon the clarification of principles of self-cultivation, but upon formulating theories of justice within which maximum freedom is granted the individual to pursue *any* version of self-development. With the transition to Bourgeois Liberalism, the whole notion of a standard for self-formation, and indeed even of a universally valid philosophical anthropology, is lost.

This transition from an Aristocratic to a Bourgeois Liberalism was one of the central themes of Romano Guardini's *The End of the Modern World*. Comparing the self-development of 'mass man' with the ideals of Goethe, Guardini observed:

Mass man has no desire for independence or originality in either the management or the conduct of his life. Nor does he seek to create an environment belonging only to himself, reflecting only his self. The gadgets and technics forced upon him by the patterns of machine production and of abstract planning he accepts quite simply; they are the forms of life itself ... Neither liberty of external action nor freedom of internal judgement seem for him to have unique value. And understandably so, for he has never experienced them.[17]

Thus, just as in the absence of a non-relativist account of the good and the beautiful, Aristocratic Liberalism is powerless to counter its disintegration to a Bourgeois form, so too, in the absence of a non-emotivist account of any of the transcendentals, the Bourgeois form is powerless to prevent its own descent into nihilism. There are however at least three versions of nihilism:

1 the despair of the 'mass man' who has no understanding of his potential for a life of grace, to which reference has been made above;
2 the behaviour of the Sartrean rebel to which reference was made in the previous chapter; and
3 the projects of those who aspire to transcend the predicament of 'mass man' by living 'beyond good and evil'.

The following section seeks to present the principles of self-cultivation found within the third of these, exemplified in the work of Nietzsche.

The Nietzschean model

In the encyclical *Veritatis Splendor*, reference was made to the fact that, once the idea of universal truth about the good is lost, there is also a consequent failure to identify and to recognise that in human nature which makes our freedom a real possibility, and beyond this sometimes a denial of the reality of a determinate human nature.[18] Such a denial is a fundamental principle of the Nietzschean conception of 'developing oneself culturally'. E. B. F. Midgley calls this the 'ontological instability' of the Nietzschean self.[19] For Nietzsche, developing oneself culturally does not mean that one strives to meet a particular pre-given standard of excellence, but rather to engage in a quest for authenticity. The Nietzschean perspective thus shares the Aristocratic Liberal interest in authenticity, but differs from the Aristocratic Liberal perspective in emphasising that such a quest is closed to plain persons; and whereas the Aristocratic Liberals still regard truth and goodness as desirable ideals, Nietzsche in his aspiration to live 'beyond good and evil' abandons truth and goodness for a neo-pagan conception of beauty as power.[20]

Also consistent with the Aristocratic Liberal tradition is the fact that the Nietzschean conception of authenticity lacks any substantive content. Jacob

Golomb describes it as a *pathos* of incessant change, as opposed to a passive subordination to one particular ethic.[21] Authenticity is a predicate not of character or the self, but of acts and *pathos*, and 'all types of pathos are of equal epistemological legitimacy'.[22] Golomb concludes that it follows from the central notion of Nietzsche's philosophy that there is no will, or what is called the 'will' is no more than a 'fluid collection of effects and a bundle of different types of pathos'.[23]

Throughout this quest for an 'authentic' self-formation, the rôle of reason is reduced to the instrumental function characterised by Hobbes as 'finding the way to the things desired'. Thoughts are treated by Nietzsche as the epiphenomena of the struggles between the competing Apollonian and Dionysian drives – they are 'signs of a play and struggle of effects'.[24] This is, of course, the complete inversion of the classical Christian model, according to which, even after the fall, the intellect retains the capacity to discern the difference between good and evil and master the emotional drives.

In addition to effectively eliminating the faculty of the will, and reducing the intellect to the status of servant of the emotional drives, Nietzsche also overturns the classical theistic accounts of the rôle of the memory. He suggests that those who seek to live beyond good and evil should 'consider the ability to experience life in a non-historical way as the most important and most original of experiences, as the foundation on which right, health, greatness, and anything truly human can be erected'.[25] They should copy the mode of life of animals, who allegedly 'forget at once'.[26] This Nietzschean prescription of a strategy of 'forgetting' anything that might circumscribe the subsequent behaviour of the self in its quest for authenticity is aided by other tendencies derived from the Enlightenment tradition(s) within the culture of modernity to discard the past. Indeed, in his commentary on Nietzsche's account of the rôle of memory, Paul de Man argued that the combined interplay of a deliberate forgetting with an action that is also a new origin reaches the full power of the idea of modernity.[27] It is, in other words, the culture of modernity's most definitive characteristic. Further, with the Liberal prescription of the compartmentalisation of the self, there is a tendency to abolish even the possibility of a collective memory. MacIntyre argues that one indicator of this is that storytelling has become a peripheral social activity.[28]

The 'prototypical' classical Christian model

In contrast to modernity's 'culture of forced (or deliberate) forgetting', the classical Christian model of self-cultivation is a specific instance of what the sociologist Paul Connerton calls a 'prototypical life' and a 'life of celebrated recurrence'.[29] The theological anthropology of *Gaudium et spes* paragraph 22 – the idea that the human person only possesses self-knowledge to the extent that he possesses knowledge of Christ, and the notion that Christ is the standard of a perfected humanity – means that the classical Christian model of self-cultivation is prototypical. Within such a life there is acknowledged a duty to sanctify time. The present is transformed into cycles of memory of past events such as saints' days and Christian feasts that confirm Christ as Lord of the temporal order – the *Alpha* and the *Omega* – while calling the remembering community to a realm which is beyond the temporal. Life is also a structure of celebrated recurrence in the sense that each life based on the classical Christian model follows through 'stages of grace' within the sacramental life of the Church, beginning with Baptism and ending with the Last Rites and Extreme Unction. Within such lives, each person possesses his or her own relationship with the Trinity, and from this relationship he or she receives a unique vocation. However, this classical Christian mode of individuality is not the object of self-cultivation, as it is in the Aristocratic Liberal and Nietzschean traditions. In the classical Christian model, 'individuality', which finds expression in a vocation, is a divine gift to be freely accepted or rejected. It is not self-created. Russell Hittinger has summarised the Thomistic and, in particular, the Balthasarian position thus:

> The perfection of human agency consists, for them [Aquinas and von Balthasar], in the participation in a mission that originates in the divine persons, and which takes concrete shape in the person of Christ. The other sub-themes of ethics (political, legal and personal) are not dissolved, but rather are keyed into a theological drama ... We are not created with intellective and volitional capacities simply in order to realise ourselves in these acts, but rather to serve a divine mission.[30]

Given the culture of modernity's anti-historical orientation and given also the Nietzschean 'erased blackboard' treatment of the faculty of the memory, any classical Christian account of the exercise of the right to culture within contemporary 'mass culture' needs to pay particular attention to the issue of the rôle of memory in this exercise. A 'prototypical life' of celebrated recurrence is unlikely to flourish within an anti-historical culture.[31] This means, in effect, that the problem identified by Paul VI as the 'split between the Gospel and culture', and by John Paul II as the 'challenge of secularism' and the trend towards a 'culture of death', cannot be adequately dealt with solely by attempting to revive the natural law doctrine and providing critiques of emotivism, utilitarianism and consequentialism. This work in defending the objectivity of the true and the good, which has been the focus of Catholic moral philosophy in the post-Conciliar era, especially during the pontificate of John Paul II, has been monumental and a necessary corrective to the widespread deference to Liberal ethical thought among 'Catholic' scholars. Nonetheless, this work has been related to the will and the intellect and needs to be supplemented with an account of the effect of 'mass culture' upon the memory and the soul's participation in the transcendental of beauty and, at a more general level, with an account of the relationships between knowledge, memory, tradition and the transcendentals.

Memory and 'sapiential experience'

In Book X of the *Confessions*, Augustine described the faculty of memory as a 'vast cloister' from which one recollects one's thoughts, and he drew attention to the relationship between memory and knowledge in his observation that the word *cogo*, meaning 'I assemble' or 'I collect', is related to *cogito*, which means 'I think', in the same way as *ago* is related to *agito*, or *facio* to *factito*.[32] In *De Trinitate* Augustine further spoke of the three powers of the soul as: *memoria*, *intellectus* and *voluntas*. St Bonaventure tied these faculties to the processions of the Trinity: 'the generating Mind, the Word, and Love are in the soul as memory, understanding and will, which are consubstantial, coequal and coeval and interpenetrate each other'.[33]

While the Augustinian–Bonaventuran accounts emphasise the analogy between memory, as one of the three faculties of the soul, and the Trinitarian processions, both St Albert in *De Bono* and St Thomas in *De Veritate* treat memory as an indispensable auxiliary of the virtue of prudence. Thus, Albert states that memory has two functions: it is a condition for what we know rationally (*habitus cognitivorum*) and a condition for making ethical judgements (*habitus moralium*). Further, memory is useful for making ethical judgements because 'memory takes in an event that is past as though it stayed ever-present in the soul as an idea and has an emotional effect on us, and so this event can be very effective for providing for the future'.[34]

Thomas, following Albert, speaks of memory as one of eight 'quasi-integral' parts of prudence: memory, understanding, docility, ingenuousness, reason, foresight, circumspection and caution.[35] Pamela Hall argues that this catalogue shows that, for the making of a prudential judgement, Aquinas required not merely deliberative skills but also an experience-gathering ability.[36] Similarly, Romanus Cessario argues that 'prudence incorporates personal experience into its own *habitus* formation' – it presupposes that a person has learned from human experience something about right dispositions.[37] The same point is made by his fellow Dominican, Servais Pinckaers: 'virtue involves all of man's faculties, including his sensibility, it develops according to a pedagogical process; it makes possible a judgement of connaturality' and 'this allows ethical sciences to approach all the nearer to concrete action, prudential judgement and experience'.[38] Cessario further observes that this emphasis on the element of human experience distinguishes Thomistic *prudentia* from both Aristotelian *phronesis* and the Kantian account of moral judgement. Contrary to Kant, there is a rôle for experience and the inclination of appetites; and contrary to Aristotelian *phronesis*, Thomistic prudence adds to the emphasis on the intellectual aspects of judgement, the rôle of the other faculties of the soul, including 'the quest of the Christian tradition – *amor meus, pondus meum*, my love, my inclination'.[39]

Speaking of the difference between Thomistic and post-Cartesian accounts of the concept of 'experience', Kenneth Schmitz argues that for Aquinas there is a kind of experience that could be classified as 'sapiential experience'. This is not a 'mere reduplication or reiteration of given facts, but includes a kind of directive for action that reaches beyond the facts towards the practice of some skill or the enactment of some conduct'.[40] This concept of 'sapiential experience' concurs with Cessario's judgement that there is a significant difference between Thomist and Aristotelian prudence, and Thomist and Kantian moral judgement, in that the Thomist position acknowledges a rôle for other faculties of the soul. It also concurs with the observation of Pinckaers that virtue involves all the soul's faculties, including its sensibility; and is in accord with Hall's argument that prudential judgements require both memory and foresight. The memory is thus the indispensable auxiliary of prudence because it is in the memory, or the 'vast cloister' as Augustine called it, that an experience of right and wrong dispositions and actions – the 'sapiential experience' – is stored.[41]

'Experience' is thus not a morally neutral phenomenon. Although Hall, Pinckaers, Schmitz and Cessario, among others, are drawing attention to the neglect within the Thomist tradition of the moral significance of experience and hence the faculty of the memory, and the effect of this neglect upon the Thomist understanding of prudential judgement, the Balthasarians may be interpreted as contributing to the development of a theological hermeneutic of culture by drawing attention to the moral significance of an experience of the transcendental properties of being – an experience which is stored in the memory:[42]

> No metaphysics of being qua being and of its transcendental determinations is separable from concrete experience, which is always sensuous. The truth and the openness of being as a whole will be seen only where a judgement is made about some precise thing that is true; the goodness of being will be experienced only where something that is good meets one, something that simultaneously brings near the good and (through its finitude, fragility, lack of goodness) takes it away again. It is from the experience of the senses that we know that the beautiful exists ... [43]

On this account, if the will is to be receptive to a virtuous development, especially to being motivated by charity or love, it must have an experience of goodness; and if the intellect is to be receptive to a virtuous use, especially to perfection by the theological virtue of faith, then it must first have some experience of truth; and if the memory is to be receptive to the theological virtue of hope, then it needs an experience of the beautiful.[44] In the case of the last one, the Transfiguration of Christ provides an example of how an experience of the beautiful can prepare the soul for the virtue of hope. St John of the Cross described the effect of hope on the memory as to 'fill it with pre-sentiments of eternal glory'.[45] A memory of an experience of beauty thereby operates to recall a despairing soul to an understanding of its true potential and nobility. Conversely, as Schmitz emphasises, Aquinas recognised that certain experiences can have an adverse impact upon the knower, since they may contribute to a loss of hope, courage or some other virtue.[46]

Although there are clearly differences in the treatments of the faculty of memory represented by Augustine and Bonaventure, on the one hand, and Albert and Thomas, on the other, it may be argued that these two ap-proaches are not only complementary but actually need to be synthesised in order to develop a richer account of 'self-cultivation' or, more precisely, the development of the soul, which is capable of providing an explanation for the apparent weakness of Christian faith and practice in contemporary culture. Specifically, it may be argued that, whereas Thomist scholarship has tended to focus on the relationship between the theological virtues and the facul-ties of the soul, and the more Augustinian Balthasarians on the relationship between the transcendental properties of being and the faculties of the soul, particularly beauty and the memory of its form, what needs to be developed is an account of 'self-cultivation' (soul formation) defined by the Trinitarian relations between theological virtues, faculties of the soul and transcenden-tal properties. In such a scheme, the intellect may retain its Thomist primacy as the faculty that is ultimately responsible for moral judgement, but none-theless the rôle of the memory and the will, and the soul's participation in the transcendental properties and perfection by theological virtues, are, in the words of Bonaventure, 'consubstantial, coequal and coeval and interpen-etrate each other'. The key relationships are set out below:

Faculty of the soul	Theological virtue	Transcendental property
Intellect	Faith	Truth
Will	Love	Goodness
Memory	Hope	Beauty

In each category the theological virtue operates upon a particular faculty of the soul to perfect its operation and participation in its corresponding transcendental property. Not only are the relationships Trinitarian in a linear sense as one goes across the columns, but the relationships are also Trinitarian as one moves down each column. The relationships could thus be better represented as a set of interlocking circles.

The Thomist tradition is replete with accounts of how souls become disor-dered when one or more of the theological virtues is lacking and the soul is thereby rendered incapable of full participation in the transcendental prop-erties.[47] What is not so developed within the tradition is an understanding of how different experiences and an immersion within different cultures and the boundaries created by different historical contexts affects the receptivity of the soul to grace. No doubt one reason for this is the legitimate concern that the tradition might be perceived to be engaging in its own version of historical determinism. However, if one adopts the metaphysical framework of William Norris Clarke (to which greater reference will be made in the following chapter) – that the human person must be understood in terms of both his or her *relationality* as well as *substantiality* – then it may be argued that it is possible to take the 'historical dimension' into account without jettisoning the non-historical.[48] Whereas John Paul II perceives there to be a 'super-imposing and mutual compenetration' of the *ontological* dimension (the flesh and spirit), the *ethical* dimension (moral good and evil) and the *pneumatological* dimension (the action of the Holy Spirit in the order of grace), one may argue that the human person is not exhaustively defined by these three dimensions, but rather that the *historical* dimension is also significant.[49] It is this historical dimension that covers the field of relationality and in which an experience of the transcendentals is found. In the words of Marcel Regnier, the human person is a 'historical being' and not simply 'a well-defined essence endowed with a principle of specific operations'.[50] Further, it may be argued that if the forms of the true, the beautiful and the good are not instantiated within this historical dimension, then the opportunities to develop what Schmitz calls 'sapiential experience' are diminished. Although John Paul II does not express the idea in terms of a neglected element within the metaphysical framework, he does acknowledge that:

> The struggle and rebellion taking place in the human heart finds in every period of history and especially in the modern era its external dimension, which takes concrete form as the content of culture and civilisation, as a philosophical system, an ideology, a programme for action and for the shaping of human behaviour.[51]

Reference has already been made to this significant passage in Chapter 2, where it was observed that it is precisely in this passage that John Paul II comes closest to a cultural critique of modernity and outright rejection of the Liberal tradition. The specific question that John Paul II did not address in this analysis is: What is the effect upon self-formation of a culture which is the result of an atheistic philosophical system, ideology and programme for action? And more specifically: What is the effect of its architecture, music, literature and indeed the whole realm of its arts, institutional practices, modes of dress and modes of social relating upon self-formation? An analysis of these questions will require an exploration of the relationships set out above.

The problem of 'mass culture'

Of the three horizontal lines, the relationship between memory, hope and beauty has been both the relationship least examined and the relationship most likely to have been adversely affected by the creation of cultures of 'forced and deliberate forgetting' and the marginalisation of beauty in their emphasis upon technology, efficiency and functionality.[52] In the absence of beauty and with a conception of the memory as, at best, a faculty for storing data, or, at its most base, a board to be erased, 'mass man' is often without hope. Romano Guardini identified the problem as a causal relationship between the lack of a 'fruitful and lofty culture' that provides the sub-soil for a healthy nature, and a spiritual life that is 'numb and narrow' and develops along 'mawkish, perverted and unlawful lines'.[53] Implicit within this judgement is the idea that the historical dimension is important for moral formation.

One major aspect of von Balthasar's project was to demonstrate that within the mass culture of modernity the Trinitarian relationship between the true, the beautiful and the good has been disintegrating, and in particular the beautiful has been close to eclipsed. In Guardini's terms, this means that the sub-soil is barren, and it explains why von Balthasar believed that this severance was not merely of significance for intellectual historians, but that it has affected the very possibilities for evangelisation. As a consequence of this 'transcendental aridity' of contemporary mass culture, 'man feels himself to be so humiliated through the disfigurement and denial of form', that he 'daily experiences the temptation to despair of the dignity of existence and to break off all association with a world which disowns and destroys its own nature as image'.[54] Although John Paul II in his Apostolic Exhortation *Ecclesia in America* identified the need to evangelise those who live in urban environments, and although statements of the Pontifical Council for Culture, to which reference was made in Chapter 2, acknowledge that atheism and a sense of social alienation are common phenomena found in urban environments, neither statement takes the further step of suggesting that 'mass culture' is itself a significant theological problem.[55] This would require a recognition that modernity is not merely a series of intellectual propositions, but an entire culture, which includes its music, architecture, literature, institutional practices, modes of dress and social relating.

In such circumstances the Church cannot remain indifferent to the various domains of culture, on the grounds that she has (in some undefined sense) recognised the 'autonomy' of such domains. Each domain will either foster or hinder the instantiation of the truth, beauty and goodness of the grace of the Incarnation, and, to the degree that persons have no experience of the transcendentals, their 'exercise of the right to culture' will be impoverishing, even self-destructive. Classical Thomism neglected an analysis of the ways in which truth, beauty and goodness are instantiated within a culture, perhaps because Aquinas wrote at a time in history when the various cultural domains, however imperfect, were self-consciously open to such an instantiation. However, in an age characterised by, in von Balthasar's words, 'the disfigurement and denial of the forms of truth, beauty and goodness', the tradition of Thomism needs to be enriched with a more developed account of the Trinitarian relationships between faculties of the soul, their formation through an experience of the transcendentals and their perfection by the theological virtues. Such an enriched anthropology would provide principles for the exercise of a 'right to culture' and principles by which to judge the effects of 'mass culture' upon the exercise of this so-called 'right'.

From this perspective the classical Christian model for the exercise of the 'right to culture' is inherently 'aristocratic', but in a different sense from Aristocratic Liberalism and Nietzscheanism. The last two presuppose that the capability of exercising the 'right to culture' is limited to those with special abilities – the 'intellectual aesthetes' to whom reference was made in Chapter 1. In this sense the classical Christian model is radically egalitarian, since it is open to all who have been baptised. However, unlike the Liberal and Nietzschean, the classical Christian model does not hold that any kind of self-cultivation is good so long as it is self-directed and not imposed by an external authority or tradition. On the contrary, the classical Christian model of culture, in terms of both artistic standards and the development of the soul, is 'aristocratic' in the sense that it is predicated on the soul's participation in the transcendentals understood as modes of being. Some artistic forms, and some human actions and relationships are better than others because they participate to a greater degree in the transcendental properties of being. This means that the classical Christian model recognises standards and gradations of cultural excellence. The classical Christian model is also 'aristocratic' in the sense that it demands behaviour of a self-sacrificial, and hence chivalrous, character, in contrast to the self-assertive demands of the Aristocratic Liberal and Nietzschean models. Accordingly, as von Balthasar believed:

> Those who withdraw to the heights to fast and pray in silence are ... the pillars bearing the spiritual weight of what happens in history. They share in the uniqueness of Christ, in the freedom which cannot be caged or put to use. Theirs is the first of all aristocracies, source and justification for all the others, and the last yet remaining to us in an unaristocratic age.[56]

The possibility of a 'modern Catholic self'

The idea that there currently exist three dominant models of self-cultivation is not only found within MacIntyre's work, but is the subject of a series of publications by Charles Taylor. These include *Sources of the Self: The Making of the Modern Identity*, *The Ethics of Authenticity*, the Marianist Award Lecture published in *A Catholic Modernity?* and a 1996 Castel Gandolfo symposium lecture delivered in the presence of John Paul II entitled *Die immanente Gegenaufklärung*.[57] In these publications, Taylor acknowledges that there exist three separate categories of concepts or 'value-menus' for the cultural development of the self:

1   those associated with pre-modern theism;
2   those associated with the Enlightenment emphasis on the authority of disengaged reason; and
3   those associated with Romantic expressivism or 'one of its modernist successor visions'.[58]

Accordingly, Taylor observes that the culture of modernity and its associate concepts of self-cultivation can be conceptualised as a 'space in which one can move in three dimensions – through the original theistic foundation and the two independent [Enlightenment and Romantic] frontiers'.[59]

If one construes the Nietzschean or the Genealogical as a variety of the Romantic dimension in post-Enlightenment philosophy, then MacIntyre and Taylor are essentially in agreement regarding the different value-menus that are available for the cultivation of the self. However, notwithstanding their agreement on the sources of the various value options, MacIntyre and Taylor differ in their judgement about the ability of these sources to be synthesised to form a framework of values for a 'modern' Catholic self. Taylor, on the one hand, suggests that 'the claims upon us of one set of (genuine) goods' – (that is, theistic, Enlightenment or Romantic) – do not 'refute the claims of a rival set', and thus suggests that a higher synthesis of all three sources is required. MacIntyre, on the other hand, believes that a higher synthesis is not possible, and asserts that it is in 'terms of some overall coherence of every genuine claim about goods with every other that the genuine good is to be distinguished from the deceptive simulacrum'.[60]

The three central properties of the Romantic tradition which Taylor believes are significant for the quest of self-cultivation are (a) the 'affirmation of ordinary life', (b) the focus on 'inwardness' and (c) the interest in the 'inner voice of nature'. Since these concepts all have a theological origin, Taylor argues that there is not necessarily any irresolvable conflict between their expression and theism, and further that the tradition of pre-modern theism has actually benefited from elements of both the Enlightenment and Romantic traditions:

> The notion is that modern culture, in breaking with the structures and beliefs of Christendom, also carried certain facets of Christian life fur-

ther than they would have been taken within Christendom. In relation to the earlier forms of Christian culture we have to face the humbling realization that the breakout was a necessary condition of development.[61]

From MacIntyre's perspective, however, the concepts of 'ordinary life', 'inwardness' and 'the inner voice of nature', like the concepts of rationality, justice and virtue, mean radically different things within different traditions; and, further, the breakout, as Taylor calls it, would not have been possible but for the Protestant severance of the secular and sacred into distinct ontological orders. The concept of 'nature', for example, is radically different in each of the Thomist, Liberal and Nietzschean traditions. In the Thomist tradition, the concept cannot be understood without reference to the concepts of grace, creation, providence, divine law and human nature; in the Liberal tradition, providence and grace either do not exist or are irrelevant and human nature has no particular telic orientation, whereas in the Nietzschean tradition, nature does determine one's destiny, but there is no universal human nature and providence and grace remain otiose. Each person is a unique bundle of emotional drives and must create him/herself.

Similarly, the concept of the spiritual value of 'ordinary life' differs quite dramatically between these traditions. Although 'ordinary life' may be affirmed from a Catholic perspective, such an affirmation is different in both theory and practice from an affirmation of ordinary life from Lutheran and post-Reformation perspectives.[62] Taylor acknowledges the close association of his concept with that of the Lutheran tradition when he states:

> What I am trying to gesture at with the term 'affirmation of ordinary life' is the cultural revolution of the early modern period, which dethroned the supposedly higher activities of contemplation and the citizen life and put the center of gravity of goodness in ordinary living, production and the family.[63]

The concept of a 'universal call to holiness', which received approval at Vatican II, and its associate concept of the sanctification of daily work, itself a transference of the Benedictine idea of the sanctification of labour from the specifically monastic sphere to the world at large, was not coupled – at least at the magisterial level – with a rejection of the value of monastic life, as it was in the Lutheran tradition. Taylor acknowledges that the concept 'underlies our contemporary bourgeois politics', and he concedes that 'the affirmation of ordinary life involves a polemical stance towards those traditional views [presumably those of the pre-Reformation monastic traditions] and their implied elitism'.[64] Indeed, Taylor implied that he agreed with the Lutheran criticism of monasticism, when he argued that 'these vocations [in monasteries] were meant to mark out elite paths of superior dedication, but were, in fact, deviations into pride and self-delusion'.[65] Any elements of the pre-modern theistic heritage that might be retained in a synthesis for a 'Catholic modernity', or 'Modern Catholic self' would thus on his account have to assimilate the typically Lutheran and Calvinist 'affirmation of ordinary life', at the probable expense of earlier views which gave priority to contemplation and doxology, and which emphasised that a participation in civic life was part of the Christian notion of the good life.

Of even greater significance are the differences between the pre-modern and subsequent Cartesian understandings of 'inwardness'. These differences are readily acknowledged by Taylor, and their development is traced in his *Sources of the Self*. The difference has also been addressed by Kenneth Schmitz in his treatment of the theological significance of nominalism. Schmitz observes that the 'principal victim' of nominalism's attack was 'not just the lumber of the scholastic framework' – the Thomistic scheme of first, formal, final and efficient causes – but the 'resident being that lived within the house':

> The interiority of modern subjectivity is vastly different in character and motive from the ontological interiority that, as traditional metaphysics appreciates, is resident in all being as the heritage of every created being ... the purpose of Christian interiority is not to find itself a refuge (whether Cartesian, Humean or Kantian, rationalist, empiricist, or transcendental) – but to place itself before the transcendent Source of whatever being, meaning, and value the human person possesses as a gift received.[66]

Schmitz concludes that this pre-Reformation process of interior reflection is characterised by an *ascesis* of self-examination, self-purgation and self-denial, rather than the Romantic emphasis on self-assertion and self-fulfilment.

Taylor acknowledges the distinction between what might be defined broadly as 'pre-modern' and 'modern' interiority when he observes that the denial (inherent in modern forms of interiority) that human life finds any point of reference beyond itself amounts to an 'eclipse of the transcendent' and gives rise to an 'exclusive humanism', that is a notion of human flourishing which recognises no valid aims beyond itself.[67] Taylor asserts that a 'denial of transcendence has penetrated far deeper and wider than simple card-carrying, village atheist style secularists', and that it also shapes the outlook of many people who see themselves as 'believers'.[68] In other words, Taylor argues that, among those in contemporary society who claim a belief in some form of theism, there is a 'climate of thought' or 'horizon of assumptions' that leads to an 'eclipse of the transcendent', which is different from an explicit self-conscious rejection of the transcendent. This gives rise to a 'spiritual hunger', which is often met by 'turning to forms that lie within the reach of an exclusive humanism' or that 'thoroughly blur the boundary between immanent and transcendent; as if this whole issue, so central to all the great religious traditions, were no longer visible to many people'.[69] Taylor believes that this condition has only arisen within the last half-century and that it has been accompanied by a heightened regard for the 'Romantic' ethic of authenticity. In place of the pre-modern theistic quest for participation in the transcendental properties of being, there is now the following constellation of attitudes:

1   the supreme value of human life is found in the elimination of suffering and the driving back of the frontiers of death;
2   owing to the religious emphasis upon the higher goals of spiritual perfection, this approach to life was not characteristic of pre-modern cultures; and
3   that we have arrived at point 1 by an overcoming and critique of such pre-modern religion.[70]

Notwithstanding this denial or eclipse of transcendence within the culture of modernity, Taylor believes that there exists a possibility that the ethic of authenticity may at some future time become open to an acknowledgement of the importance of the transcendental realm – that there might be a reconciliation between the theistic and romantic heritage and a synthesis of their values. Taylor defends his optimism for such a synthesis with the argument that 'the obstacles to belief in Western modernity are primarily moral and spiritual, rather than epistemic'.[71] In other words, he argues that the hostility to the theistic heritage within the culture of modernity is not based on epistemological foundations but rather on a prejudice of a 'post-revolutionary climate'. Taylor defines a post-revolutionary climate as one that is 'extremely sensitive to anything which smacks of the *ancien régime*, and sees backsliding even in relatively innocent concessions to generalised human preferences'.[72] He gives as an example of this the Puritan aversion to liturgical practices, which were evocative of Catholic ritual, and the Bolshevik proscription of the title 'Mister', which was symbolic of bourgeois manners. Taylor's thesis is thus that the contemporary hostility of the culture of modernity to aspects of the theistic heritage, including the realm of the transcendent, is but an aspect of the attitude that it was pre-modern religion which was responsible for the alleged lack of interest in human welfare. In a post-revolutionary climate, all aspects of the theistic heritage are understandably, if erroneously, treated in a hostile manner, regardless of whether they were, as a matter of fact, responsible for those aspects of the former heritage now deemed to be obscurantist. However, in a post-post-revolutionary culture we may be able to appreciate both the human and the transcendent.

Contrary to Taylor, MacIntyre's position is that the hostility *does* have an epistemic basis and further that it may be found in the Reformers' attack on the epistemic authority of 'Tradition' and the hierarchical ecclesiology of the Catholic Church. The Lutheran dogma of 'faith alone', 'Scripture alone' and 'God alone' introduced subjectivity and diversity into an order which was based on tradition, sacraments and hierarchy, for which 'certainty' and 'objectivity' and 'universalism' were the inherent values. This Reformation attack itself followed a period of 'decadent' scholasticism, which culminated in the Suarezian interpretation of Aquinas that MacIntyre holds as a 'modern' distortion of classical Thomism.[73] The synthesis of Patristic theology and Aristotelian philosophy effected by Aquinas was systematically dismantled in the period of late scholastic philosophy and Reformation theology and was finally debased by Cartesian philosophy and Jansenist theology. Therefore, for MacIntyre, the hostility to theism within the culture of modernity is *essentially* epistemic, even though he may well agree with Taylor that we live in a 'post-revolutionary climate', that is an era of 'forced forgetting', and that this carries within it an extreme sensitivity to anything evocative of the old order, and that this sensitivity is frequently without any rational basis.

In his account of the sources of the modern self, Taylor does not treat the distinctions between the Catholic and Protestant contributions to the theistic heritage as being of great significance. When Taylor uses the expression 'Judeo-Christian' he appears to include the Reformation traditions, whereas MacIntyre prefers the narrower terms of 'Augustinian Tradition', 'Thomist Tradition' and the 'Mosaic Law'. In *A Short History of Ethics*, MacIntyre went so far as to treat Luther with Machiavelli, Hobbes and Spinoza, rather than dealing with his ideas in the preceding chapter entitled 'Christianity'. As Schmitz has emphasised, the whole Reformation theological framework was heavily influenced by nominalism and its attack on the Patristic Thomistic understanding of the individual soul's ability to participate in the transcendental properties of being and the life of the Trinity. This distinction between pre- and post-Reformation Christianity is therefore of crucial significance in understanding the distinction between the classical Christian and the modern notions of self-cultivation. Indeed, Schmitz has drawn attention to the fact that Hegel dubbed the modern inward turn 'the Protestant Principle'.[74]

The difference between MacIntyre and Taylor can thus be explained as a particular instance of the issue of the value to be given to what sociologists and intellectual historians call 'Protestant culture'. Taylor argues that the 'breakout' was good for the purposes of a theistic form of self-cultivation, whereas MacIntyre views the breakout as a transition from an order in which both rationality and self-cultivation are linked to the concepts of tradition, sacraments and a sacerdotal hierarchy, to one based upon a rival conception of self-cultivation unmediated by a priestly and sacramental order or any matrix of culturally embodied practices.[75]

Conclusion

The ambit of the notion of self-development or self-cultivation, or what in German is called *Bildung* and in Greek *Paideia*, is almost infinite. All such notions have in common, however, what Przywara calls the 'fundamental engagements of the soul'. Different conceptions of the exercise of the 'right to culture' are thus predicated upon different understandings of the soul, its faculties and, it has been argued, their relationship to the transcendentals in the contemporary world.

Both 'wings' of the Liberal tradition – the Aristocratic and the Bourgeois – have served to foster the Nietzschean conception of self-cultivation. On the one hand, the Aristocratic focus on the concept of *die schöne Seele* may be construed as the precursor to Nietzsche's *Übermenschen* concept, and, on the other, Nietzsche's contempt for Bourgeois Liberalism's preference for utility and functionality rather than originality, individuality and greatness may be credited with generating a kind of 'Thermidorian reaction' in Nietzsche and his followers. Certain kinds of Thomists (the non-Whig variety) and Nietzscheans are thus united in their opposition to bourgeois cultures, and united in fostering what Werner Sombart and Christopher Dawson called an 'erotic' culture. Where the two traditions differ, however, is over the ends to which the *eros* is directed, and the competence of plain persons to be involved in the project at all. However, whereas the classical Christian and the Nietzschean conceptions of self-cultivation share an opposition to Bourgeois Liberal conceptions, both the Bourgeois Liberal conceptions and the Nietzschean share a tendency, in opposition to the classical Christian, to suppress the faculty of memory in this process of self-cultivation, and to reduce the rôle of the intellect to that of an instrumental service of the passions or 'drives'. Above all they are united in the promotion of a 'culture of forced or deliberate forgetting'. By contrast, the faculty of memory is significant from the Augustinian–Bonaventurian–Balthasarian perspectives for recollecting the true, the beautiful and the good, and thereby providing the soul with standards of cultural excellence, and it is significant from the Albertine Thomist perspective for the development of the virtue of prudence.[76]

According to this analysis, the difficulty with any endorsement of 'mass culture' is that it gives the Church's blessing to a 'low' and non-erotic culture that stifles the exercise of the right to culture; the difficulty with Lambert's rejection of the 'aristocratic ideal of culture' is that it can mean anything from a conception which takes its bearings from the ideas of the Fathers and the Scholastics, and their classical Greek, Roman or Hebrew precursors, through to the Enlightenment-style conception of the Earl of Shaftesbury, the neo-Dionysian conceptions of Nietzsche or the ideas of a number of nineteenth- and early-twentieth-century authors on the subject of culture – including Matthew Arnold, Samuel Taylor Coleridge, T. S. Eliot and John Ruskin. All of these authors have in common the idea that cultural formation is characterised by the quest to achieve ideals. The ideals differ according to the theological perspectives of the authors, but they all agree that *some* persons, *some* societies and *some* institutions may be more or less successful in this quest than others. Thus all these different perspectives can be described as 'aristocratic'. Any negative references to 'aristocratic culture' found within theological discourse thus need to be clear about precisely which version of 'aristocratic culture' is to be condemned.

Although it is correct to describe 'mass culture' as a 'genuine contemporary cultural creation', as Dondeyne does, this merely means that it is a specific type of *Kultur*. It does not follow from this, as a matter of logic, that such a *Kultur* is fertile soil for the flourishing of Christian practices. The 'democratic' nature of 'mass culture' means that although it may be a culture in the *Kultur* sense, the essence of this *Kultur* is to be an anti-culture, that is a *Kultur* without a corresponding conception of *Bildung*. This was essentially Guardini's insight when he spoke of a 'non-cultural culture'.[77] In the sense developed here, it is a 'bourgeois' rather than an 'erotic' *Kultur*: it prefers uniformity and conventionality to individuality, as it is variously understood in the Aristocratic Liberal, Nietzschean and classical Christian traditions.

Finally, the proposal of Taylor – to work towards a synthesis of the various sources of the self to effect a 'Modern Catholic self' – can only succeed if certain presuppositions of the rival sources are assimilated to classical Thomism, especially the Lutheran–Calvinist version of the 'affirmation of ordinary life'. Such a project would however appear to foster the sociological phenomenon of persons being 'Catholic in faith, but Protestant in practice', or, more precisely, Catholic in denominational allegiance, but Protestant in both theory and practice. Taylor's project may therefore be construed as one which runs parallel to that of Whig Thomism. Whereas the Whig Thomists are focused on a reconciliation of the Enlightenment and Thomist traditions in the context of political and economic philosophy, and, thus, culture as *Kultur* – Taylor's work is focused on a similar synthesis but with the emphasis upon culture as a form of self-cultivation or *Bildung*. In the following chapter it will be argued that the logic of Whig Thomism also impels the Thomist tradition in the direction of an endorsement of a Protestant form of culture.

Finally, although Taylor focused on three particular properties of the Romantic movement, each of which are problematic from the perspective of classical Thomism, he did not focus on those aspects of the Romantic movement that relate to an opposition to Enlightenment conceptions of rationality, especially the tendency to denigrate the rôle of memory and tradition in the formation of the soul. These elements of the Romantic movement are consistent with the general orientation of postmodern Augustinian Thomist scholarship, but they are not treated by its proponents as new elements of the Thomist tradition. Rather, they are regarded as elements that have been neglected within the post-seventeenth-century tradition, and the neglect is explained by the focus of the tradition's masters upon the intellect in an effort to meet the epistemological standards of the Enlightenment(s).

5

THE *LOGOS* OF THE *KULTUR* OF MODERNITY

Whereas Chapter 3 dealt with the issue of the *ethos* or *Geist* of institutional practices and the epistemic authority of experts, bureaucratic managers and ostensibly neutral public institutions, and Chapter 4 with the effect of modernity's mass culture upon the opportunities for a classical Christian *Bildung*, this fifth chapter will focus on critiques of the form or 'logic' of the culture (*Kultur*) of modernity.[1] These critiques all converge on the argument that the construction of a theory of culture consistent with the Christocentrism of paragraph 22 of *Gaudium et spes* requires the rejection of the idea that cultures are 'theologically neutral'. From a Christocentric perspective, 'every created entity of the cosmos, every aspect of every entity, is, from the beginning of its existence, related to God in Christ'.[2] In other words, 'Christ affects the cosmos not only efficiently and finally but also formally'.[3] As a matter of logic it follows from this that cultures cannot be 'autonomous' in the popular sense of the word. Rather, as von Balthasar acknowledged, 'the interpretation of the grace–nature distinction affects one's understanding of the structure of metaphysics, ethics, apologetics, politics, and the entire praxis of human life', which of course includes the realms of institutional practices, conceptions of self-formation, and the logic of cultural forms.[4] This incarnational theology is explained in short-hand form by David Schindler as the idea that every *ethos* always needs a *logos* that precedes it and gives it meaning.[5]

Another way of presenting these ideas is to say that, whereas the treatment of culture in *Gaudium et spes* and in the articles of *periti* such as Bernard Lambert is consistent with an extrinsicist construction of the grace–nature relationship, the critiques of the *logos* of the culture of modernity to be presented in this chapter are all predicated upon a rejection of this construction in favour of de Lubac's reading of the relationship. For this reason the chapter will begin with an account of the intellectual history of de Lubac's project and its development in the works of David Schindler and Kenneth Schmitz. It will further be argued that the theological critiques of Schindler and Schmitz, and account of the *logos* of the culture of modernity as the form of the machine, are needed to provide a theological foundation to MacIntyre's otherwise philosophical and sociological insights; and that, taken together, the critiques of the 'culture of America' to be found in the works of, *inter alios*, MacIntyre, Schindler and Schmitz, lead to the conclusion, contrary to that of the Whig Thomists, that this culture is hostile to both the flourishing of virtue and the reception of grace.

Invalidations of the secular

Although MacIntyre has examined the failure of the Enlightenment's attempt to construct a conception of human flourishing upon an allegedly theologically disengaged rationality, he has not examined the theological counterpoint to this project, namely the attempted severance of the orders of nature and grace.[6] This work has been undertaken by Henri de Lubac and contemporary scholars who draw upon de Lubac's heritage, particularly the members of the Communio school. The possibility of an assimilation of the insights of this school to MacIntyre's critique has however already been prepared for by MacIntyre's identification of the severance of reality into secular and sacred realms as problematic. In *Marxism: An Introduction*, he wrote:

> When the sacred and the secular are divided, then religion becomes one more department of human life, one activity among others ... then the natural becomes an end, not the hallowing of the world, but in itself. Likewise if our religion is fundamentally irrelevant to our politics, then we are recognising the political as a realm outside of God. To divide the sacred from the secular is to recognise God's action only within the narrowest limits.[7]

Thus, at the time when the Rahnerian reading of the culture of modernity as a 'must be' was the common reading of *Gaudium et spes* and the issues raised therein, MacIntyre regarded such readings as inherently anti-religious. Writing as a Marxist sociologist in 1968 he stated that 'nothing has been more startling than to note how much contemporary Christian theology is concerned with trying to perform Feuerbach's work all over again'.[8] He further observed that in secular society Christianity has a tendency to present itself as having a *relevant* content and function by presenting itself as having a *secular* content and function, and this in turn gives rise to the many attempts to demythologise Christianity – 'to disentangle the relevant kernel from the irrelevant husk'.[9] In effect this means:

> The function of religion which consisted in providing a radical criticism of the secular present is lost by those contemporary demythologizers whose goal is to assimilate Christianity to the secular present.[10]

At the same time as this 'secularising' project was going on, however, the project of 'invalidating the secular order', which had begun early in the twentieth century with the scholarship of Maurice Blondel and Henri de Lubac, was continuing apace and drawing Christian theology in the opposite direction. Inherent within de Lubac's theology of grace was the rejection of an understanding of the grace–nature relationship as one of an extrinsic relation of two completely separate orders. The word 'extrinsicism' was coined by Blondel in *History and Dogma* to describe the neo-scholastic position, in contrast to the term 'historicism' which he used to characterise the modernist view.[11] De Lubac argued that the extrinsicist understanding rested on a false (late mediaeval and counter-Reformation) interpretation of the position of St Thomas. In his account of this argument in *Passage to Modernity*, Louis Dupré explains that, while Aquinas recognised a purely philosophical conception of nature as an object of rational reflection independent of revelation, in the concrete order of reality this was for him merely an abstraction.[12] The validation of an autonomous 'secular' order in late scholasticism by scholars preparing commentaries of the work of Aquinas was based on an unintentional failure to distinguish between 'pure nature' as an object of philosophical speculation, and pure nature in the order of concrete reality. As Georges Chantraine explains the intellectual history, 'Thomists had become accustomed to reading St Thomas's texts on this topic with the eyes of nineteenth century rationalists, paradoxically fascinated by sixteenth century scholasticism, itself already stamped with rationalism'.[13]

For de Lubac, the idea of a pure nature contained dangerous Pelagian tendencies, since it meant that it would be possible to sever grace from nature and marginalise it under the category of the 'supernatural'. The supernatural could subsequently be privatised and social life would then proceed on the basis of the common pursuit of goods associated solely with the 'natural' order. The next step would be for the perfection of the natural order to be treated as synonymous with the Christian project. Once the achievement of worldly perfection becomes an end in itself the 'Christian project' becomes indistinguishable from the Enlightenment project, and humanity, once again, seeks perfection by relying on its own powers. In MacIntyre's words, 'the natural becomes an end, not the hallowing of the world'. Paradoxically, the belief in the existence of a 'pure nature' can also foster Jansenism since there is no longer a 'natural' orientation or longing for the supernatural. With such an 'extrinsic' account of the relationship of nature to grace, the interpretation of the human *telos* thereby ends up at either of two extremes – Pelagian or Jansenist – depending on whether one is optimistic or pessimistic about the potential of nature without grace.

Dupré argues that one reason for the popularity of the extrinsicist interpretation is that the concept of 'pure nature' is very Aristotelian: 'Aristotle's concept of nature followed a strictly immanentist teleology in which the end had to be strictly proportionate to the available human means'.[14] Although Aquinas agreed with Aristotle that nature contained some immanent teleology – for example, virtue and contemplation in the good city – this defined only part of the whole reality for Aquinas. As a pre-Christian account of human nature, it left unexplored the whole dimension of grace. Dupré and de Lubac argued that, while Aquinas was sensitive to this missing dimension, and supplied for it in various ways in his complex system, later commentators on his work, for example Suarez and Sylvester of Ferrara, were less alert to this distinction between the thought of Aquinas and Aristotle. Accepting Aristotle's principle concerning the proportion of ends to means, they denied that nature was capable of any supernatural desire or end at all. The rejection of this concept of a really existing pure nature by de Lubac and others associated with the Nouvelle Théologie thus effected a major shift in the interpretation of the relationship between nature and grace within classical Thomism as it is read in contemporary times.[15]

The logic of identities in relation

Schindler agrees that the use of Aristotelian categories to explain the grace–nature problematic has added to rather than lightened the burden of that task. He argues that the creature's relation to God is not 'substantial': not inscribed in the essence or nature of the creature, such that the divine nature and created nature would be confused – or one or the other eliminated. But that relation likewise is not 'accidental': it is not something that 'happens to' the already-constituted nature of the creature, and thus remains extrinsic to that nature.[16] Schindler therefore eschews the use of the substance/accident terminology of Aristotle to describe the relationship between nature and grace and in its place he offers a theory of relations.[17] In particular his 'logic of relation' requires a rejection of the principle of simple identity – the principle according to which x, whatever be its content, has its identity in itself, apart from or outside of relation to non-x.[18] In this he follows the Heideggerian critique of Cartesian rationality which has been embraced by postmodern scholars.[19] He does not, however, eschew the concept of substantiality altogether, as postmoderns frequently do. Rather he follows the argument of William Norris Clarke that 'relationality and substantiality go together as two distinct but inseparable modes of reality', analogous to that of the identities-in-relation within the Trinity.[20] Norris Clarke presents the argument thus:

> Within the divine being, the relations of procession between the Three Persons are not accidental but constitutive of the very nature of the divine substance. Substantiality and relationality are here equally primordial and necessary dimensions of being itself at its highest intensity.[21]

While the development of a metaphysical framework wherein relationality and substantiality are treated as equally primordial aspects of being has been the focus of the work of Norris Clarke, and has been adopted by Schindler, the idea is also evident in the works of Ratzinger and Kasper. Ratzinger has argued that the 'undivided sway of thinking in terms of substance is ended', while Kasper endorses a 'Trinitarian ontology' wherein 'ultimate reality is conceivable not in terms of a self-subsistent substance but of a person who is fulfilled only in a selfless relationality of giving and receiving'.[22] Furthermore, Schindler implicitly agrees with MacIntyre that all conceptions of rationality are tradition dependent when he suggests that there are at least two distinct 'logics' of intelligence: one secular, one credal Christian.

The 'secular' logic has as its hallmark the principle of simple identity. Its features come to expression in the manner in which causal activity is understood primarily in terms of effectivity; in the manner in which episte-mological primacy is accorded to negation, doubt and control, over affirma-tion, faith and openness; and in the manner in which meaning is derived by breaking the action or question into ever smaller bits for an analysis of the simplest conceptual units, or by the addition of differences.[23] In contrast, the 'credal' logic has as its hallmark the principle of identities already in relation. Its features come to expression in several different ways: causal activity understood first as forceful gives way to activity that is from within and to effective activity now understood to be creative and generous rather than self-assertive; the primacy of negation, doubt and control gives way to a primacy of affirmation, receptivity and responsiveness.[24] Schindler is not arguing that these two logics are mutually exclusive or that the first is to be rejected altogether, but rather that for the fortunes of Christianity it is crucial which logic is accorded primacy.[25] This is because the presupposition of the principle of simple identity as a first principle forces inclusion by way of dualistic addition, whereas the presupposition of the principle of relation leads to inclusion by way of integration.[26]

Schindler further argues that there needs to be a recognition that all 'log-ics' are guided at the outset by some presupposed truth. For a secularised 'Cartesian' logic, the truth is the principle of simple identity; for the 'credal Christian' logic, the truth is the principle of Trinitarian processions. From this he concludes that the appropriate question is 'not whether one will weight intellectual enquiry in advance but *how* one will do so'[27] On this view:

> The Christian then, precisely as Christian, is committed to showing the how and where and in what ways relation (openness and interiority) show up ... in the natural and human entities of the cosmos. This requires on-tological (cosmological, anthropological) inquiry which is distinct from theology, even as it is never to be separate from theology.[28]

This description parallels that of members of the Radical Orthodoxy circle, who have described their project as one of re-envisaging the particular cultural spheres from a theological perspective. In effect, such a view calls for an entirely new synthesis, not merely of the orders of nature and grace, faith and reason, but of the entire realm of culture, understood as the *ethos* of our institutions, the principles or *nomoi* for the development of the soul, and the *logos* of the *Kultur* of all societies which have been evangelised. Fundamental to such a project will be the analysis of the various spheres of culture with something like Schindler's logic of 'identities in relation'. Its orientation is the opposite of the Cartesian methodology, according to which meaning is first and essentially discrete, arrived at by breaking up identities-in-relation into identities perceived in isolation from their relationships and gained by the addition of differences. This methodology explains in part the tension between the school of 'Analytical Thomism', whose method tends to follow the standard Cartesian approach, and the Balthasarians, who rely upon a conception of truth and rationality which is 'symphonic'.

The mechanical form of the 'secular logic'

An example of the 'mechanical form' of a 'secular logic', especially the characteristics of deriving meaning from the analysis of the smallest conceptual units of a tradition and synthesis by way of the addition of differences, may be found in an article by Timothy Chappell. Chappell boldly claims that 'in political philosophy and in ethics, Thomism has not come to abolish the Enlightenment project, but to fulfil it'.[29] He concedes that 'the ethics of the Enlightenment lacks coherence', but only because it 'lacks a good account of the human *telos*' (this idea he claims to take from MacIntyre), and he further concludes that Thomists should 'secure the magnificent achievements of the Enlightenment project in forwarding social justice and human well-being by giving it a good account of the human *telos*'.[30] This is an example of what Schindler calls synthesis by way of the addition of differences. One takes the political and economic philosophies of the Enlightenment traditions and tacks them onto a 'good account of the human *telos*'. In doing so, one presupposes that the principles to be found in the political and economic philosophies of the Enlightenment traditions will not displace or otherwise be inconsistent with the long-standing elements of the Thomist account of the human *telos*.

Among the 'magnificent achievements' of the Enlightenment traditions, Chappell lists 'liberalism, individualism, rights theory, and the welfare state'. These are listed without any acknowledgement of the extensive criticisms of each of these concepts to be found within the corpus of Thomist scholarship. Chappell further states that we should '*never mind the pedigree*' of each of these concepts, '*just look at its results*'.[31]

Schindler, however, along with MacIntyre, is not only deeply sceptical about the Enlightenment's 'magnificent' achievements but also regards the pedigree of concepts to be of the first importance. This is because he believes that concepts are not value neutral but are always related to the philosophical–theological presuppositions of the tradition in which they have been embedded:

> If it is true that what has prevailed in modernity has been a logic of secularisation whose central principle is that of simple identity or identification, then it also seems true that the achievements of modernity, notably in medicine and technology – not to mention in the politico-social order with its emergence of liberal-democracy – are likewise a function of that same principle.[32]

These statements bring into relief the divergence of position within the Thomist tradition regarding Liberalism. From Schindler's perspective, Chappell's belief in the affinity of the Thomist and Liberal traditions is paradigmatic of everything that is wrong with the 'secular logic' approach. First, there is a complete lack of concern about the theological principles that underlie each of these concepts – '*never mind the pedigree*', '*just look at its results*'. Second, the same maxim highlights the pragmatic orientation of the methodology. Third, there is the tendency to analyse each concept in isolation from the others, which has the effect of ignoring the impact of the cultural embodiment of these concepts – an intellectual practice that MacIntyre describes as 'a kind of unsystematic conceptual archeology'.[33] Take, for example, the concept of 'individualism'. The intellectual history of this concept is strongly rooted in voluntarist philosophy and post-Reformation theology. Before a scholar claiming allegiance to the Thomist tradition endorsed it, one would expect such a person to give an account of how this concept can be incorporated into a tradition that emphasises rival concepts, such as 'social solidarity', in the context of economic and political philosophy, the self-surrender of the soul to God in the context of spirituality, and a hierarchical sacerdotal order in the context of ecclesiology. Similarly, it is difficult to see how a Thomist scholar could offer an uncritical endorsement of the idea of 'the welfare state', without making reference to criticisms of certain sorts of welfarism to be found in the encyclical *Centesimus Annus*. Chappell is correct to observe that both Aquinas and Kant share a belief that rationality is the key to moral judgement, but, as scholars of the two have long observed, Aquinas and Kant presume very different conceptions of rationality. In MacIntyre's parlance there is a rationality related to a tradition, including the tradition of Christian Revelation, and there is rationality conceived *in vacuo*, reputedly cut off from an association with any tradition. In Schindler's parlance there is a logic of credal rationality, and a logic of Cartesian rationality.

Thus, from the MacIntyre–Schindler perspective, there is a presumption that any version of rationality that is based upon a rejection or marginalisation of grace or revelation is defective. Moreover, even if one accepts the methodology of 'never mind the pedigree, just look at the results', MacIntyre and Schindler converge on the conclusion that the results are 'tragic' not 'magnificent'. In MacIntyre's analysis, the tragedy is generated by the predicament of the plain person trying to cobble together a moral framework from the rubble of the classical theistic synthesis while participating in institutions which purport to operate according to certain moral principles that, when examined, are found to be nothing more than an ideology designed to conceal the points of conflict and dysfunctionality within those institutions. In Schindler's analysis, the tragedy is found in the banality of the mechanical/post-Enlightenment understanding of human practices. In modern culture:

> Sexual relations hollowed out into their material shell become lustful manipulation; political relations hollowed out into their material shell become brutal power; market relations hollowed out into their material shell become hedonistic consumerism; and music and architecture governed by the laws of such market relations become noise and harsh ugliness.[34]

If one takes each of these examples, it is possible to see how a post-Enlightenment mode of analysis that severs the truths of revelation from the domain of reason has evacuated human practices of their depth of meaning, or at least severely impoverished them. Thus, sexual relations are all too often reduced to their most basic mechanical form as a physiological engagement; in the context of political and market relations, the bonds between subjects or citizens are reduced to contractual engagements by which each seeks to achieve his/her own interests, and in the context of the principles of modern aesthetics what matters is 'what is functional' and 'what will sell'. Thus the whole theology of the body, including the notion of sexual relationships as a 'gift' of one person to another, replete with significance such as a commitment to the other's good, is marginalised under a category of subjective opinion or religious imposition. Similarly, the rich conception of the common good in political and market relations is implicitly denied. And in the context of architecture and music, the idea that these and other art forms should have some association with objective beauty is again marginalised under a category of subjective opinion or individual taste.

Kenneth Schmitz links this 'subjective turn' to the Cartesian distinction between primary and secondary qualities. Post-Cartesian epistemology conferred objective status upon primary qualities (dimensions and size), but objective status was denied to secondary qualities such as colour and sound:

> At the level of perception, secondary qualities are made to retreat from the field surrendering the constitution of objective relations; while at the

level of concepts, the philosophy of mechanism is left to define the limits and the character of the objectively real.[35]

The pedigree of concepts therefore does matter, because the *specifica differentia* of the *genus* is the construction of the grace–nature relationship, which, as von Balthasar argued, affects ethics, politics and the entire *praxis* of human life. If one's pedigree is an Enlightenment pedigree, then it may represent a cross between nominalist philosophy and Lutheran theology (in the German context), Aristotelian philosophy and Calvinist theology (in the Scottish context) and Cartesian philosophy coupled with atheism (in the French context), to name but some of the more common permutations in the seventeenth and eighteenth centuries. In Matthew Lamb's terminology, the relationship between Thomism and these projects is dialectical rather than complementary or genetic, because at the very foundation of the various Enlightenment projects, and the Thomist tradition, are different and dialectical ways of relating nature to grace. Indeed, it is characteristic of some Enlightenment projects not to relate them at all but to start with nature without grace. As Schindler argues, for as long as the theological presuppositions of the Enlightenment traditions are left unchallenged, their deeper logic of 'self-centricity and externality, and the consequent reliance on technique and control and manipulation' – that is, the mechanical logic which follows from the severance of faith and reason, nature and grace, the sacred and the secular – 'will also go unchallenged'.[36]

The 'culture of America'

Not only do MacIntyre and Schindler reject the idea of the autonomy of culture from theology, they also reject the principle that the various provinces of culture are autonomous in relation to one another, in the manner of mechanical parts.[37] Central to their 'Augustinian Thomist' alternative is the belief that there exists a relation between the *ethos* of institutions, the principles or *nomoi* of individual self-formation and the *logos* of a given *Kultur*, and that the relationship is intrinsic. It is these *relations* that need to be understood in order for the Thomist tradition to provide an accurate judgement regarding the openness or otherwise of modern and postmodern cultures to Christian practices. In his work *Christendom Awake*, Aidan Nichols makes essentially the same argument but frames it in the language of Trinitarian analogies and appropriations:

> First, a culture should be conscious of transcendence as its true origin and goal, and this we can call culture's tacit 'paterological' dimension, its implicit reference to the Father. Second, the forms which a culture employs should manifest integrity – wholeness and interconnectedness; clarity – transparency to meaning; and harmony – a due proportion in

the ways that its constituent elements relate to the culture as a whole. And since these qualities – integrity, clarity and harmony – are appropriated in classical theology to the divine Son, the 'Art' of God and Splendour of the Father, we can call such qualities of the beautiful form the specifically Christological aspects of culture ... And thirdly, then, in the Trinitarian taxis, the spiritually vital and health-giving character of the moral *ethos* of our culture yields up culture's pneumatological dimension, its relation to the Holy Spirit, of whom we sing in the *Veni Sancte Spiritus: Sine tuo numine, nihil est in homine, nihil est innoxium.*[38]

The issue is thus not merely whether the culture of America permits, in a juridical sense, the practice of the Catholic faith, but whether the paterological dimension, as Nichols calls it, can be properly integrated into the other dimensions. If the Christological aspects of the culture are missing, that is if there is an absence of integrity, clarity and harmony, or if there is something defective about the pneumatological dimension, for example the moral *ethos* of corporate institutions, then the culture cannot be judged as one worthy of endorsement by the Thomist tradition.

Within the literature on this issue, the parties to the debate (including MacIntyre, Schindler and the Whig Thomists) tend to use the expression 'the culture of America' as a theoretical construct. MacIntyre states that not only is 'America' the 'name of the modern world' but it is also 'a metaphysical entity, an intangible abstraction always imperfectly embodied in natural reality'.[39] MacIntyre and Schindler argue that this 'metaphysical entity' embodies the Liberal principle of the autonomy of one sphere of culture from all the others, and, further, that this mechanical reading fosters a particular type of self whose mode of thought is that of a 'secular logic'. In Nichols's terms, they are arguing that the Christological dimension is inadequate to support the flourishing of a culture based upon the principles of the Thomist tradition.

A common criticism of this judgement of the intrinsically secular logic of American culture takes the form of references to the high levels of denominational identification in American society. This kind of criticism was addressed by Marcel Gauchet in his work *The Disenchantment of the World: A Political History of Religion.*[40] Gauchet concludes that the cultures of France and the United States are *essentially* secular, notwithstanding the fact that a relatively high percentage of the population maintains some degree of denominational identification. Gauchet argues this position by drawing a distinction between 'infrastructural religion' and 'superstructural religion'. Infrastructural religion is that which provides a society with the large part of its framework of values and is the basis of its self-understanding. Superstructural religion, in contradistinction, relates to a realm of private belief and 'Sunday/Sabbath practice'. Gauchet concludes:

The United States shows us how spiritual and cultural influence was preserved by denominational membership within a society whose workings, orientations, and values were just as far removed from the structure of dependency toward the other as the older, superficially more de-Christianized or laicized, European societies.[41]

This is essentially the conclusion of Nichols:

A culture, even if in its dominant conceptuality, its standards of behaviour, its artistic images, and the institutions in which its public life unfolds, it accepts, at any rate nominally, the reference-point of God, may at the same time be ontologically non-perspicacious and lacking in internal integration of an organic or architechtonic kind.[42]

Whereas Nichols speaks of a lack of an internal integration of Christian principles, and Gauchet of principles which are merely 'superstructural', in a speech delivered on a tour of the United States in 1968, Henri de Lubac traced what in Gauchet's terms is the division between the infrastructural and superstructural qualities of Christianity, to the neo-scholastic conception of the relationship between nature and grace, according to which the natural and the supernatural each constituted a complete and distinct order. The first effect of this conception was that the supernatural came to be seen as 'an artificial and arbitrary superstructure'; and 'while theologians were striving to protect the supernatural from all contamination, it became isolated from the life of the mind, and from social life, and the field was left clear for the invasion of secularism'.[43] De Lubac observed that one of the guiding ideas behind this construction of the two orders was that it would help to facilitate general agreement between theists and atheists about the natural order. The two could work together on the front of 'natural' or 'humanist' projects, while the more socially contentious supernatural aspirations could be relegated to the privacy of the individual soul.[44] De Lubac concluded that the cumulative effect of this construction is a conception of Christian progress according to which progress is realised in 'a total secularisation that would banish God not only from social life but from culture and even from the relationships of private life'.[45] When this occurs the infrastructural properties of religious faith (to use Gauchet's terminology) have been dissolved and all that remains is a privatised superstructural religious sentiment which may sometimes find expression in privatised religious practices and tribal denominational loyalties. Once again a culture might look Christian and its adherents appear to have a life of the soul but this may be largely fragmentary, formalistic and vacuous.

Consistent with the analyses of MacIntyre, Nichols, Gauchet and de Lubac is Schindler's judgement that 'Americans explicitly intend to practice religion faithfully even as this intention and practice are mediated implicitly by a theory of theism that already contains the seeds of atheism'.[46] Notwithstanding its 'intentional sincerity and moral generosity', the 'religion of Americans contains within it a largely unconscious logical framework consisting of notions of the self, of human being and action, drawn mostly from Post-Enlightenment, democratic–capitalist institutions'.[47] Dupré makes the same charge when he states that 'the enemy is within' – 'believers have become atheists in the original attitudinal sense, since their faith has been constrained to a frame of mind that allows no real transcendence'.[48]

Kenneth Schmitz has listed the values and concepts in this unconscious or tacit logical framework as liberty in the form of individual autonomy, economic, social and political liberalism, utility and modern progress, pragmatic morality and the work ethic.[49] The fact that the pedigree of these concepts is frequently to be found in the union of voluntarist philosophy and post-Reformation theology and, even worse, derived from philosophical traditions which have expressly excluded the dimension of theological analysis is not considered by the Whig Thomists as prima facie evidence that the principles of this logical framework may be incompatible with the Thomist tradition. For example, in the following statement by Michael Novak, a leading proponent of Whig Thomism, the Calvinist pedigree of capitalist practices is clearly acknowledged in the reference to the Scottish Enlightenment:

> The thinkers of the Scottish Enlightenment achieved a revolution in the human *ethos*, a revolution whose spiritual possibilities have yet to be realized. It is my hope that moral and cultural leaders, philosophers and poets, theologians and prelates, will grasp these possibilities, and fashion from them the maxims of practical moral guidance for which so many economic activists are manifestly thirsty.[50]

No one has ever suggested that the Scottish Enlightenment was a great moment in Catholic thought and practice, and Novak implicitly recognises this in his statement that 'democratic capitalism is not just a system but a way of life' and that 'the order of democratic capitalism calls forth not only a new theology but a new type of religion'.[51] On this last point Schindler and Novak are in agreement. Schindler frequently emphasises the fact that in any acceptance of liberal capitalist practices there follows not merely an adoption of these specific economic and political practices but 'a definite theology and spirituality' and thus 'a particular *ethos* or way of life'. He differs from Novak and other proponents of Whig Thomism in his judgement that this *ethos* is hostile to the development of a Catholic culture and what was called in the previous chapter the cultivation of a 'classical Christian self'. There is, he argues, a 'double autonomy' at work within Liberal cultures: the autonomy of the self vis-à-vis others and an autonomy from a living sense of God.[52] Such cultures are thus defined as a 'structure of sin' formed by a double dualism:

In its understanding of nature (being), our culture separates form – the meaning which gives shape to the culture's institutions and patterns of life – from love; and this separation within nature between form and love presupposes a more primitive separation of nature itself from the incarnate God who is the unity of form and love. This double separation then results in an inadequate sense of both form and love: form, abstracted from love, becomes externalized, manipulative, and forceful; and love, abstracted from form, now becomes blind, empty of order. Objectivity takes the shape of a machine, while subjectivity becomes arbitrary freedom.[53]

Schindler further classifies Liberalism into three primary types, depending on whether the dualism it fosters begins from a stance of 'direct opposition' to theism, a 'hard dichotomy' of the realms of the sacred and the secular or a 'soft dichotomy' of the same realms.[54] These three subdivisions correspond to MacIntyre's categories of radical, liberal and conservative Liberalisms, and have an analogue in Matthew Lamb's distinction between complementary, genetic and dialectical relationships. Thus the explicitly atheistic type of Liberalism derives from a dualism of direct opposition; the second category is exemplified by the dualisms of Descartes and the third by the tendency to subordinate the truths of Revelation to the principles of a philosophical rationalism 'as though divine revelation had to accommodate itself to fixed philosophical conceptual containers that admitted of no expansion'.[55] Schindler concludes that the contemporary culture of America is a 'culture of death' derived from a dualism of direct opposition, but that a 'liberalism more consistent with the third and especially the second types has prevailed more often throughout the history of America'.[56] Hence, 'America's modernity, having begun in conservative and liberal liberalism's timid (methodological) abstraction from God, is ending in radical liberalism's energetic (ontological) elimination of God'.[57] Within these subdivisions, Schindler locates the problem with John Courtney Murray's defence of the American polity as being a version of the third type of dualism. Specifically, he argues that Murray conflated the sacred–secular distinction typical of neo-scholastic thought into a Church–state distinction typical of the theology of the Reformers, and included within was an understanding of the Church as a purely juridical entity. Such an ecclesiology is inconsistent with the 'mystical body' theology of the Church and more generally the ecclesiology of the Communio school favoured by prelates such as Ratzinger and Scola.

The priority of doxology

The issue of whether the relationship of the Thomist and Liberal traditions is dialectical, genetic or complementary can be related to the other issue which we concluded in Chapter 2 has been left open in the cultural analysis of John

Paul II – that of the difference between Protestant and Catholic cultures. Sociologists agree that a major difference between the two is the order of priority given to good works (and work in general) and contemplation. Although Schindler has not himself made reference to the sociological distinctions between Protestant and Catholic cultures, he does argue that an assimilation to the Thomist tradition of ideas derived from the Scottish Enlightenment is impossible, not merely because the theology of the Reformers fosters the autonomy of the economic and political, but because it gives priority to doing over being, to 'good works' over doxology:

> What is at stake, then, is whether we can have a spirituality wherein 'being' is prior to 'doing' or 'having'; where contemplation-immanent activity is an anterior condition for all action-transitive/transcendent activity; and where the interiority of the former activity therefore keeps the latter activity from sliding off into extroversion and simple externality.[58]

In justice to the Whig Thomists, it can be argued that this relationship between 'contemplation-immanent activity' and 'action-transitive activity' is another aspect of the unresolved 'explosive problematic' of *Gaudium et spes*. This is because the reading of *Gaudium et spes*, which emphasises Christ as *Omega*, has tended to turn the focus of post-Conciliar theology upon the eschatological significance of action-transitive activities. There is, however, no statement within *Gaudium et spes*, or another Conciliar or post-Conciliar document, which suggests that the priority which the Thomist tradition has historically accorded to 'contemplation-immanent' activities should be abandoned; on the contrary, in both the fields of the theology of labour practices and the sacramental theology of marriage, John Paul II has emphasised the intransitive over the transitive. This issue of a more developed theological understanding of the relationship between the two forms of practices (contemplation-immanent and action-transitive) may thus be construed as another project requiring analysis in order to resolve some of the tensions within *Gaudium et spes*, and post-Conciliar theology in general.[59] In any such deeper analysis, the differences to be found between classical Thomism and Patristic thought, on the one hand, and late scholasticism and Enlightenment thought, on the other, is again likely to be significant. Peter Henrici has alluded to this in his argument that inherent within Tridentine Catholicism were modernist tendencies derived from the Protestant emphasis upon action over contemplation:

> A specifically modern Catholic theology existed between Trent and Vatican II. The practice of Christian life was unduly burdened by the idea of 'making'. Christian life consisted largely of duties that are performed because one is obliged to do so. Kant has become a secret father of the Church. For many Christians, perfection is seen as something 'do-

able'. Moved by a kind of Christian Pharisaism, Christian existence is viewed as a meritorious achievement that God commands and by virtue of which one is able to please him.[60]

In this context, the letter *Testem benevolentiae*, from Leo XIII to Cardinal Gibbons, may be construed as lending authority to Henrici's argument and the anti-American culture position of, *inter alios*, de Lubac, Schindler, Schmitz, Lamb and MacIntyre. In this letter, Leo XIII identified in 'Americanism' a tendency to emphasise the natural virtues while privatising the supernatural ones, and a related habit of dividing Christian virtues into passive and active categories, coupled with the argument that the former were better suited for past times whereas the latter are more in keeping with the needs of the present.[61] This approach fosters a tendency to marginalise the place of contemplation and prayer in the economy of salvation and to emphasise good works. Such tendencies would thus assist the assimilation of Catholics to mainstream American life but at the price of the diminution of precisely those characteristics of Catholic culture that distinguish it from the various versions of Protestant culture. As Peter Joseph has noted, it is ironic that the Protestant principle of 'faith alone' emphasised works, whereas the Catholic principle of faith and works still emphasised contemplation.

In any analysis of the relationship between contemplation-immanent and active-transitive practices, Schindler argues that the critical theological issue becomes that of defining what is meant by the concept of human 'dominion' over the order of creation as it appears in the Genesis account and as it is used in *Gaudium et spes*; and, further, when properly understood, 'dominion' consists in ordering things in light of the person's capacity for worship. [62] This idea that there is a relationship between social and economic practices and liturgy, and that it is important to which is accorded primacy, is radically anti-modern and finds its contemporary magisterial endorsement in the argument of Ratzinger that in Catholic theology the person is a liturgist before he/she is a worker.[63] In *The Spirit of the Liturgy*, Ratzinger argues that the 'only goal of the Exodus is shown to be worship, which can only take place according to God's measure'.[64] In other words, the reason that God liberated the Jews from servitude to the Egyptians was not so that they could enjoy 'self-determination' but so that they could order their lives in accordance with His precept of the priority of worship. They had to be 'snatched from their obstinate attachment to their own work' and freed from the 'domination of activity'.[65] It is perhaps for this reason that one finds in the work of Catherine Pickstock the judgement that 'traditional communities governed by liturgical patterns are likely to be the only source of resistance to capitalist and bureaucratic norms today'.[66]

The question thus becomes: How is the situation of a Whig Thomist self participating in the economic and political practices of the culture of America different from what Francis George has described as the tendency to be 'Catholic in faith', 'Protestant in culture', or different from what Dupré has described as a person 'constrained to a frame of mind which allows no real transcendence'? To the Whig Thomists, whom he calls neo-conservatives, Schindler poses the question thus:

> The question is not whether the neo-conservatives see the cross, confession, and grace as indispensable in Christian life. Of course they do. The question is whether, nonetheless, they do not effectively 'privatise' these realities.[67]

Again it can be argued that the ambivalent treatment of culture in *Gaudium et spes* is in part responsible for this development, although the tendency pre-dates the Council, as Henrici acknowledges. The recommendation in Conciliar documents that missionaries accommodate themselves to local practices and cultures has been popularly construed as an invitation to the clergy in the Sees of metropolitan modernity to do the same, that is to accommodate their practices to those of the culture of modernity. This occurred at precisely a time when, largely due to the efforts of teaching Orders of religious, the Catholic population in countries of the New World was upwardly socially mobile. The Catholic elites within this generation desperately wanted respectability and legitimacy within the dominant 'modern' and 'Protestant culture', and the very loose account of the nature of the cultural realm and undefined references to concepts such as 'modern man' and 'modern world' and the 'autonomy of culture' in *Gaudium et spes* gave them the theoretical justification for the accommodationist stance they desired. E. Michael Jones, in his work on modernist architecture, described the 1960s in countries such as the United States, Canada and Australia as the 'high-noon of the Catholic inferiority complex' – a time when Catholic intellectuals 'lusted after modernity'.[68]

The form of love

In the final analysis, Schindler concludes that the process of transcending the culture of America requires 'the recovery of the centrality of the liturgy and sacrament as form, as form of the Church, and finally of the world'.[69] Such a recovery however would require a rejection of the autonomy of the spheres of culture in relation to one another, and in particular the idea of their autonomy in relation to theology. It would also require that priority be given to doxology over work, to being over doing. Schindler describes this sacramental form as the 'form of love' and he describes it thus:

> The love which is the inner condition and form of all Christian action and production is not a principle which we ever possess or control, and from which we can then deduce programs of action. Rather, as Balthasar insists, we do not so much organise in terms of that principle as it 'organ-

izes' us. In fact, that 'principle of organization' is precisely a love which, in the paradox that is the heart of Christianity, takes the form of the Cross, of *kenosis*, of self-emptying gift … . Alternatively, action marked by rigid concern for management and mastery, and by self-assertion, is just so far indicative of a form more like that carried in mechanism and liberalism.[70]

This provision of an 'objective' standard of love bridges the hitherto asymptotic worlds of history and tradition. The problematic relationship between history and tradition has been described in terms of 'historical awareness remaining backward wherever tradition persists and, conversely, tradition crumbling wherever historical awareness takes hold'.[71] De Lubac and von Balthasar, and in contemporary scholarship, Schindler, Schmitz, and Scola, among others, argue that this classically Hegelian either/or predicament – that is, history *or* tradition – can be resolved by positing the Second Person of the Trinity as the archetype of perfected humanity. In de Lubac's words, 'in revealing the Father and being revealed by Him, Christ completes [achève] the revelation of man to himself'.[72] Christ is thus the transcultural, transhistorical *logos* – the *Alpha* and *Omega* – in which the tradition of the Old Testament finds its fulfilment, the tradition of the New Testament finds its source and future consummation, and the Socratic tradition of the Greeks finds the tension between *mythos* and *logos* resolved. In von Balthasar's terminology, the Incarnation unites two spans of a bridge representing a historical revelation on the one side and a tradition-dependent reason on the other. Contrary to the methodological presuppositions of the Enlightenment, it is through immersion in the tradition that one comes to an objective understanding of one's position in history, and through an examination of history that one comes to an appreciation of the rationality of the tradition.

This juxtaposition of the *form of love* with the *form of the machine* and the emphasis on an intrinsic relationship between nature and grace is not only the theological foundation that MacIntyre's critique of the culture of modernity requires, but also gives new depth to his interest in the nature of *praxis* and his aversion to practices regulated by bureaucratic criteria. In Chapter 3 we saw that, in contradistinction to bureaucratic modes of regulating social institutions more or less for their own sake, MacIntyre promotes a concept of a practice as something which is of its nature *intransitive*. In other words, a practice must be ordered towards the achievement of, or participation in, some genuine 'good of human flourishing' and will thereby foster the self-development of the person engaged in the practice, as well as those whom he or she serves. Schindler deepens this argument with the insight that because of the intransitive dimension practices will always involve an ontology, or an onto-logic, which is inclusive of a spirituality, and the form of the practice will thereby be unavoidably religious or anti-religious in character.[73] If the form of the practice is mechanical, its onto-logic will be atheistic. Such a practice is closed to the operation of grace, and the practitioner is imprisoned within a cycle identified by MacIntyre as alternating between being the manipulator and being manipulated. Although the mechanical form of modern culture is manifested in different functions – sexual, political, economic, aesthetic – the 'substance' of the form is always the same: autonomy and self-asser-tion, control and manipulation. One can be a manipulator to achieve one's own goals or the manipulated as an instrument in the achievement of the objectives of another. Schindler stresses that what is most objectionable about such bureaucratic proceduralism 'is not so much that it grants prior-ity to (putatively empty) form over substance, but that the priority it grants to form itself already *hiddenly contains* (however unwillingly) the *substance of mechanism*'.[74]

In reaching this conclusion, Schindler is not taking an idiosyncratic posi-tion. Earlier in the twentieth century, Georges Bernanos and von Balthasar had both drawn attention to the mechanical *logos* of the culture of modernity, while more recently Oliver O'Donovan has argued that 'the appearance of a social secularity could be created by understanding society as a quasi-me-chanical system, incapable of moral and spiritual acts' and hence 'the false consciousness of the would-be secular society lies in its determination to conceal the religious judgements that it has made'.[75] Schindler's conclusions are also in accord with the judgement of William T. Cavanaugh that, far from being neutral in matters of theology, the modern state is best understood as a source of an alternative soteriology to that of the Church.[76] In Pickstock's terms, the modern Liberal state is a 'polity of death', while in the Trinitarian language of Nichols, the argument against the modern Liberal state and the 'culture of America' is that any desire for the promotion of the paterological dimension is undermined by the lack of a Christological dimension and a very weak pneumatological dimension.

Thus where MacIntyre has focused on the manner in which the ideolo-gies underpinning modern institutional practices require those associated with them to adopt a number of different postures or 'selves', and to change moral frameworks according to changes in rôle and the dominant *ethos* of an institution, Schindler 'radicalises' MacIntyre's philosophical and sociological analysis by concluding that these practices are impervious to grace: 'appeals to morality and social justice, insofar as they are made in conventional terms, and hence in terms of the form of our culture, will just so far miss the form which is given in grace'.[77] Only the 'form of love' has the capacity to go to the root of the intransitive dimension of human actions and transform it. MacIntyre's argument is that the dichotomy between relationships governed by bargaining undertaken for mutual advantage and affective relationships omits an alternative understanding of relationships characterised in terms of alternating practices of giving and receiving. It is consistent with Schindler's logic of identities-in-relation, Anthony Fisher's call for practices which con-tain a sacramental dimension, and, more generally, with the analogies drawn by Norris Clarke between relationality and substantiality in the human person and in the processions of the Trinity. All four projects are seeking to overcome the mechanical form in the service of the integrity of the self and the form of love.

Conclusion

The implications of this multistranded critique of the culture (*Kultur*) of modernity are 'radical'. Schmitz concludes that 'the meeting of Catholicism and Americanism is the meeting of two different liberties', and, moreover, they are 'ordered liberties' ordered in two very different directions.[78] The fact that they are 'ordered liberties' means that the arguments of Timothy Chappell, and the proponents of Whig Thomism, will not suffice to demonstrate the possibility or desirability of a true synthesis of the Thomist and Liberal traditions. Although Thomism may share concepts in common with other traditions, what matters is how and where these concepts are placed within the architectonic order of each tradition and the kind of *Geist*, *Bildung* and *Kultur* they generate when embedded in personal and institutional practices. This will be determined by the onto-logic of the tradition from which they have been derived.

In reaching his conclusion that the 'culture of America' is what John Paul II would identify as a 'structure of sin', built upon 'a philosophical system, an ideology and a programme for action and for the shaping of human behaviour', Schindler makes the qualification that it is not part of his claim that American culture or liberal cultures in general are 'any more or less sinful in a subjective sense than any other cultures in history'.[79] Rather, his argument is that the institutional structures, practices and technologies are governed by an ideology that is 'wrongly disposed towards power-relations', and, further, that this state of affairs *disposes* those living within such cultures to behave in a particular way for reasons of social survival and advancement – and this way has the form or *logos* of the machine.[80]

It is because the institutional practices and ideologies which sustain them *dispose* persons living within the culture of modernity to behave in a particular way that it can be argued that many Catholics in the United States and other countries of the Western world have a tendency to be 'Catholic in faith' but 'Protestant in culture'. Members of the laity come to conclude that a life in which the good of religion is infrastructural is open only to those who live celibate lives within religious orders. Von Balthasar observed that this mentality tends to foster the Protestant secular–sacred dichotomy. In *Love Alone*, he argued:

> The form of Christian love in the sign of Christ is indivisible, it can never be subjected to a sort of division of labour, some Christians specializing in a transcendent aspect (which is then called 'eschatological' or con-

templative), others specializing in the immanent aspect (the active life, turned towards the world). Any hint of that dichotomy tears the image of Christ in two and makes it unrecognisable and incomprehensible in both aspects.[81]

A similar argument to that of von Balthasar can be found in John Paul II's Apostolic Exhortation, *Christifideles Laici*, in which he states that Catholic laity may not live two parallel lives – on the one hand, the so-called spiritual life with its values and demands, and, on the other, the so-called 'secular life' with its values and demands.[82] In the final analysis, the burden of Whig Thomism is that of defending the argument that its promotion of the institutional and economic practices of the Liberal polity does not in practice require such a division of the secular and sacred, the eschatological and the immanent. As Duprè argues, the logic of the critique of the infrastructural secularism within the 'culture of America' is that, in order to 'restore meaning to [this] culture, it is not sufficient to profess a belief in God and to observe specific rules of ritual and conduct'.[83] Rather, there needs to be a regaining of an authentically Augustinian Thomist sense of 'inwardness' – not its subjectivist Kantian–Lutheran alternative – and with this the opening of practices to grace and self-transcendence, that is to the form of love. This would necessarily entail a recognition of the importance of the contemplation-immanent dimension of human practices, and the related principle that the person is a liturgist before he or she is a worker. This focus upon doxology should lead in turn to a greater awareness of the layers of meaning within human practices, and the manner in which the identity of any participant in a practice is formed through his or her relations with other persons – a stance that Schindler defines by the primacy of 'affirmation, receptivity and responsiveness'.

Part III

A POSTMODERN DEVELOPMENT OF THE TRADITION

6

CULTURE AND THE RATIONALITY
OF THE TRADITION

Whereas Part II focused upon an examination of the hostility of modern culture to the instantiation of the principles of the Thomist tradition, Part III focuses upon an examination of how the Thomist tradition is being developed by proponents of a postmodern Augustinian Thomism to incorporate within it an account of the significance of culture for moral and intellectual formation. This has been made necessary by the crisis created within the tradition by the emergence of the culture of modernity, and by the emphasis placed within the Genealogical tradition on the significance of rival cultures and traditions and the rôle of culture in the formation of the soul, or, as Liberals and Genealogists would say, 'self'. Since such an account of the theological significance of culture was in part completely missing from classical Thomism and in part only latently present, this lacuna needs to be 'filled in' if the Thomist tradition is to have any hope of engaging the arguments of the rival Liberal and Genealogical traditions.

In the following two chapters, it will be argued that the central postmodern element of postmodern Augustinian Thomism is the idea of a narrative tradition and its associate concept of a tradition-constituted rationality. Concomitant with the argument in Chapter 5 that 'no culture is really neutral' is MacIntyre's agreement with the proponents of the Genealogical tradition that no conception of rationality is ever really neutral in its relation to theism. MacIntyre acknowledges the Genealogical claims that all forms of rationality are 'tradition dependent', but holds that although reason may not be neutral it can be universal. Indeed, in *Three Rival Versions of Moral Enquiry*, MacIntyre argued that 'reason can only move towards being genuinely universal and impersonal in so far as it is neither neutral nor disinterested'.[1]

Such a conception of rationality represents a dramatic break with the strategy of the neo-Thomists to defend their tradition by reference to Enlightenment conceptions of rationality. Criticisms of their strategy may be found in the works of scholars associated with the Nouvelle Théologie, and in Etienne Gilson's histories of Thomist thought. In a letter to de Lubac, Gilson criticised the Dominican theologians from Hervé Nedellec right up to Cajetan and beyond of 'emasculating' the doctrine of St Thomas and of making his theology a 'brew of watered-down *philosophica aristotelico thomistica* concocted to give off a vague deism fit only for the use of right-thinking candidates for high school diplomas and Arts degrees'.[2] Similarly, Yves Simon observed:

> Today we consider it a paradox that Thomists have ever accepted a division of philosophy which was initiated by Wolff, consolidated by Kant, popularized by the Eclectics of the school of Cousin and was fundamentally at variance with that upheld by Saint Thomas.[3]

Thus while all Thomists agree that there is a relationship between faith and reason and that it is a perennial interest of their tradition to defend the complementarity of the two orders, the contemporary challenge of postmodern scholarship is forcing Thomist scholars to think more deeply about how their understanding of rationality differs from the Enlightenment-derived alternatives on the one hand, and from the Genealogical tradition on the other. This chapter therefore focuses on an account of how Alasdair MacIntyre's notion of a narrative tradition contributes to meeting this challenge.

The influence of R. G. Collingwood

MacIntyre's notion of a tradition-dependent rationality derives in part from the early influence of historiographer R. G. Collingwood. Although Collingwood was sympathetic to the kind of Continental Liberalism espoused by Guido de Ruggiero, it was not Collingwood's political philosophy that inspired MacIntyre but rather his theory of history. Collingwood argued that past ideas could not be studied without reference to the historical context in which the ideas originated, and thus that historians should reconstruct in their own minds the situations in which the great philosophers found themselves.[4] MacIntyre presents the issue as one of understanding the 'social embodiment of concepts' and argues that 'to abstract any type of concept, but notably moral concepts, from the contexts of the tradition which they inform and through which they are transmitted is to risk damaging misunderstandings'.[5] From this perspective, the task of philosophy is to articulate for a particular social order 'its concepts and beliefs in a manner which enables those who inhabit that culture to learn both what criticisms of those concepts and beliefs require a rational answer and to what degree such an answer can be provided'.[6] In an essay on Aquinas's critique of education, MacIntyre summarises this methodology thus:

> [W]ith Aquinas's texts as with those of many philosophers a crucial question is always: Against whom is he writing here? Within what controversy is this or that particular contention to be situated? Philosophers characteristically invite us not simply to assert p, but to assert p rather

than q or r, and we will often only understand the point of asserting p, if we know what q and r are.[7]

Concretely, MacIntyre argues that the position in which Aquinas found himself when a young teacher at the University of Paris was not merely that of having to reconcile the theological tradition of the Fathers (principally Augustine and his *credo ut intelligam* principle) with the philosophical tradition of Aristotle; but also of having to formulate jurisprudential principles to deal with the jurisdictional conflicts of the time. These included the power of the papacy, the powers of the sainted Louis IX in France and the ex-communicated anti-Papal Frederick II in Sicily, and the powers of the episcopacy.[8] For MacIntyre, the fact that Louis IX sent royal archers to the University of Paris in 1255 to ensure that a Dominican master could safely deliver his inaugural lecture was one of a myriad of historical events in the life of St Thomas that would have provided the background data against which he formulated his theses. Moreover, when providing an account of Aquinas's treatise on law, MacIntyre develops his arguments by reference to the contrasting attitudes of Louis IX, Frederick II and Aquinas on the social influence of *jongleurs* (medieval minstrels). These provide MacIntyre with a case study in which to examine Aquinas's approach to the question: 'To what extent ought a ruler enforce the practices of Christian morality?'

Another illustration of MacIntyre's methodology can be found in his treatment of the Scottish Enlightenment. Just as the scholastic system was forged by Aquinas's synthesis of Aristotelian philosophy with the theology of Augustine, MacIntyre views the main dynamic of the Scottish Enlightenment as an attempted synthesis of Aristotelian philosophy with the theology of Calvin. And just as MacIntyre argues in the above example that the principles endorsed by Aquinas are better understood by reference to the jurisdictional conflicts of his time, he argues that it is important to understand that the educated class which effected the Scottish Enlightenment was torn between English culture on the one side and Highland Gaelic culture on the other. It had to formulate principles for a common moral system, based on an authority completely independent of the rival cultures of Scotland. And while the ideas of Louis IX and Frederick II were used by MacIntyre in the *jongleurs* case study to bring into sharper focus the nuances and complexities in Aquinas's thought, so too in the Scottish context MacIntyre refers to the ideas of English and Anglo-Hibernian writers (Blackstone and Burke) to highlight the distinctive features of the position in Scotland.

This use of the historical methodology of Collingwood by a Thomist is not as arbitrary or eccentric as it might at first appear. Aspects of Collingwood's theory of the history of ideas were also shared by Werner Stark (1909–85), a Thomist sociologist and economic historian. Stark developed the theme that, in order to examine the seminal ideas within different systems of thought, it was necessary to consider how these ideas made sense within the framework of the social conditions out of which they grew.[9] In the context of the sociology of knowledge, Stark was in a position very similar to MacIntyre in that he was trying to reconcile theories of the 'social determination of knowledge' with a quest for transhistorical truth. Other Thomist scholars in the twentieth century who sought to acquire a better historical understanding of the work of St Thomas included Martin Grabmann, Pierre Mandonnet, Fernand van Steenberghen and James Weisheipl, each of whom is acknowledged by MacIntyre in his Gifford Lectures as adopting a methodology with affinities to his own.[10]

A reference to the tension between a Collingwood-style approach to intellectual history and the Thomist quest for a transhistorical truth may be found in a recent address by Joseph Ratzinger. After giving an outline of historicist approaches, Ratzinger went on to say that 'behind this form of historical interpretation lies a philosophy, a fundamental perspective on reality, which says that it is in fact pointless to ask about what is; we can only ask ourselves what we are able to do with things' and further, that 'this philosophy contains a false humility that does not recognise in the human person the capacity for the truth'.[11] MacIntyre's position, however, like that of Stark, does not deny the capacity for knowledge of the truth. Rather he asserts that:

1   the quest for truth always takes place within a particular tradition, that is that conceptions of truth are tradition dependent;
2   traditions can be tested for rational coherence;
3   there is a universal human nature and consequently a transcultural standard of human flourishing otherwise defined by the principles of the natural law; and
4   the Thomist tradition is the only tradition which is rationally coherent and able to yield an account of the principles of the natural moral law.

The following sections seek to synthesise these apparently conflicting principles and thereby assimilate insights from Collingwood's methodology to the Thomist tradition, without sacrificing the idea of a transhistorical truth. This is necessary if MacIntyre's postmodern development of the tradition is not to repudiate the natural law doctrine or otherwise suffer from specific flaws to which reference has been made in the criticism of historicism in *Fides et ratio*.

The concept of a narrative tradition

Implicit within the methodological parameters outlined above is a rejection of the idea that it is possible to understand concepts in laboratory conditions, as it were, abstracted from the traditions in which they were originally formulated. Rather, MacIntyre promotes a conception of rational inquiry as one *embodied* within a tradition.[12] Significantly, his understanding of a tradition is much richer than that of a mere conceptual framework. Just as the sociologist Paul Connerton argued in his account of a life of celebrated recurrence, to which reference was made in Chapter 4, that meaning can be conveyed not just by writing or speaking, but also by gestures, modes of dress and rituals; so, too, MacIntyre argues that 'beliefs are expressed in and through rituals and ritual dramas, masks and modes of dress, the ways in which houses are structured and villages and towns laid out, and of course by actions in general'. As a consequence, 'the reformulations of belief are not to be thought of only in intellectual terms; or rather the intellect is not to be thought of as either a Cartesian mind or a materialist brain; but as that through which thinking individuals relate themselves to each other'.[13]

Such an understanding of the elements of a tradition builds upon ideas that were already developed in the latter half of the nineteenth century and the first half of the twentieth century by John Henry Newman and Maurice Blondel. In particular, MacIntyre's account of a tradition shares the typically Blondelian emphasis on the relationship between doctrine and practices as two essential elements of a tradition, but adds to this emphasis Newman's interest in the rôle of masters of a tradition in handing on the theory and practices of a tradition and in the resolution of crises within the tradition.[14] The idea that traditions develop through the resolution of crises is acknowledged by MacIntyre to be one of the central themes in John Henry Newman's *Essay on the Development of Doctrine*.[15] Blondel defined a tradition as the 'living synthesis of all the speculative and ascetic, historical and theological forces', that is 'the data of history, the efforts of reason and the experience of faithful action'.[16] He further argued:

> Christian practice nourishes man's knowledge of the divine and bears within its action what is progressively discerned by the theologian's initiative. The synthesis of dogma and facts is scientifically effected because there is a synthesis of thought and grace in the life of the believer, a union of man and God, reproducing in the individual consciousness the history of Christianity itself.[17]

The alternative idea – that truth can be pursued outside the framework of a tradition – is attributed by MacIntyre to an account of rationality going back to the Sophists. With reference to Plato's warning in the *Phaedrus* about those whose relationships depend upon writing, MacIntyre suggests that '[w]hat is condemned is all writing that has become detached from the author who speaks in and through it, so that the author as author cannot be put to the questions along with her or his text'.[18] MacIntyre then considers whether this means that all writing is to be condemned once the author is dead, and concludes that the answer is 'perhaps not, if someone else is able to stand in the author's place, to supply the needed authorial voice, and to respond to interrogation by others'.[19] From this judgement, MacIntyre formulates the following theses:

1   if writing is to escape condemnation, it must function as subordinated to and only within the context of a spoken dialogue; and
2   thinking always involves thinking in the context of some particular and specific public, with its own institutional structure.[20]

From these theses he concludes that the key question is: 'Within what kind of public, with what kind of institutionalised structures will we be able to identify the limitations imposed on our particular inquiries as a prelude to transcending those limitations in pursuit of the goods of reason?'[21]

Notwithstanding magisterial warnings about historicism and cultural relativism in certain approaches to philosophical questions, the fact that it is possible to consider the historical dimensions of an issue without ending in a position of historical and/or ethical relativism is reflected in the recent International Theological Commission statement entitled *Memory and Reconciliation: The Church and the Faults of the Past*. This statement recommends a methodology consistent with MacIntyre's two theses. The authors of the document summarise their methodology thus:

> Bringing to light the communality between interpreter and the object of interpretation requires taking into account the questions that motivate the research and their effect on the answers that are found, the living context in which the work is undertaken, and the interpreting community whose language is spoken and to whom one intends to speak.[22]

Such a methodology and account of rationality rejects the idea that knowledge can be transmitted in a cultural vacuum. It highlights the importance of institutional cultures and personal relationships for the transmission of knowledge, and, in particular, for the transmission of a knowledge of the practices of a tradition and the meaning of doctrinal propositions upon whose authority, or to which end, the practices were founded and are directed. Its significance can be illustrated by reference to elements of the 'explosive problematic' of *Gaudium et spes*.

First, it suggests that the document's authors were naive in their assumption that the key concepts in the document would be accorded the same content regardless of whether they were read by plain persons or philosophers, Catholics or non-Catholics, Easterners or Westerners.[23] Thus, for example, the word 'humanism', on its own, without the adjective 'Christocentric' 'theocentric' or even 'Christian' placed before it, is likely to be construed quite differently by a plain person than by someone with a knowledge of Maritain's *Humanisme intégrale*. Similarly, the concept of 'authenticity' will mean something different to a person with a knowledge of Heidegger's philosophy than it will to someone who lacks a knowledge of Heideggerian concepts. This kind of knowledge depends upon an immersion within a tradition – an education which cannot be presumed of many of those to whom the Conciliar documents were in part directed. Moreover, in making the point that post-Conciliar history cannot be read as *wholly* determined by interpretations of Conciliar documents, Mark S. Massa has recently observed that part of the problem is the presumption that 'ordinary Catholics, even well-educated ones, read and understood the theology of Roman-promulgated documents and organized their lives accordingly'.[24] However, in so many cases, what individual members of the faithful presume the teaching of the Church to be has been acquired tacitly in the institutions and publications of liberal modernity, rather than by a careful reading of magisterial documents against the background of contemporary philosophy and theology.

Second, MacIntyre's account of a tradition highlights the problems with John XXIII's assumption that it is not difficult to distinguish between 'the substance of the ancient doctrine of the *depositum fidei* and the formulation of its presentation' or, in other words, the idea that it is always possible to distil doctrines from the tradition which embodies them and then represent them in the idiom of an alternative tradition – in this context, the idiom of 'modern man' – without in any way changing the meaning of the doctrines.[25] The post-Conciliar trend which derives from these assumptions is characterised by Aidan Nichols as the belief that it is possible to 'hand down authentic Tradition while manifesting insouciance towards the forms in which Tradition is embodied'.[26] This particular aspect of the problematic has also been addressed by Francis George:

> Implicitly, Pope John's statement seems to support an instrumental view of language, regarding language as the means whereby a speaker gives expression to thoughts which exist independently of language, through employment of words whose meanings are the object of explicit agreement between prospective speakers. By contrast, an expressivist view of language holds that thought has no determinate content until it is expressed in a shared language.[27]

In the particular context of the liturgy, George has stated that 'only if, in fact, the Catholic faith has helped to shape the culture will that culture provide a language and customs that can be an apt vehicle for worship'.[28] Implicit within this statement is an expressivist view of language, that is a view which connects the meaning of linguistic terms to the culture out of which they grew.

An illustration of the expressivist theory may be found in texts that require persons of one culture to explain the texts of another in which a common language is apparently shared but not a common culture. For example, the following words from the first verse of 'Waltzing Matilda', Australia's

121

unofficial national anthem, are all English words but are almost inexplicable to non-Australians:

> Once a jolly swagman, camped by a billabong, under the shade of a coolibah tree
> And he sang as he watched and waited till his billy boiled
> Who'll come a-waltzing Matilda with me?

The terms, 'billy' 'billabong', 'swagman' and later in the song, 'troopers' 'squatters', 'jumbuck' and 'tuckerbag' can to some degree be translated as water can, water hole, tramp, police, farmers, sheep and lunchbox, but the rich nuances are lost. A squatter, for example, is not merely a farmer, but a person who occupied a very particular and socially controversial place within Australian history.

MacIntyre's preference for the expressivist view is evident in his argument that to 'abstract any type of concept, but notably moral concepts, from the traditions which they inform and through which they are transmitted is to risk damaging misunderstandings'.[29] The alternative position – the instrumental view of language – may be criticised, as George acknowledges, as rationalistic. George concludes that:

> Cultural forms and linguistic expressions are, in fact, not distinguished from the thoughts and message they carry as accidents are distinguished from substance in classical philosophy. A change in form inevitably entails also some change in content. A change in words changes in some fashion the way we think.[30]

Not only was a rationalistic or instrumental account of language implicit in some pronouncements and pastoral strategies of John XXIII and Paul VI, but, as Fergus Kerr has demonstrated, there are similarly Cartesian presuppositions in the linguistic philosophy of the most influential theologian of the Conciliar period, Karl Rahner. Kerr observes that 'Rahner's natural assumption – that communication comes after language, and language comes after having concepts – is precisely what the Cartesian tradition has reinforced'.[31]

What this means in effect is that the tendency in post-Conciliar thought and practice, especially in the fields of catechetics and liturgy, to attempt a transposition of Catholic doctrine and practice into 'modern' and 'contemporary' idioms, has been naive and has risked a diminution of the rich complexity of the narrative tradition, that is of those elements of the tradition for which there is no equivalent in the non-specialist, non-philosophical, non-theological, non-Thomist and non-liturgical language of 'modern man'. An understanding of elements of the narrative tradition may also be lost through mistranslation in circumstances where different traditions apparently share some linguistic concepts, but actually invest those concepts or words with a partly or wholly different substance or nuance.

In an article written prior to his election to the papacy, John Paul II made reference to this kind of problem in the context of the debate over *Humanae Vitae*. Speaking of a 'kind of shifting and transposing of concepts which goes on all the time', he observed that in *Humanae Vitae*, 'natural law was taken to mean merely the biological regularity we find in people in the area of sexual actualisation'. He concluded that:

> Authors of various articles and publications spoke out on behalf of such a misguided concept, and in turn imposed upon the Holy Father, and along with him upon the magisterium of the Church, an understanding of natural law that in no way corresponds to the Church's understanding of it.[32]

More recently, John Paul II has expressed concern over contemporary society's inability to receive and understand magisterial documents. He acknowledged that there is a 'problem of transmission of the fundamental truths that these documents address to all the faithful, more than that, to all people, and, in particular, to theologians and people of learning'.[33] He raised the questions: 'To what degree does the dynamic of the media affect these difficulties?' and 'To what degree do particular historical situations affect them?'[34] A MacIntyrean response to such questions is that in order to be transmitted the fundamental truths need to be embodied within a narrative tradition which in turn informs a culture and, further, that the forms of such a culture need to be clearly visible to both plain persons and people of learning. Moreover, the subjection of the Catholic tradition to what John Paul II called the 'kind of shifting and transposing of concepts which goes on all the time', and in particular to the project of transposing the fundamental truths of the tradition into the idioms of the culture of modernity, means, in effect, that the elements of the narrative tradition are constantly in a state of flux, and this has resulted in wide-scale confusion among plain persons and, ultimately, to their lack of interest in the various projects.

The significance of this critical concept of a 'narrative tradition' should thus not be underestimated in any evaluation of MacIntyre's contribution to the recent and future development of the Thomist tradition. Perhaps more effectively than any before him he has demonstrated the need for broadening the concept of a tradition to include much more than just timeless, spaceless doctrinal principles, so as to include the time- and place-bound practices which embody and are directed towards the achievement of the principles. He has also emphasised the importance of 'masters', or 'scholar-saints', within such a narrative tradition, in whom there is found the 'perfect synthesis of thought and grace', and to whom the responsibility of resolving the crises within the tradition falls.[35] As Hibbs has observed, the 'Christian tradition embraces and extends the ancient view of pedagogy, which required as its starting point submission to a teacher, to a tradition of inquiry, and to the discipline of dialectic'.[36] From this perspective, authority is not an impediment to inquiry; rather, it is a necessary element of it.[37] In re-emphasising the importance of a narrative tradition, and a conception of pedagogy which requires the student's submission to the authority of the teacher, MacIntyre steers Thomism away from the lure of the Kantian conception of enlightenment free from constricting traditions and authorities, towards a position which is in accord with that of the theologians associated with the Nouvelle Théologie. Von Balthasar, for example, consistently emphasised the importance of scholar-saints as bearers and developers – the masters – of the tradition. The following quotation illustrates this point as well as encapsulating much of the above analysis about the importance of speech and language in the transmission of a tradition:

> Christianity is not strictly speaking a 'Blood religion'; it is the religion of the Word, but not uniquely, not even primarily, of the Word in its written form; it is the religion of the Logos, not written and mute, but the incarnate and living *Logos*.[38]

Furthermore, the idea of individual self-enlightenment penetrating the meaning of free-floating concepts is inconsistent with a theological framework such as Schindler's identities-in-relation logic. The genius of Plato's Academy and the medieval universities and religious orders is that they provided a culture which facilitated the transmission of the tradition in their institutional relationships and practices. Plato had the culture of the Academy, Augustine the Episcopacy, and Aquinas the Dominican Order. MacIntyre argues that each of these institutional cultures embodied four principles:

1   a conception of truth beyond and ordering all particular truths;
2   a conception of a range of senses in the light of which utterances to be judged true or false and so placed within that ordering are to be construed;
3   a conception of a range of genres of utterance, dramatic, lyrical, historical and the like, by reference to which utterances may be classified so that we may then proceed to identify their true senses; and
4   a contrast between those uses of genres in which in one way or another truth is at stake and those governed only by standards of rhetorical effectiveness.[39]

Within such institutions, a *Geist* or *ethos* was generated by practices formulated with reference to the internal ends of the tradition, which included the transmission of the practical and intellectual elements of the tradition to up coming generations. The practices also had their own onto-logic or *logos* consistent with the ends of the tradition, and thus fostered a particular type of self-formation or *Bildung, Paideia* or self-formation based upon the tradition's own philosophical and theological anthropology. In such communities there was an 'acknowledgment of truth as a measure independent of the tradition which aspires to measure itself by truth', but there was nonetheless 'no thesis, argument, or doctrine to be so measured which was not presented as the thesis of this particular historically successive set of tradition-informed and tradition-directed individuals and groups'.[40]

The kind of community which is here described is not merely that of a group of individuals united around a few common objectives, such as health care for the aged, or shelter for the poor, but of an entire order in which certain practices exist simultaneously as elements of the tradition and of the culture in which novices would be formed and masters perfected. Tradition and culture are therefore symbiotic. For the flourishing of such a community nothing could be more toxic than the introduction of a counter-culture of 'forced or deliberate forgetting'. The idea that each successive generation of novices needs to recreate the tradition, rather than merely develop it, so that they can claim to be 'autonomous' in the sense promoted by the theories of Rousseau and Kant, or so that they can be 'authentic' and 'relevant' to the needs of 'modern man' in the sense promoted by Heidegger and Rahner, is hostile to an Augustinian Thomist understanding of the processes of rational and cultural formation. According to the classical conception, part of what is transmitted by the masters to the novices is the truth contained in the historical memory of the community: to reject the value of historical memories is thus to reject the truth itself.

To argue that a culture of 'forced or deliberate forgetting' is hostile to intellectual and moral, and hence cultural, formation is not, however, to promote a nostalgic or static conception of tradition. With each successive generation the tradition matures and develops to deal with new issues which arise. In the present context, the 'new historical situation' is the predicament of aspirant Thomist selves caught within the contradictions of the culture of modernity. It is this particular problematic that the masters of the tradition need to address and resolve.

'Smudging the boundaries' between philosophy and theology

This introduction of the concept of a narrative tradition into the Thomistic framework, or highlighting of where it was already implicit, raises the question of the implications of such a concept for the relationship between philosophy and theology. In the following subsection it will be argued that

MacIntyre's mature works exhibit a tendency to 'smudge the boundaries between theology and philosophy' and that it is precisely this notion of a narrative tradition that brings the boundaries together and overlaps both.

In *Difficulties in Christian Belief*, published in 1959, MacIntyre drew a very sharp distinction between 'secular' and 'Christian morality'. The first, which he associated with the work of Kant, he quickly dismissed as not having *any* affinity with the Christian position. There is not, he argued, 'any neutral standpoint from which we can judge between Christianity and its alternatives', or any 'neutral standing ground between Christian morality and other moralities'.[41] However, once MacIntyre moved beyond Barthian Presbyterianism, his work began to exhibit what Deal Hudson calls the 'Romantic tendency' to 'smudge the boundaries between philosophy and theology'.[42] In doing this, he does not reject the 'no neutrality' thesis, but he does allow room for some overlap between an Aristotelian 'open to Revelation' position and a fully developed Thomism. This is particularly evident in his interview with Dmitri Nikulin. In response to questions from Nikulin regarding the possibility of an ethic of virtue without a concept of God, MacIntyre replied that he followed Aquinas in the assertion that human nature has the capacity to acquire the natural virtues, without understanding that they bring with them special theological obligations. However, he also followed the Thomistic argument that the supernatural life is the form of all the virtues, and that such a life is impossible without love and grace. Accordingly, he concluded that 'the virtues can only be complete with a theological understanding, however the practice of the natural virtues and the understanding of them, of what makes for their excellence, is compatible with atheism'.[43] Such a position is further developed in his 1998 John Coffin Memorial Lecture, wherein he argued that embedded within Christianity are the elements of a moral philosophy which can be detached from theological claims to revealed truth on moral matters.[44]

In other words, MacIntyre acknowledges that, at least to some degree, there is a rôle for philosophical analysis which is not directly dependent upon theological claims. However, in other contexts, MacIntyre appears to concur with the Nietzschean claim that there is no philosophical position which is neutral in its stance towards the question of the existence of God, and that the mere belief in the principle of non-contradiction is an inherently pro-theistic position. In response to Nikulin's question 'Can the highest good that the end of the virtuous life offers be without a specific reference to God?', MacIntyre responds that 'the consequence of an Aristotelian virtue-ethics is the obligation to remain open to the possibility of divine existence'.[45] The difficult theoretical issue is that of how one can accept simultaneously the Nietzschean argument that the mere belief in logic, for example, is itself a pro-theistic position, that is the 'no neutrality' thesis, along with the idea that there is a 'way of understanding morality that can be detached from theological claims to revealed truth on moral matters'.

One possible way of asserting both propositions is to adopt what Aidan Nichols has identified as a common Catholic position. According to Nichols:

> From the point of view of theological fruitfulness, a good philosophy will consist of, formally speaking, the best purely natural reasoning available, but that materially speaking or content-wise, revelation could help to identify the areas which natural reasoning could most profitably be directed. Thus the form of philosophy as practised by Christians would have no reference to revelation, but its content would.[46]

In other words, MacIntyre's belief that an Aristotelian virtue ethic requires one to 'remain open to the possibility of divine existence' means that one's philosophical standpoint cannot be neutral in relation to the claims of revelation, even though no specific reference to the claims of revelation need ever be made in the formulation of a philosophical virtue ethic. The same resolution of the problem has been indicated by Schindler. Schindler asserts that 'philosophy in its starting point and all along the way, will always – willy-nilly – bear a relation to theology (to what has been revealed) that is intrinsic: that relation can be either negative or it can be positive, but in either case it will be a relation'.[47] However, this does not mean that the philosopher who is aware of the truth revealed in Scripture can argue deductively or inferentially from that truth.

Fides et ratio

These issues have, to some degree, been treated in John Paul II's encyclical *Fides et ratio*. In this work he asserts that there exists a kind of 'implicit philosophy' shared by people in a 'general and unreflective way'.[48] MacIntyre would call the principles of this 'implicit philosophy' the 'basic intuitions of plain persons'. John Paul II offers as examples the principles of non-contradiction, finality and causality, as well as a concept of the person as a 'free and intelligent subject, with the capacity to know God, truth and goodness'.[49] From MacIntyre's perspective, such basic principles of an 'implicit philosophy' are those upon which his own philosophical projects are based, and those upon which the judgements of plain persons need to be based.

Nonetheless, MacIntyre concedes the claim of the Genealogical tradition, to which John Paul II makes no explicit reference, that these principles are not 'neutral' but loaded in a pro-theistic direction, since they assume that there is an order to the universe. Although plain persons may arrive at a concept of the person as a free and intelligent subject, with the capacity to know God, truth and goodness through the exercise of reason, they may equally conclude, through the exercise of reason unperfected by the theological virtues, that there is little empirical evidence for the proposition that persons are free and intelligent subjects with a capacity for truth, goodness and friendship with God. The widespread occurrence of determinism, atheism and nihilism in Western societies following World Wars I and II is a complex phenomenon that may in part be because the evil of these social conflagrations has destroyed the 'self-evident' nature of the principles of an 'implicit philosophy'. Leo Strauss alluded to this when he contrasted pagan atheism with modern atheism. The former he described as motivated by a desire for freedom from the responsibilities imposed by the gods, the latter as a kind of stoic intellectual probity.[50]

Not only can the supposedly self-evident principles of an 'implicit philosophy' be undermined by the overwhelming knowledge of the human capacity for irrational behaviour, but the ability to reach an understanding of these principles may also be impaired by personal 'sin' (weakness, confusion, self-interest and self-delusion) and by, in John Paul II's terms, 'the content of culture and civilization, as a philosophical system, an ideology, a programme for action and for the shaping of human behaviour'. Another way of putting this is to say that the basic principles of practical reasoning, which the Thomist tradition holds are *per se nota* accessible to all persons of goodwill and right reason regardless of whether they have accepted Christian Revelation, will not be immediately accessible to persons whose thought and behaviour have been shaped by a 'philosophical system, an ideology, or programme for action' that is atheistic, or anti-realist or irrational. A will whose appetite for goodness has been dulled by the habitual performance of practices that are neither virtue requiring nor virtue rewarding, or an intellect that is directed towards power rather than truth, or an imagination satisfied by the bland and ugly rather than reaching out for the beautiful, or a memory which is tormented by despair and foreclosed against the virtue of hope, pre-disposes the person against knowing and applying the basic principles of John Paul II's 'implicit philosophy'. In Schindler's terms, the starting point of such a will, intellect, memory or imagination, is a relation of opposition to revelation, whereas, in MacIntyre's discourse, the predicament of such faculties highlights the problem of the relationship between virtue and the discernment of the principles of an 'implicit philosophy'. It emphasises the fact that the discernment of the principles of practical reasoning and ultimately of the natural law is not simply a matter of ratiocination, like finding a solution to a quadratic equation, but requires the cooperation of all the faculties of the soul. If any faculty has been perverted through such practices and dispositions (including despair and presumption), the ability of plain persons and even philosophers to discern the basic precepts will be impaired. Rational inquiry 'depends for its success on the virtues of those who engage in it, and it requires relationships and evaluative commitments of a particular kind'.[51] Schindler and Nichols would add that these 'evaluative commitments' include a commitment to a view of life centred upon participation in the forms of the true, the good and the beautiful – forms so little experienced in 'mass culture' as to make many people almost impervious to evangelisation. This is essentially the argument of Aidan Nichols in the following passage:

> To appreciate a form aright, to receive aright its message, depends in some way or other on our having appropriate dispositions. Without a basic readiness to receive what the form has to offer, a willingness to entertain its message, the dialogue between the eloquent appearing of being and human language is more than likely to be at cross-purposes.[52]

Thus, with reference to the arguments in Chapter 4 it can be concluded that the 'sapiential experience' which flows from participation in the transcendentals is not only necessary for the development of the virtue of prudence, but is also required for the discernment of the principles of an 'implicit philosophy'.

MacIntyre therefore acknowledges, in a manner consistent with principles espoused in *Fides et ratio*, a legitimate realm for the work of philosophy. He rejects the Calvinist interpretation of Aquinas as a proto-modernist who conceded too much ground to philosophy; but he also believes that even conceptions of finality, causality and non-contradiction, and the human capacity for knowledge of God, truth and goodness, will differ according to the tradition from which they are derived. Some traditions are fundamentally 'open to the possibility of divine existence', others are fundamentally closed to the same possibility. Even among those who are open to the 'possibility of divine existence', the conclusions that are likely to be reached regarding the principles of an 'implicit philosophy' will differ according to whether, for example, one takes a Lutheran or Thomist interpretation of the effect of the Fall on the human capacity for knowledge of God, truth, beauty and goodness. These problems are not directly addressed in the encyclical and in this respect it fails to engage the Nietzschean and postmodern Thomist and Augustinian arguments.[53] What would seem to be required by the Thomist tradition at this juncture in its history is a deeper understanding of the extent to which the tradition agrees with the Genealogists that conceptions of rationality are tradition dependent; and, further, a deeper understanding of how an immersion within a cultural order that is more or less resistant to grace and hostile to virtue undermines the ability of plain persons to reach an understanding of the principles of John Paul II's 'implicit philosophy'. Although MacIntyre has not provided a conclusive treatment of the issue, his work has at least drawn attention to the problematic and indicated the areas in which research needs to be undertaken.

At a more general level of analysis, John Paul II has suggested that the relationship between theology and philosophy should be construed as circular.[54] Looked at in this manner, MacIntyre's tendency to 'smudge the boundaries' between philosophy and theology occurs at points on the circle where the two converge. Moreover, MacIntyre's apparent untidiness with respect to such demarcations may well stem from two important factors. First, MacIntyre believes that traditions need to be taken as a whole and not severed into component parts which assume the status of unbridgeable disciplines. Second, there is the tension inherent within the Thomist tradition between its Aristotelian and Patristic elements. The Patristic elements are responsible for the more historicist and revelation-specific dimensions of MacIntyre's work, whereas the Aristotelian elements are responsible for his insistence that there is a normative way of being human and a philosophically discernible list of basic goods of human flourishing and of norms of human action.

Harmonising Aristotelian and Patristic elements

When speaking of the methodology of moral discernment, MacIntyre has a tendency to emphasise the Aristotelian aspects of the Thomist tradition, but when speaking of the moral formation of plain persons, it is the Patristic elements that are brought to the fore. This is not to say that MacIntyre is in any sense a modern disciple of Averroës. He does not subscribe to a position of a philosophic truth for the philosophers and the principles of Revelation for plain persons, since he believes that plain persons need to be 'enough of a philosopher' to work out the first principles of practical reasoning for themselves, and philosophers need to be formed within a narrative tradition before embarking on their own developments or critiques of the tradition. There are not two different truths, but merely two different approaches to the one truth. Therefore, depending on the context, MacIntyre alternates between an emphasis on the Aristotelian and Patristic, especially the Augustinian, dimensions of Thomism. The Patristic elements are stronger when the issue is the importance of cultural factors in moral formation, whereas the Aristotelian aspects tend to dominate in considerations of what might be called the 'practices of philosophy'. The first type of issue is encapsulated by the term *Bildung*, whereas the second is more narrowly defined as 'moral philosophy as an intellectual practice'.

In his exposition of the difference between the Augustinian and Aristotelian approaches to philosophical questions, MacIntyre makes the following observations:

> The **Augustinian** is committed to one central negative thesis about all actually or potentially rival positions: that no substantive rationality, independent of faith, will be able to provide an adequate vindication of its claims.[55]

> From the **Aristotelian** point of view an understanding of oneself as having an essential nature and the discovery of what in one belongs to that nature and what is merely *per accidens* enters into the progress of the self

... even though that understanding and discovery may take place in a way that presupposes rather than explicitly formulates the philosophical theses and arguments involved.[56]

MacIntyre's Augustinian claim that all alternative 'rationalities' will either 'fall into ineradicable incoherence or be compelled to acknowledge points at which there is an unavoidable resort to attitudes of unjustified and unjustifiable belief' is exemplified in the Augustinian analysis of John Milbank's *Beyond Secular Reason*, wherein he deconstructs so-called 'scientific' sociologies into their mythic components.[57] It is also consistent with the argument of, *inter alios*, Vatican II, de Lubac, John Paul II, Schindler and Scola that the human person only attains full self-knowledge through an understanding of Christ as the archetype of perfected humanity. Without this understanding, those plain persons who are proto-Aristotelians may, through the exercise of the principles of an 'implicit rationality', grope their way towards the truth, but they will always reach an impasse without the knowledge acquired through Revelation mediated by Christian Scripture and tradition. However, at the same time, MacIntyre's description of Aristotelian analytical processes is compatible with the idea that it is through participation in virtue-requiring and virtue-engendering practices that one most quickly grasps an understanding of one's own form, potential and *telos*. With Aristotle, one can get at least as far as the *praeparatio fidei*. As MacIntyre acknowledges, '[a] Pauline and Augustinian account retrospectively vindicates that in Aristotle which had provided a first understanding of the core of the moral life'.[58]

Although MacIntyre does not offer a systematic account of precisely how one is to transcend the contradictions of the culture of modernity – that is, whether one starts in an Augustinian fashion, submitting one's intellect and will to the truths of the Christian (especially Thomist) tradition, or whether one is simply immersed in a culture and through a more Aristotelian reflection upon its practices comes to an appreciation of the value of the truths and/or ideologies forming the substance of that culture – the appropriate approach would seem to vary according to how one is placed in life, that is in history. Those who are immersed within the *praxis* of the Augustinian Thomist tradition from childhood will come to an appreciation of the principles of that tradition, partly through a process of self-conscious reflection, and partly through what Michael Polanyi called the 'acquisition of tacit knowledge'. Historically this is how many 'plain persons' acquired an appreciation of the Augustinian Thomist tradition. However, MacIntyre also acknowledges that one can come to an understanding of the tradition through a dialectical process of the elimination of all other traditions. This is more typically the route of the philosopher and the convert. Indeed, the extraordinary number of leading twentieth-century philosophers, theologians and artists who actually came to Thomism from outside the tradition by a process of intellectual discernment in cooperation with the work of grace bears testimony to the value of what MacIntyre calls 'culture transcend-ing tradition dependent rationality'. A roll call, by no means exhaustive, includes Elizabeth Anscombe, Benedict Ashley OP, Frederick Copleston SJ, Christopher Dawson, Michael Dummett, John Finnis, Peter Geach, Eric Gill, Peter Kreeft, Jacques Maritain, Raissa Maritain, Aidan Nichols OP, Max Scheler, Edith Stein and, to some degree, MacIntyre himself.[59]

Either way, it is clear that for MacIntyre the notion of a tradition, and of a particular *ethos* associated with this tradition, is essential. Theory and prac-tice cannot be separated and one understood apart from the other. Hence, MacIntyre's statement that any particular tradition must be capable of a social expression, that is of being embedded within a particular community, and his argument that even philosophers can only come to an understand-ing of the arguments of a tradition by an association with communities in which those arguments or principles are embodied. Milbank makes a related point when he observes that the argument for the Christian tradition is not merely a series of theoretical propositions, but also the 'story of preachings, journeyings, miracles, martyrdoms, vocations, marriages, icons painted and liturgies sung, as well as intrigues, sins and warfare'.[60] This perspective is also encapsulated in von Balthasar's statement that 'the saints are Tradition at its most living', and John Paul II's statements in *Fides et ratio* that 'the mar-tyrs are the most authentic witnesses to the truth about existence' and that 'truth is attained not only by reason but also through trusting acquiescence to other persons who can guarantee the authenticity and certainty of the truth itself'.[61]

Certainty as 'rational coherence'

This conception of certainty differs from the kind of certainty based upon mathematical proofs typical of post-Cartesian thought. It is best described as a kind of 'rational coherence'. Since MacIntyre set out to analyse the culture of modernity and, in particular, the effect of this culture on the formation of the self, he arrived at the conclusion of the certainty of the truth of the Thomist tradition only after a consideration of all the common theoretical alternatives. Here there is a relationship between MacIntyre's idea that Thomism is philosophically vindicated by being the only tradition which renders the integrity of the self a possibility, and the *modus operandi* of Newman. Newman argued that when all the evidence points to one conclu-sion, converges on one exclusive explanation, then the mind should assent to that one conclusion without fear of the truth of its opposite. Similarly, for Belloc, although no one factor determines history, only one tradition – the Christian Greco-Roman tradition – renders history intelligible.[62]

Such a methodology that does not begin with the principles of Christian Revelation, but rather from an examination of the contradictions of the culture of modernity and a search for an escape route from the either/or tragic options offered by the modern 'severance' or 'mutation' or 'heretical reconstruction' of the classical theistic order, is one of the factors which gives MacIntyre's Thomism its 'postmodern' quality. Such an approach was fore-shadowed by the Italian Thomist Cornelio Fabro in his monumental history of modern atheism entitled *God in Exile* wherein he observed:

> Just as the Christian message of salvation could appear more radiant to the man of classical tragedy, it may without presumption be hoped that the free highway of a better-founded hope, may open up to present-day man out of the holocaust-mottled dead end in which he sees the *cogito* consuming itself.[63]

MacIntyre himself acknowledged the difference between his own ap-proach and that of classical Thomism in his 1990 Aquinas Lecture:

> We inhabit a time in the history of philosophy in which Thomism can only develop adequate responses to the rejections of its central positions in what must seem initially at least to be un-Thomistic ways ... in order to restate and defend those [Thomistic] positions in something like their original integrity through an internal critique of those theses and argu-ments which have displaced them, a critique dictated by Thomistic ends, but to be carried through in part at least by somewhat un-Thomistic means.[64]

The 'un-Thomistic means' is arguably MacIntyre's approach of starting from the 'self' rather than from God, and working out the principles by which the self can possibly retain its integrity. In the final analysis, MacIntyre's strongest argument for the Thomist tradition is that the self that embod-ies the principles of any other tradition is destined to fragmentation and even vacuity. To some degree this lends credence to the judgement of John Milbank that the truths of Christianity cannot ultimately be defended at the bar of reason, but rather that the scientific *mythos* of the Enlightenment and any alternative neo-pagan *mythos* employed by the Genealogical tradition can be out-narrated. MacIntyre's position is not, however, that it is either impos-sible or hubristic to seek to mount a philosophical defence of the rationality of the Thomist or, more generally, Christian tradition.[65] Rather, he seeks to broaden the notion of a tradition to include both its theoretical and practi-cal dimensions. On the one hand, when emphasising the practical dimen-sion, MacIntyre would agree with Milbank that Christian practices are an argument for the tradition or, as Andrew Louth argues, the tradition of the Church is not like the traditions to which the Gnostics appealed, simply some message, truth or ideology, but 'the whole character of the Christian commu-nity, its rites, its ceremonies, its practices, and its life'.[66] However, MacIntyre also argues that the belief that the human intellect is rational (albeit fallen and less than angelic) is a fundamental element of that tradition, and, further, the fact that the Thomist tradition can be rationally demonstrated to be the only tradition which offers any hope for the formation of an integral self, is itself a very strong argument for both the truth of the tradition and the merit of philosophy as an intellectual practice. The tradition of Thomism is not merely a history of dialectical encounters; but dialectical encounters are one important aspect of the tradition that seeks an intellectual explication and defence of Christianity. It should be emphasised however that although MacIntyre's defence of the Thomist tradition begins from the perspective of the self, his account of the process of self-formation requires, as a principle of epistemic priority, the existence of a narrative tradition and the self's immersion within that tradition. This means that while MacIntyre employs a very Aristotelian 'reflection upon practice' methodology in his examinations of the predicament of the various types of modern self, his solution to the predicament is quintessentially Augustinian.

Conclusion

The concept of the tradition-constituted rationality embedded within social practices and transmitted from generation to generation by the masters of the narrative tradition is the key postmodern concept in MacIntyre's postmodern Augustinian Thomism. Unlike much of neo-Thomist scholarship, which sought to engage the proponents of the Encyclopaedist tradition with arguments drawn exclusively from the Aristotelian currents in Thomism, MacIntyre's idea of a tradition-dependent rationality differentiates the Thomist understanding of rationality from the Encyclopaedist conception, and thus sides with the Genealogists in their argument that, at the basis of any account of rationality, and indeed of any philosophy, is a mythology or theology. Nonetheless, MacIntyre does not concede the Nietzschean argument that the choice for or against Christianity is a mere matter of preference – of differences in personal temperament. Through his explanation of the operation of a narrative tradition he seeks to unite the theoretical and participatory levels of human experience, as well as the realms of faith and reason. If the notion of the narrative tradition is taken away, and philosophy and theology are pursued as completely separate disciplines, then the tradition of Thomism begins to fragment. Theoretically it may be possible to distinguish philosophy and theology, but those who consistently work only within the philosophical field risk adopting the logic of 'secular rationality' as they lose sight of where their philosophical questions fit within a theological framework. An example of this problem was analysed in Chapter 5 with reference to Timothy Chappell's endorsement of Enlightenment traditions regardless of their theological pedigree. Alternatively, those who eschew any rôle for philosophy in theological analysis run the risk of ending in a position of pure fideism. This has historically not been a problem within the Thomist tradition, but it remains a risk for any self-consciously Christian philosophy.

MacIntyre's tendency to 'smudge the boundaries' between philosophy and theology should thus be perceived not as an intellectual inconsistency, but rather as the result of his argument that both are intrinsically related, although they may take different priorities depending upon the intellectual context. Further, in engagements with the Genealogical tradition, a reference to the theological dimensions of Thomism will not give rise to the same problems as it has in engagements with the Encyclopaedist tradition. Whereas the Encyclopaedists deny epistemological legitimacy to theological arguments, the Genealogists believe that philosophical arguments are at root inescapably mythological. The battle lines thereby change to a focus on the theological dimensions of an issue. In this sense, MacIntyre's tendency to 'smudge the boundaries' may be a necessary corrective to the overly zealous attempts of the neo-Thomists and others to narrow the horizons of the tradition so as to meet the epistemic standards of the Encyclopaedists.

What are the practical consequences of this analysis for the Thomist tradition? It raises the question of the prudence of the strategy that has been pursued of adopting elements of the conceptual apparatus of the rival Liberal tradition. In particular, MacIntyre's analysis raises the question of whether there can be any such things as 'universal values', understood not in a natural law sense, but rather in the second sense to which reference was made in Chapter 2 – the idea that there is a set of values which are of general appeal across a range of traditions, including the Nietzschean, Thomist and Liberal traditions.

Among many Thomist scholars, any reference to tradition-constituted or tradition-dependent rationality, or to the barriers posed by alternative traditions to a comprehension of the principles of the natural moral law, raises fears of cultural relativism and historicism. However, MacIntyre rejects cultural and ethical relativism, while conceding to the Genealogical tradition the argument that the universalism of the Thomist tradition is far from neutral in its relation to theological questions. In the following chapter it will be argued that this concession does not destroy the natural law doctrine which lies at the heart of the Thomist tradition's claims to offer a universally valid moral framework. It simply shifts the focus of ethical debates to an examination of the theological presuppositions of contending ethical systems, including the 'Christian roots' of the ideal of the human person implicit within natural law arguments.

7

NATURAL LAW AND THE CULTURE
OF THE TRADITION

As was explained in the Introduction, there has been some reluctance among proponents of natural law jurisprudence to consider the rôle of culture in moral formation and prudential judgement. This is because of the concern that any such consideration would undermine the claim that the precepts of the natural law are discernible by all persons regardless of cultural background. This chapter is therefore focused on an account of how a postmodern Augustinian Thomism need not, and, in fact, does not, undermine the natural law doctrine within the Thomist tradition. Since the New Natural Law school pioneered by Germain Grisez, John Finnis and Joseph Boyle is currently the dominant school of natural law theory within the Thomist tradition, this chapter begins with an analysis of the relationship between MacIntyre's account of natural law and that of the New Natural Law school. It will be concluded that, just as different conceptions of the grace–nature relationship have effected different readings of the compatibility of Liberal political philosophy and the Thomist account of the human *telos*, so too the neo-Thomist and Nouvelle Théologie readings of the grace–nature relationship also lead to two different approaches to natural law. Again it will be argued that MacIntyre's reading is consistent with those theologians associated with the Nouvelle Théologie, especially Schindler and Scola, and differs from the New Natural Law school in recognising some qualifications to Hume's 'no ought from is' principle in emphasising the rôle of a narrative tradition in the discernment of the principles of the natural law, and in rejecting the idea that elements of the Enlightenment tradition can or ought to be synthesised with classical Thomism. In particular, MacIntyre regards the strategy of adopting elements of the conceptual apparatus of Liberal jurisprudence as highly problematic. With reference to ideas of von Balthasar, the final section of this chapter will defend MacIntyre's judgement on this issue.

MacIntyre's project and the New Natural Law theory

The first point that MacIntyre makes about Thomistic natural law is that it is important to consider Aquinas's arguments within the context of his work as a whole. The tendency of scholars to focus on questions 90–97 of the *Prima secundae* of the *Summa Theologiae*, as though a knowledge of these sections is all that is required, is dismissed as an example of the flawed intellectual practices which were the subject of criticism by R. G. Collingwood.[1] In particular, MacIntyre argues that such an approach leads to difficulties with the interpretation of 'principium' in question 94, wherein Aquinas states that 'the first principle [*principium*] of natural law is that good is to be done and evil avoided'. Since both Kant and Hume were post Aquinas, MacIntyre regards it as anachronistic to read Kantian and Humean constructions into Aquinas, and applies instead a Platonic and Aristotelian reading of *principium*.

Such a reading has two dimensions: an epistemological dimension by which the *principium* refers to the first principle of a thesis, and an ontological dimension which refers to the formative order of something, in this context the human person.[2] *Principium* understood in this ontological sense is construed by reference to questions 1–89 of the *Summa*. In this section of the analysis, MacIntyre is critical of the adoption by Finnis and Grisez of the Humean argument that no 'ought' can be derived from an 'is'.[3] MacIntyre does not regard the argument as completely wrong but qualifies Hume's principle, claiming that there *are* 'several types of valid argument in which some element may appear in the conclusion which is not present in the premises' and that 'the alleged unrestrictedly general logic principle on which everything is being made to hang is bogus'.[4] Significantly, the one example given by MacIntyre of a valid argument in which an element appears in the conclusion which was not present in the premise is that where the 'is' in the premise refers to the nature of the human person. Although he does not develop an extensive defence of his premise that the idea of 'man' is a functional concept, from a theological perspective he states that the 'moral scheme of Christianity is one according to which the law which God utters to us is entirely congruent with the nature that He created in us and with the ends which that nature pursues' and that 'the deontology of the commandments is embedded in the teleology of the doctrine of creation'.[5]

From a more classically Aristotelian perspective, MacIntyre argues that for every species there is something that constitutes the flourishing of the members of that species. For example, 'the flourishing of dolphins is one thing, the flourishing of gorillas another, the flourishing of bacteria a third, and the flourishing of human beings as rational animals a fourth'.[6] From this perspective, when MacIntyre speaks of human nature he means 'the properties of the human person in virtue of which individuals are able to flourish as members of the human species'.[7] Evaluative judgements about the goods of human flourishing are therefore 'a species of factual judgement concerning the final and formal causes of activity of members of a particular species'.[8]

However, while MacIntyre argues against Grisez and Finnis that where human nature is concerned it is possible to work from 'is' to 'ought', he nonetheless agrees with Grisez and Finnis that in the formulation of the principles of the natural law it is not the case that first we must decide whether some theory of human nature or cosmology is true and only secondly pass a verdict upon an account of the virtues which is based upon it.[9] In the following passage, Finnis acknowledged the affinity of MacIntyre's methodology for discerning the goods of human flourishing with that of his own:

> In reflecting on this abstract formulation of morality's first principle, one will bear in mind the remarks of Alasdair MacIntyre ... It is a Cartesian error, fostered by a misunderstanding of Euclidean geometry, to suppose that first by an initial act of apprehension we can comprehend the full meaning of the premises of a deductive system and then only secondly proceed to inquire what follows from them. In fact it is only insofar as we understand what follows from those premises that we understand the premises themselves.[10]

However, it is also consistent with MacIntyre's starting point, and uncharacteristic of the New Natural Law project, that MacIntyre argues that no progress in moral enquiry is possible without first committing oneself to a particular narrative tradition. In this sense he valorises the Augustinian current within the Thomist synthesis.[11] Although 'religion' is classified as a 'good of human flourishing' by members of the New Natural Law school, it is merely one of seven incommensurable goods, and it is defined by Finnis rather opaquely as 'harmony with God', or 'the search for ultimate explanations of the universal order of things and of human life and destiny' and 'the attempt to bring human affairs into harmony, actual or ritualistic, with the source of such explanations'.[12] These definitions might include participation within a narrative tradition but this is not an obvious reading of the expressions. Rather, it would seem more obvious to say that there is no analogue within the New Natural Law school for the concept of a narrative tradition.

Although members of the New Natural Law school acknowledge that virtuous habits are a necessary element of moral formation, they rarely raise the typically MacIntyrean questions about the relationship between virtue and culture, and, in particular, whether the whole form of the culture of modernity is hostile to the kind of formation required for the development of a fully flourishing Thomist or classical Christian self, and, if so, the impact of such a judgement upon the premises of their own intellectual project.[13] MacIntyre's position, however, is that even the methodological premise that one can work back from conceptions of human flourishing to conceptions of human nature presupposes a common human ontology and thus a normative way of developing one's human potential, and this latent normativity is consistent with *some* narrative traditions that are embedded within *some* institutional cultures and not others. While the proponents of New Natural Law theory would probably agree with MacIntyre's principle, they have not applied it to a consideration of the relationship between the Liberal tradition, the culture of modernity, and the prospects for plain persons discerning the principles of the natural law.

As stated in Chapter 1, the precise nature of the relationship between the New Natural Law project and the Liberal tradition has not been made explicit in the corpus of New Natural Law literature. This is notwithstanding their trenchant criticisms of Liberal ethics, and Finnis's acknowledgement of the inter-relationship of ethics, political philosophy and jurisprudence in the preface to *Natural Law and Natural Rights*.[14] In his Linacre lecture of 1997, Finnis asserted that the term 'Liberal' has 'no core meaning sufficiently stable and clear for use in a general political philosophy or theory', and that we should do 'our general critical political reflection without attempting to employ "Liberalism" as a framework category'.[15] Nonetheless, in the same paper, Finnis argues that we can embrace the idea that Aquinas was the 'first Whig' because:

> ... although he rightly defended institutions and practices important in public life on the basis that they are required or authorised by certain moral and metaphysical truths, he at the same time insisted that the proper functions of the state's laws and rulers do not include making people morally good by requiring them to abstain from immorality. The rôle of state government and law, according to Aquinas, is to uphold peace and justice; the requirements imposed, supervised, and enforced by state government and law concern only those sorts of choice and action which affect other people.[16]

In one sense MacIntyre is in agreement with this statement – that Aquinas limited the extent to which the state should suppress immorality. MacIntyre treated this issue in his discussion of Aquinas's reaction to the behaviour of *jongleurs* who congregated around the Sorbonne singing anti-Dominican ditties.[17] MacIntyre argues that, when Aquinas posed the question whether it belongs to human law to repress all vices, he replies trenchantly in the negative, since 'law is designed for the instruction and correction of those who are still deeply imperfect in the virtues, and of them too much should not be asked too soon'.[18] As a consequence, 'moral legislation should concern itself with only the more grievous vices'. From this MacIntyre concludes that Aquinas 'disagrees with both later Puritans and with Liberals', for 'like Puritans and unlike Liberals he understands the law as an instrument for moral education, but like Liberals and unlike Puritans he is against making the law by itself an attempt to repress all vice'.[19]

Notwithstanding MacIntyre's agreement with Finnis that Aquinas 'limited the extent to which the state should interfere with the suppression of immorality', he does not hold, as Finnis does, that this position qualifies him to be classified as the 'first Whig', or indeed any kind of 'Whig'. A spirit of generosity towards those who are still imperfect in virtue does not make one a 'Whig' or a Liberal in MacIntyre's understanding of those terms. As was stated in previous chapters, MacIntyre believes that Liberalism is a tradition and as such has its own canon of authorities, its own history of disputed questions, its own classification and rank ordering of goods, as well as its own conceptions of justice and rationality. The significance of the difference in methodology between those who describe themselves as analytical Thomists and those who think in terms of competing conceptions of 'rationality', 'traditions' and 'cultures' is evident in this difference between Finnis and MacIntyre on the reputed 'Whiggery' of Aquinas.

MacIntyre demonstrates an awareness of the importance of this methodological distinction in his statement that it is not in 'respect of their individual theses, considered item by item, but only in respect of those theses understood in their relationship to some specific mode of enquiry' that the 'true nature of the conflict between Thomism and modern standpoints can be adequately explored'.[20] For example, where Finnis in the above quotation ascribes to Aquinas the belief that the 'requirements imposed, supervised, and enforced by state government and law concern only those sorts of choice and action which affect other people', MacIntyre might well respond: 'Yes, but a Thomist and a Liberal would have a different interpretation of what it means to 'affect other people'.

Nigel Biggar drew attention to this issue in his comparison of the accounts of the human good in the works of Karl Barth and Germain Grisez. He explains that the argument is not that the content of theistic and atheistic moralities is always entirely different, but rather that 'the particular moral beliefs that they share are differently located in larger wholes that qualify – sometimes slightly, sometimes radically – the significance of each of their parts'.[21] In any analysis of the question of whether the relationship between any two traditions is complementary, dialectical or genetic, this factor of the location of moral concepts within a larger architectonic tradition can be decisive.

The ambivalent nature of the relationship between the New Natural Law project and the Liberal tradition has been the subject of criticism in a number of articles. Ernest Fortin went so far as to assert that the constant recurrence of such characteristic expressions as 'personal authenticity', 'creativity', 'values' and 'lifestyles' to be found within the scholarship of the New Natural Law school are but a modern substitute for the classical notion of the good life, and that the intellectual pedigree of such concepts reveals the degree to which the enterprise remains 'in thrall to the dominant spiritual and political consciousness of the times'.[22] Similarly, Charles Covell has drawn attention to the disjunction between Finnis's criticisms of elements of post-Enlightenment philosophy and his endorsement of the public values embodied in the institutional organisation of modern Liberal society:

> Fuller, Oakeshott, Hayek and Finnis were uniformly critical of the intellectual and cultural tradition associated with the European

Enlightenment. Even so, the theorists were simultaneously defenders of the Enlightenment, by reason of a common, if frequently unacknowledged, allegiance to the public values embodied in the legal and constitutional organisation of modern Liberal society. The basic fidelity of the theorists to these values was in no way qualified by their shared conviction that the political morality of secular liberal constitutionalism could no longer be supported in terms of the specific ideologies constructed during the actual historical period of the Enlightenment.[23]

On the Covell reading, the New Natural Law project is an example of what Charles Taylor calls the 'untenable position' of picking certain fruits of modernity, such as human rights, and making them a part of one's intellectual framework, but then condemning the whole movement of thought and practice that underlies them.[24] Implicit within such an intellectual 'practice' is the tendency, common to so much post-Conciliar thought, to regard the relationship between 'form' and 'substance' as unproblematic.

In summary, while MacIntyre and the proponents of New Natural Law share some of the same epistemological priorities in the context of the task of defining the goods of human flourishing, the current trajectory of the MacIntyre project, especially MacIntyre's emphasis upon the Augustinian elements within Thomism, suggests that his account of natural law differs from the New Natural Law school in four important respects:

1 MacIntyre allows for some arguments from 'is' to 'ought'.
2 There is within the New Natural Law project no obvious analogue for MacIntyre's notion of a narrative tradition.
3 The logic of MacIntyre's Augustinian Thomist position, although he has not explicitly stated this, is that the good of religion should be treated as the infrastructural and even primary good, rather than the goods being, in Finnis's terminology, 'equally fundamental' and 'incommensurable'.
4 Within MacIntyre's jurisprudence there is no ambivalence regarding the Liberal tradition. He completely rejects this tradition and, in particular, the project of transposing Thomist natural law into the rhetoric of Liberal natural right.

The absence of a narrative tradition

As a consequence of the centrality of the rôle of a narrative tradition within the work of MacIntyre, Joseph Boyle has dismissed the idea that the MacIntyrean and New Natural Law projects may be capable of synthesis. Boyle argues that the foundations of moral life and judgement are in the moral law, and moral laws are propositional realities, 'dictates of reason', not 'character traits, practices, or cultural creations'.[25] In further opposition to MacIntyre's position he adds, 'whatever unifies those who think about moral questions within the natural law tradition it is not a community of shared lived values'.[26]

However, MacIntyre would not in fact take objection to Boyle's principle that 'the foundations of moral life and judgement are in the moral law' and, further, that 'moral laws are propositional realities'. Not only has MacIntyre defended the place of rationality in ethics in his various critiques of emotivism, but at least as early as 1979 MacIntyre defined a 'moral judgement' as 'one that is to hold equally for Frenchman or Italians, for Athenians or Corinthians'.[27] Merely because MacIntyre is interested in the rôle which culture plays in moral formation does not mean that he believes that culture provides the criteria for truth. However, Boyle was correct in his assertion that MacIntyre would disagree with the statement that 'whatever unifies those who think about moral questions within the natural law tradition it is not a community of shared, lived, values'. This is because the emphasis of the MacIntyre project is on understanding the social processes which are significant for moral formation; in particular, the manner in which the *ethos* of a given community influences the acquisition of virtues necessary for the making of prudential judgements.[28] MacIntyre's project can thus best be understood as a specific example of what Anthony Matteo calls a 'pre-modern epistemological *modus operandi* capacious enough to do justice to both the detached and participatory levels of experience'.[29] MacIntyre's account of virtue-ethics relates to the participatory level of experience, whereas his treatment of natural law relates to the more abstract level of intellectual discernment, or what MacIntyre calls 'reflection upon practice'.

The particular philosophical anthropology at the root of this account of the relationship between natural law and a culturally embodied narrative tradition is encapsulated in MacIntyre's definition of the human person as a 'culture-transcending dependent rational animal'. Such a definition goes beyond the classical Boethian definition of the person as an individual substance of a rational nature as it emphasises the rôle which community life and practice has upon the moral formation of the person. This is consistent with the metaphysical project of William Norris Clarke, elements of which are shared by, *inter alios*, Ratzinger, Kasper, Schindler and Schmitz, as discussed in Chapter 5, in that it draws attention to the fact that a person is only fully understood in terms of both relationality and substantiality – a principle that is also central to the philosophical anthropology of John Paul II and which informs such concepts as 'solidarity' and communio. MacIntyre summarises the relationship between the 'detached and participatory levels of experience' of the culture-transcending dependent rational animal thus:

It is only of course in terms provided for each of us by our own culture that human beings can initially formulate whatever truths we may apprehend about human nature and about the natural law. And it is from the resources provided by our own culture that we first set about trying to provide 'the most adequate formulation' for those truths. (cf. *Veritatis Splendor* paragraph 53). But insofar as the conception of human nature which we arrive at is indeed that of human nature as structured by the Natural Law, we will have succeeded in transcending what is peculiar to our own or any other culture. It will have become a conception of that which 'is itself a measure of culture' of that in human beings which shows that they are 'not exhaustively defined' by their culture and not its prisoner.[30]

Since the starting point is a reflection upon the practices inherent within the given social and institutional cultures, those whose cultural 'sub-soil', to use Guardini's expression, has already been formed by reference to the principles of the natural law will find the whole process of transcendence easier than those who have been immersed within the barren sub-soil of mass culture and its ideological institutions. As was discussed in Chapter 6, MacIntyre believes that participation within a narrative tradition is a necessary element of moral formation. Someone without an experience of religion, or functional family and community life, or beauty, is likely to find the whole notion of natural law incomprehensible. Again, Nigel Biggar has made reference to this problem in his comparison of Barth and Grisez's accounts of the human good. He observes that, in a world in which there appears to be no God and no hope of what New Natural Lawyers call 'integral human fulfilment', the requirements of 'practical reasonableness', by ceasing to appear practicable, thereby come to seem practically *un*reasonable'.[31] Biggar concludes that 'the presence or absence of faith in God and hope for the realisation of integral human fulfilment determines what seems morally reasonable'.[32] This is consistent with the conclusion of Rufus Black that New Natural Law theory 'emerges as a conceptual framework for ethical analysis, the actual character and content of which will be determined by the understanding of reality – that is, the world-view of the person who is using it'.[33]

Although MacIntyre agrees with Finnis and Grisez that the best approach to an analysis of the goods of human flourishing is via a reflection upon practices – his argument, as was developed in Chapter 3, is that some practices are so dysfunctional that those who participate in them retard their potential to develop as moral persons and that such morally retarding or 'emotivist' practices are dominant in modern institutions. A narrative tradition is thus a crucial medium in which to participate in the goods of human flourishing and serves an epistemological function in the discernment of the goods. Since the goods of religion, knowledge, play, work and aesthetic experience are largely cultural inheritances, they could be developed along 'narrative lines'. However, this would require a recognition by the New Natural Law theorists of the epistemological significance of traditions and the 'forms' in which traditions are embodied, and this in turn would introduce a tension into the New Natural Law framework, which remains closer to the Liberal–Kantian idea of 'pure reason' than to the pre-modern and postmodern idea of 'tradition-constituted rationality'.

Religion as an 'infrastructural' and 'primary' good

The question of whether the goods of human flourishing are equally fundamental and incommensurable or whether the good of religion occupies a special infrastructural position has been recognised as a problem by a number of authors. For example, James Schall argues that 'the crux of the problem has to do with the relation of the first principles of practical reasoning to metaphysics', or, in other words, 'to what degree is practical reasoning itself dependent on an order of being that is not simply arbitrary but one with its own intrinsic order in nature, in human nature?'[34] This is a return to the problem, mentioned in Chapter 6, of the dependence of rationality on a created order in the world. In his *Critique of the New Natural Law*, Russell Hittinger argues that, if there is no proper telic completions to humanity and the goods sought, 'then there is no compelling reason to opt for Aristotle rather than Nietzsche'.[35] Essentially the same position is taken by Ian Markham. Markham argues that, while modernity has made belief in God an 'appendage belief', Christians cannot in fact 'tag God on to their system', since 'both Aquinas and Nietzsche show us that God is a transforming belief, central to how we view everything':

> You cannot assume a rationality and argue that there is no foundation to that rationality. Either God and rationality go or God and rationality stay. Either Nietzsche or Aquinas, that is our choice.[36]

Ernest Fortin presents the issue as the question of whether the two tables of the Ten Commandments bear any intrinsic relationship to each other, that is does the first table serve as a mandatory ground of the second? He suggests that a Thomist theory of natural law requires 'not only that the content of the natural law be naturally known to all human beings', but that it be known precisely as 'belonging to a law which is both promulgated and enforced by God as the author of nature'.[37]

Although MacIntyre has not addressed this issue directly, the notion that religion must be, in a sense, infrastructural is consistent with his Augustinian emphasis upon the formative rôle of a narrative tradition in moral and hence cultural formation and with his rejection of the idea of an autonomous secular realm. In a statement which echoes Fortin, he observes that 'a knowledge of God is, on Aquinas's view, available to us from the outset of our moral enquiry and plays a crucial part in our progress in that enquiry'.[38] Alternatively, the absence of an analogue for a narrative tradition within the New Natural Law school is consistent with an account of religion as merely one of seven unranked goods. By treating the goods of human flourishing as 'incommensurable', one can maintain some degree of association with a particular religious community without making its principles formative in other dimensions of life. There can be, in other words, the kind of 'division of labour' approach criticised by von Balthasar in *Love Alone*, to which reference was made in Chapter 5. However, in MacIntyre's account of a narrative tradition that includes not merely intellectual propositions but the entire realm of social practices, including the layout of towns and villages, one's religious principles are formative of the other dimensions. For example, theology affects architecture or, in the language of the goods of human flourishing, religion affects aesthetics. Once one begins to think in terms of narrative traditions, the good of religion begins to be seen as the infrastructural principle of the narrative tradition and its culture, including one's mode of participation in the goods.[39] Thus, the MacIntyrean reading would seem to be that a narrative tradition is not technically a good in itself, but rather another category to the goods, one which properly informs all experiences of and choices regarding the goods; and, further, because of the centrality of the Catholic faith to the Thomist tradition, the good of religion within this particular narrative tradition enjoys a certain priority. Moreover, if one takes into account the Trinitarian 'form of love', it can be argued that the theological virtues of faith, hope and charity properly inform all the goods, including, but not only, the good of religion.

In a recent article which suggests that the 'incommensurability principle' may be under review within the New Natural Law school, Joseph Boyle acknowledges that religion may be what he calls a 'supervenient motive' for other actions, and that some persons may choose to organise their lives around such a 'single, supervenient motive'.[40] In this case, the good of religion might be construed as infrastructural. Boyle does not reach this particular conclusion but gestures towards it with the statement: 'because of religion's object, the divine source of meaning and reality, it has pride of place even among the reflexive goods'.[41]

In the context of the grace–nature problematic examined in Chapter 5, only an extrinsicist account of the relationship permits a reading of the good of religion as a merely superstructural good. Although members of the New Natural Law school have not engaged in the debates regarding interpretations of the grace–nature relationship, in an early article on the 'Natural End of Man', Grisez indicated his preference for the pre-de Lubac extrinsicist position.[42] This is consistent with his explicit rejection of the Augustinian account of the human good, and the argument of the New Natural Law school that the end of man is 'integral human fulfilment'.[43] This means in effect that, if the de Lubacian so-called Nouvelle Théologie construction is adopted, then there automatically arises a tension between 'new theology' and 'New Natural Law'. This is evident in the commentary on *Veritatis Splendor* by Angelo Scola, who works within the tradition of de Lubac. Scola begins his analysis of the encyclical by drawing attention to John Paul II's reference to

John 1:17 – 'the law was given through Moses; grace and truth come through Jesus Christ'.[44] Scola locates the prime cause of the contemporary rejection of the possibility of a natural moral law in an 'inability to recognise Jesus Christ as the universal and concrete norm'. He argues that from a theoretical standpoint, 'this means the continuation of the Enlightenment challenge rigorously formulated by Kant, which claimed that a historical event (Jesus Christ) could not be the formulation and proof of universal, necessary truths'.[45] Indeed, Scola speaks of a problem of a double extrinsicism – the reduction of ethics to a pure norm on the one side, and the idea of *sola scriptura* on the other.[46] The first is typical of the Kantian tendency to narrow the optic of ethics to what can be viewed without recourse to Revelation, while the latter is typical of the Barthian tendency to narrow the optic of morality to a focus upon Scripture. Scola wants a natural law theory which integrates these apparent antinomies.

Schindler adds to Scola's judgements the argument that if 'Catholics persist in proposing a natural law doctrine severed from the data of Revelation, what they do is to give us something very like the abstract nature that is the centrepiece of the Liberal establishment':[47]

> What needs to be underscored here is that the demand for a neutral form of natural law argument, for a form of natural law which would seek a common ground outside of the history of the dialogue partners, is as a matter of principle a demand for a Liberal form of natural law argument. It is a demand for exactly the sort of abstraction of form which is characteristic of Cartesianism.[48]

As a consequence, Schindler proposes that there can be a universal appeal to ethics in the sense of natural law; however, any such universal appeal must be oriented, in its beginning and all along the way, to the concrete form that the universal takes in the personal life of Christ and the sacramental life of the Church.[49] This would seem to suggest that for Scola and Schindler, and less overtly, but also logically, for MacIntyre, the good of religion would need to be given an infrastructural position in any list of goods of human flourishing.

In addition to its infrastructural properties, it may also be argued that the good of religion must be given the highest or primary ranking in the Thomist framework, because of the importance of contemplation within the tradition. This is the position taken by Pamela Hall in the following passage:

> the inclusive natural end is also hierarchical in the structure of its constituent goods. Thomas speaks of the 'order' of precepts following the 'order' of inclinations. Those goods to which we are inclined as rational creatures have greatest value. Among these, knowledge about God, even within the limited search of natural contemplation, is the highest and best good.[50]

Whereas Finnis argues that 'each of us has a subjective order of priority amongst the basic values' and Grisez states that 'the fact that they [the goods] may seem more important to an individual or a group simply reflects the cultural conditioning or psychological leaning of that individual or group' and thus that 'hierarchies are simply a matter of subjective choice and temperament', the argument that a major distinction between Catholic and Protestant cultures is the order given to doxology and work, to being and doing, means that, in terms of the list of goods of human flourishing, the good of religion must at least take priority over the good of work.[51] The notion of religion as infrastructural means that it is religion which is the provider of the *logos* of a given *Kultur*. At present, however, contributors to the New Natural Law project are prescribing principles of human flourishing for persons who have very little opportunity to follow a plan of 'integral human fulfilment' because they live and work within the institutions of the culture of modernity for which the infrastructural *logos* is provided by the Liberal tradition, central to which is the notion of the compartmentalization of the self, and characteristic of which is the 'rival sacrality' of the culture and polity of death with its priority of economic productivity and mechanical *logos*. Unless religion is given the highest ranking within the hierarchy of goods, the priority of contemplation over work and of being over doing and having can be displaced with the practical consequence that persons adopt strategies – to which reference was made in Chapter 5 – of bifurcating life into religious and secular compartments. When this occurs, the good of religion is often perceived as a very inferior compartment confined to ceremonial and liturgical practices and a few moral principles.

In stating that an individual's rank ordering of the goods 'simply reflects the cultural conditioning or psychological leaning of that individual or group', Grisez is making a very MacIntyrean point. However, the Dawsonian–MacIntyrean response is that the rank ordering of goods within a given culture (*Kultur*) will differ according to its infrastructural *logos* and that it is precisely because not every culture is infrastructurally Catholic that persons need to be not merely dependent rational animals, but culture-transcending animals as well. If, for example, the infrastructural *logos* is provided by a Protestant understanding of the relationship between nature and grace, then the rank ordering of the goods is likely to be different from that of a *Kultur* fostered by a Catholic reading of the two orders. However, one can argue that although the *rank ordering* of the goods may not be simply a matter of subjective choice, the *mode of participation* in the goods is, in a sense, a matter of individual choice. In Balthasarian terms, it is a matter of different lay and clerical 'styles'. The individual's choice of a spiritual style is a key element in the drama of the soul's participation in the life of the Trinity. It is 'subjective' in the sense that there is not just one blueprint or one path to holiness, but rather different paths according to the different gifts and the different crosses individuals carry. However, if an individual's choice represents a 'style' of vocation received and accepted as a Divine gift, then it is not simply another 'lifestyle choice' but a moral action analogous to the Marian fiat.

The rhetoric of rights

The natural rights doctrine is the key element of the rhetorical framework of Liberal jurisprudence. As was stated in Chapter 1, the proponents of the New Natural Law project and Whig Thomism favour the adoption of this rhetoric. John Finnis, for example, has stated that

> If its logic and its place in practical reasonableness about human flour-ishing are kept in mind, the modern usage of claims of right as the prin-ciple counter in political discourse should be recognized (despite its du-bious seventeenth-century origins and its abuse by fanatics, adventurers, and self-interested persons from the eighteenth century until today) as a valuable addition to the received vocabulary of practical reasonableness (i.e. to the tradition of 'natural law' doctrine).[52]

MacIntyre would no doubt acknowledge that the substance of Finnisian natural right is tied to natural law; however, MacIntyre regards the idea of trying to pack the substance of a Thomist conception of justice into a Liberal conceptual apparatus as 'not practically reasonable'. In a statement which is diametrically opposite to that offered by Finnis, MacIntyre asserts:

> The dominant contemporary idiom and rhetoric of rights cannot serve genuinely rational purposes, and we ought not to conduct our moral and political arguments in terms derived from that idiom and rhetoric. In so saying, I formulate a position at odds not only with Liberal proponents of the United Nation's *Declaration of Human Rights*, but also with utter-ances of, for example, the National Conference of Catholic Bishops. My quarrel in this latter case is not, or not necessarily, with the substance of what the bishops have intended to assert on a variety of moral and po-litical matters; but in so far as the form of their assertions has involved an appeal, or has appeared to involve an appeal, to a dubious idiom and rhetoric of rights, I believe that the bishops, quite inadvertently, may have injured their own case.[53]

MacIntyre's scepticism is directly related to his premise that rationality is tradition dependent. In concrete terms, he cannot see how a jurist formed within the Liberal tradition will ever accord a Thomist substance to a right. Liberals and Thomists might use the same terminology, but they mean radi-cally different things. MacIntyre makes frequent reference to Aristotle's ar-gument that rational enquiry in politics and ethics, and rationality in action require membership of a community which shares allegiance to some specific conception of the common good. In the absence of such a shared allegiance and specific conception of the common good, MacIntyre believes that appeals to the rhetoric of rights will be nothing more than ideological shadow-boxing.[54] MacIntyre acknowledges that what 'Maritain wished to affirm in his endorsement of the rights rhetoric of the United Nations was a modern version of Aquinas's thesis that every human being has within him or herself a natural knowledge of divine law', but he further argues that Maritain failed to reckon with the fact that 'in many cultures and notably in that of modernity plain persons are misled into giving moral expression to those capacities through assent to false [i.e. emotivist] philosophical theories'.[55] By analogy, the same criticism can be made of the New Natural Law attempt to transpose natural law principles into the idiom of natural right. In the absence of shared conceptions of the good, MacIntyre believes that it is not possible for modern political institutions to foster the common good – 'a compartmentalized society imposes a fragmented ethics', and politics is thereby rendered unphilosophical and, hence, ideological.[56]

As was explained in Chapter 3, MacIntyre argues that ideological rhetoric serves a political purpose of concealing areas of conflict between competing conceptions of the good. Where words and phrases mean different things in different traditions and there is a radical conflict between traditions over the very ideas signified by the words and phrases, the resort to ideological terms has the effect of covering over the underlying ethical differences. For example, there is a tendency to replace the word 'spouse', which carries a large amount of baggage from the Judeo-Christian theologies of marriage, with the word 'partner', which can signify anything from a 'spouse' to a prostitute hired from an escort agency. Invitations addressed to 'x and partner' thus have the ideological effect of rendering one's marital status socially irrelevant. MacIntyre's argument is that the rights rhetoric, although more complex, operates in the same ideological fashion. MacIntyre describes the process as the attempt to 'translate from a language of one community whose language-in-use is expressive of and presupposes a particular system of well-defined beliefs – [in this case the natural law doctrine] – into one of the internationalised languages of modernity'.[57] The defining property of these 'internationalised languages' is their dissociation of concepts from the traditions in which they were originally embedded:

> When texts from a tradition with their own strong, substantive criteria of truth and rationality, as well as with a strong historical dimension, are translated into one of the languages of modernity, they are presented in a way that neutralises the conceptions of truth and rationality and historical context ... The conceptions of truth and rationality become not part of a presupposed framework of beliefs to which the author appeals in addressing an audience who shares or shared that same framework but are relegated to an explanation to an audience characterized as not possessing any such framework.[58]

In effect, this means that every time one of the masters of the Thomist tradition agrees to adopt elements of the 'language of modernity' they contribute to the social marginalisation of their own narrative tradition. Further, insofar as their narrative tradition is marginalised, the medium in which the plain person acquired an appreciation of the principles of the natural law is 'thinned'. This issue relates back to the ideas in Chapter 3 regarding the plain person's tacit acquisition of a knowledge of moral principles, and the ideas in Chapter 6 regarding an expressivist theory of language. Although a few Christian intellectuals may be able to give an account of how the concept of rights in Finnis or John Paul II differs, for example, from Locke's or Dworkin's account of rights, those who are not scholars of jurisprudence, ethics or political philosophy, including, in many cases, members of the episcopacy and theologians, do not possess the requisite intellectual formation to know that the specific content to be given to rights differs according to the jurisprudential tradition in which they were framed. The dominance of the Liberal interpretation in popular discourse means that those whose knowledge of concepts is tacitly acquired end up thinking within a Liberal ideological framework.

A similar point was recently made by James Schall with respect to the projects of Jacques Maritain. Schall wrote that 'reading Maritain on rights and values requires a constant internal correction to recognise that what he means by these terms is something very different from what is generally meant by them in the culture'.[59] However, the capacity for such 'constant internal correction' requires a knowledge of the intellectual history of natural law and natural right doctrines and their rival interpretations within rival intellectual traditions. If this knowledge cannot be presupposed, even among members of the episcopacy, then this means that one important element of the narrative tradition is open to misunderstanding and mistranslation. Schmitz has observed that 'even the terms "natural" and "law" are now commonly given an interpretation which is inconsistent with a Thomistic understanding and this includes the interpretations of well-disposed people who are long familiar with the Catholic faith, to say nothing of those who are unfamiliar with it'.[60] He suggests that these issues are a part of the wider phenomenon that the version of reality presented in popular journals and news reports has gained acceptance and now shapes the very reality it purports to describe. The only persons he regards as capable of a correct Thomistic understanding of the terms are those who are 'familiar in a special way with the traditional meanings'. In MacIntyre's parlance this is like saying that only those who have been immersed within the Christian narrative tradition and instructed by its masters are likely to give a Thomist interpretation of the terms.

Evidence of this misunderstanding can be seen in the arguments of those who criticise John Paul II's governance of the Church, particularly his stance against homosexual acts and the ordination of women, on the grounds that he should apply his human rights rhetoric to the internal government of the Church. For example, referring directly to the authority of *Gaudium et spes* paragraph 41 – that 'modern man' is on the way to a more thorough development of his personality – John Langan has rhetorically asked whether human development proceeds along radically different lines once we enter the ecclesial sphere, and suggests that the tension between the Church's endorsement of human rights and her actions may 'produce problems of ungovernability within the Church and a reaction of incredulity in the face of its teaching'.[61] Conversely, from a position of support for the papacy of John Paul II, Robert P. Kraynak argues that 'the endorsement of democracy and human rights as a moral imperative of human dignity is undoubtedly the major cause of confusion today about the authority of the Church and the Catholic priesthood in particular'.[62] In his assessment of the strategy, Schall concluded:

> Whether Maritain's tactic to retain the use of the words, while reformulating their meaning, is the best one seems less viable in the years since his death in 1973. Both rights and values are generally understood in a subjective manner that allows no objective component that would examine the meaning or content of the values or rights proposed by comparing them with natural law, the content of which is not solely formulated by the subjective will.[63]

This issue is thus a specific instance of the difference between an instrumentalist and expressivist account of language. MacIntyre's expressivist argument is that the Church's teaching on natural law can only be understood when it is placed within the context of the Church's own narrative tradition, and that when attempts are made to translate the sacred teachings of the faith into one of the 'languages of modernity', in this case the idioms of the rival tradition of Liberalism, something of the substance of the doctrine is at risk of being lost in the translation. As Kenneth Schmitz argues, 'the expression of meaning demands an embodiment of thought in language in such a way that neither language nor thought remains indifferent to each other'.[64] It is this principle which is implicit in Francis George's criticism of the instrumentalist position found in statements of John XXIII and explicit in Fergus Kerr's observations about Karl Rahner's approach to modernity as a theological problem, to which reference was made in Chapter 6. Moreover, leaving aside such linguistic problems, the more general argument is that the distinctive property of the 'language of modernity' is its potential to be placed at the service of ideological ends.

MacIntyre acknowledges that in the short term a refusal to engage in public debates using the conceptual apparatus and rhetoric of the Liberal tradition will not have the immediate effect of turning the proponents of the culture of death and its polity towards an adoption of the values of a civilisation of love. He does not believe that there are easy remedies because, like

Taylor, his understanding of modernity is that of a cultural formation which has evolved over several centuries. The 'culture of death' and its polity represents the convergence and apotheosis of a diverse array of political, legal, economic and theological movements. However, unlike Taylor, MacIntyre does not believe that the current conflicts between traditions will be resolved by some kind of higher synthesis. Rather, he believes that the conflict will only be resolved by the social defeat of the Liberal and Genealogical traditions. In this 'civil war' of competing traditions, he asserts that it is very important to recognise that the development and defence of a Thomist conception of justice involves 'not merely conflict with particular opposing positions within large-scale public debate, but a rejection of the terms in which such debate has been framed and by reference to which it has been structured'.[65] Further, the failure to reach such a recognition will involve Thomists in the danger of inadvertently accepting the presuppositions of the ideological vocabulary, and, more generally, of defining their own positions reactively.[66] This is essentially the argument being made by Cardinal Ambrozic to which reference was made in Chapter 2, when he questioned the prudence of defending the tradition by reference to the values of Kant's 'man come of age'.[67]

In his more recent work, *Aquinas*, Finnis adds to the defence of the adoption of the natural right rhetoric in *Natural Law and Natural Rights* the argument that although Aquinas 'never uses a term translatable as "human rights", he clearly has the concept'.[68] Specifically, he argues that, when Aquinas says that *ius* is the object of justice, he means 'what justice is about, and what doing justice secures, is the right of some person or persons – what is due to them, what they are entitled to, what is rightfully theirs'.[69] However, this argument still does not get around the fact that the classical tradition gave priority to the object, that is to justice, not to the subject. As MacIntyre emphasises, on Aquinas's view, law is primary, rights are secondary, whereas for post-Enlightenment modernity, human rights provide a standard prior to all law.[70] It is precisely this issue that Archbishop Mario Conti of Glasgow was addressing when he claimed that 'the whole question of "rights" needs to be examined more deeply if our society is to make any moral progress' since 'ultimately the question is not about rights and their vindication, but about what is right'.[71]

Finnis acknowledges that between Aquinas and Suarez a 'watershed' may be found within the tradition represented by a transition from a concept of *ius* as what is just, to a concept of *ius* as a moral power (*facultas*) which every man has, either over his own property or with respect to what is due to him.[72] Nonetheless, Finnis also asserts that there is 'no cause to take sides between the older and newer usages'.[73] The emphasis on the powers of the subject found in the Suarezian interpretation is thus not held by Finnis to be a problematic factor. In contrast, Joan Lockwood O'Donovan has drawn attention to the theological significance of the different orientations of the two traditions:

> Whereas in the older patristic and mediaeval traditions God's right established a matrix of divine, natural and human laws or objective obligations that constituted the ordering justice of political community, in the newer traditions, God's right established discrete rights possessed by individuals originally and by communities derivatively that determined civil order and justice.[74]

This argument of O'Donovan, which is consistent with MacIntyre's genealogy of the natural rights doctrine, also concurs with Schindler's criticism that the notion of a 'right', as conventionally understood, is a claim which the self has on the other.[75] In opposition to Schindler's ontology of identities-in-relation, the 'logic' of the natural right approach is one of self-centricity 'which presupposes a primitive (ontological) externality of relation between the self and others'.[76] In O'Donovan's words, the orientation of the rights-bearing subject to his or her environment is 'essentially controlling, acquisitive and competitive'.[77] Underlying this line of thought, which is critical of the project of transposing natural law into natural rights on the grounds that it emphasises the priority of the rights-bearing subject over that of justice, is a more general opposition to the transition from a common law based upon specifically Christian jurisprudential foundations with some Roman law influence, to a legal system that derives its jurisprudential foundations primarily from the Liberal tradition. While a notion of a 'right' as a claim against another does in fact form part of the common law tradition, such as a right to the use of an easement, it is not such a usage of the concept of 'right' to which MacIntyre and others are opposed. Such 'rights' were not primary but derivative, and did not attach to human beings as such, but to particular persons because of some other attribute. Accordingly, Kraynak has argued that a distinction needs to be drawn between rights (*iura*) as grants of power from higher authorities – for example, the 'right' of a priest to preach the Gospel and administer the sacraments and a 'natural' or 'subjective' right.[78]

Moreover, the 'rights' doctrine is problematic in so far as it commonly connects respect for human life and its integrity with the notion of autonomy.[79] As explained in Chapter 5, Schindler argues that it is 'the conception of the self as primitively constructive or self-creative that is at the source of the autonomy that must be challenged if we are to have principled ontological protection against atheism'.[80] Conversely, the classical Christian model of self-development is, as was argued in Chapter 4, anteriorly receptive. The idea that a classical Christian mode of self-formation takes the form of a participation in the life of the Trinity wherein a person receives a vocation as a gift of grace is difficult to assimilate to a principle which holds that human dignity rests upon the capacity for autonomy and self-creation.

Finnis in fact acknowledges that the Liberal notion of a right is tied to the idea of an autonomous self-fulfilment. He emphasises that the New Natural Law conception, by contrast, is that human aspirations are based not on juridically conceived relations with other men, but on our created nature, the 'set of aptitudes and qualities granted to each man by birth, in the design of God, for him to bring to fruition'.[81] However, he regards the adoption of the human rights rhetoric from the Liberal tradition as a contemporary example of the Patristic habit of 'plundering the spoils of the Egyptians', that is taking concepts with a profane origin and 'baptising' them by incorporating them into a Christian philosophical framework.[82] A major difference, however, between the Classical traditions and the modern Liberal tradition is that the former were at least open to theism, whereas the latter has as its methodological presuppositions a closure to theism (or at best an agnosticism which results in a constructive atheism) and related well-developed rival philosophical anthropologies. It is not therefore *any* of the treasures of the pagans that Thomists may wish to plunder, but rather those which already carry within them an openness to theism, and to created natures. If the standard notion of a right is tied to the idea of an autonomous self-fulfilment, then the attempt to keep the concept but alter its substance may end up being an example of a development by what Schindler calls 'the addition of incompatible differences'.

Speaking of the metaphor of the *Spolia Aegyptorum,* von Balthasar commented that any theft from the Egyptian camp that is carried out by 'genuine thinkers' will not be 'a mere mechanical adoption of alien chains of thought with which one can adorn and garland the Christian understanding externally'.[83] In this statement he appears to be arguing that there needs to be something in the substance of the pagan idea which is of value. The reason for adopting the rights rhetoric must be more than its popularity in contemporary discourse – it must actually add something to the tradition without which the tradition remains in some sense inadequate. To adopt particular linguistic forms simply because they are in popular usage could be construed as an example of taking the new forms as a garland to adorn an otherwise already fully developed Christian framework.[84] Von Balthasar further describes acts of adoption of ideas from alien traditions as acts of 'clarifying transposition'.[85] In this particular instance, the judgements that need to be made are:

1 whether the work of the New Natural Law school takes anything of the substance from the Liberal rights tradition, and, if so, how these element(s) fit within the architectonic order of the Thomist tradition;
2 if only the rhetoric or conceptual framework was taken, whether this is anything more than what von Balthasar calls 'taking a garland'; and
3 if only the conceptual framework was taken, is its alleged value to be found in the fact that every public institution in Western society, that is, every court and parliament, uses this rhetoric, and without it Thomists would be without the necessary linguistic currency with which to deal in those institutions?

In other words, is the value of the alien linguistic currency to be understood in *political* rather than *philosophical* terms? If the motivation for the adoption is political then not only is the transposition merely apparent, but, since political conditions come and go, the tradition runs the risk of developing a conceptual form and idiom which becomes a liability in changing political circumstances.

Finnis accepts that 'the picking-out of a word from the great babble of human intercourse involves risks that Christianity has, from the beginning, been willing to run, but not to run unconditionally'.[86] He thereby acknowledges that these adoptions or 'baptisms' involve a risk. The risk in this case would seem to be, in the short term, that the dominance of the Liberal tradition within popular Western culture is such as to marginalise and contaminate any alternative definitional substance given to the concept. As O'Donovan argues:

> Christian political thought (both Catholic and Protestant) that is not wholly complacent with this fabric [of democratic, pluralistic, technological liberalism] recognises the need to divest the concept of rights of its offensive theoretical material, but when it attempts to rescue conceptual threads from the fabric the result inevitably falls short: either too much of the fabric adheres to the threads or they lose their coherent texture.[87]

In the longer term, the danger is that the Liberal discourse will itself be marginalised and displaced by the discourse of its Genealogical competitor, and the Thomists will be left fighting a battle against the Genealogists with concepts borrowed from the marginalised Liberal tradition.

If only the conceptual forms of the Liberal natural right tradition are adopted, then this is an instance of 'taking a garland', and its alleged merit can only be rhetorical, that is political rather than philosophical. Moreover, it can be argued that as a political strategy the attempted transposition has been a failure. Even John Paul II has acknowledged that it is difficult not to conclude that 'the very affirmation of the rights of individuals and peoples made in distinguished international assemblies is a merely futile exercise in rhetoric'.[88] A MacIntyrean response to such a judgement would be: 'How could it be anything else when the genealogy of the rights project begins as an attack on classical Thomism and is then adopted as part of an ideological project to reach a political consensus in circumstances in which there was no commonly agreed upon anthropology'? In other words, it is part of the very nature of ideological projects that they exist for the rhetorical purpose of concealing ethical conflict. Those leaders of public institutions whose values derive from the Liberal tradition will not change their positions on any of the controversial issues which divide theists from Liberals and Nietzscheans simply because those who reject the values of the 'culture of death' frame the principles of their alternative 'civilisation of love' in the rhetoric of the Liberal tradition. Its rhetorical power is limited by the weight of its Thomist, Christian, or more generally pro-theistic and pro-life substance. It is not merely Liberal rhetoric to which Liberals are attracted, but a whole package of values about the good, the person and the cosmos.

Paradoxically, those who are most likely to conclude that the Liberal form signifies a Liberal substance are those members of the Catholic laity who are, in a sense, internal to the Thomist tradition, but affected by the surrounding Liberal culture. They are living through a period in the history of the tradition when, in von Balthasar's words, the forms of the tradition have lost the background against which they could be understood and in which the particular issue of the stance of the tradition towards the culture of modernity and its dominant Liberal tradition represents, in MacIntyre's terms, an 'epistemological crisis'. Moreover, one important aspect of this crisis is the popular belief that the Second Vatican Council, and in particular *Gaudium et spes*, endorsed the culture of modernity. Given such a state of affairs, the conclusion of some plain persons that the magisterial use of the rhetoric of the Liberal tradition signifies its adoption of the philosophical substance of Liberal jurisprudence is not unreasonable. Further, as argued in Chapter 5, the upward social mobility of Catholics in Western countries is actually fostered by their adoption of the rhetoric of the Liberal tradition. In circumstances where public institutions are a 'site of civil war' of competing ethical traditions, the pragmatic approach for those who aspire to be upwardly socially mobile is to avoid a strong identification with any of the contending traditions, or at least to be flexible about one's moral persona, supporting different traditions in different social contexts. The adoption by the magisterium of the rhetoric of rights thus unwittingly provides pragmatic 'Catholics' with a cover to conceal or make ambivalent their positions in circumstances where the 'cost of discipleship' should be a willingness to defend the values of the 'civilisation of love' explicitly.

Ultimately, the judgements to be made in any act of plundering the spoils of the Egyptians are of a prudential nature. What the above analysis concludes is that the act of clarifying transposition is not a simple intellectual exercise undertaken by the masters of the tradition for the other masters. It is an exercise whose nature cannot be understood outside a metaphysical framework which explains the relationship between form and substance, outside issues in linguistic philosophy regarding the relative merits of the instrumental and expressivist theories of language, and outside issues in epistemology regarding the tacit acquisition of knowledge; in particular, the manner in which plain persons rely upon their tacit understandings of the content of philosophical and theological concepts. Further, in this particular context of the adoption of the conceptual apparatus of the Liberal tradition, there is the issue of the genealogy or, in Timothy Chappell's parlance, the 'pedigree' of the conceptual apparatus. The 'pedigree' is an issue; first, because it is not so easy to distinguish form from substance as a Cartesian mode of rationality might suggest; and, second, because, in the case of the Liberal tradition, the pedigree is regarded by many scholars as a cross between Scotist nominalism and Protestant individualism with their affinity deriving from their common aversion to the analogy of being. This in itself is a major reason that the Thomist tradition's stance towards the Liberal tradition is such a crucial issue. If St Thomas was not the first 'Whig' as Lord Acton and contemporary Whig Thomists argue and if, rather, the Liberal tradition derives from the union of nominalism and certain versions of Protestantism, then the Liberal tradition cannot be conceived as standing in the same relationship to the Thomist tradition as the Thomist or Patristic traditions stood in relation to ancient Greek and Latin learning. The Fathers encountered a civilisation which had no knowledge of the Incarnation, but which was open to the transcendent and the absolute. To use a Balthasarian metaphor again, the Greeks had constructed part of a bridge which was heading in the direction of Christian Revelation while the Jews had partially constructed that bridge from the other side of the Mediterranean. The Incarnation united the spans of the bridge – it brought the cultures of Athens and Jerusalem together. However, a MacIntyrean reading of the Liberal tradition, such as proposed here, cannot be united with the Christian: it is from a posture which demands that one chooses between faith and reason, and that insists that in public life, at least, faith has no currency. In Schindler's parlance, it is a stance foreclosed to the cultural infrastructural significance of the Incarnation and its form of love. This argument – that the Liberal tradition was developed in opposition to the classical Christian synthesis, or is an 'heretical reconstruction' or 'mutated' form of it – is also consistent with von Balthasar's assertion that today Christian thinkers must acknowledge the *spoliatio Christianorum* which has taken place – the plundering of the classical Christian synthesis by neo-pagans for ideas which are re-presented in a secularised form that expressly excludes the dimension of grace.[89]

Conclusion

Within MacIntyre's account of moral discernment, the intellect still enjoys primacy as the faculty that makes moral judgements, and so moral judgements are in the final analysis what Boyle calls 'dictates of reason'. However, MacIntyre's philosophical anthropology is more developed than the classical notion of the person as the substance of a rational intellect. MacIntyre's person is a 'culture-transcending dependent rational animal' and this philosophical anthropology and associated view of the social dimensions of moral and intellectual formation is consistent with Schindler's 'credal logic' of identities-in-relation. It argues persuasively that the culture in which a person is immersed can either hinder or enhance the ability of the person to come to an understanding of the goods of human flourishing and the appropriate means to them and priorities among them; and it provides another example of the manner in which Schindler's 'Communio theology' may be used to provide a theological grounding for MacIntyre's otherwise primarily philosophical and sociological Thomism. Further, sound arguments from the de Lubac school, that religion must be an infrastructural good, and from MacIntyre's notion of a narrative tradition, suggest that, contrary to the attempts of the New Natural Law school to accommodate the Thomist tradition to Liberal categories, the good of religion must enjoy a special primary and infrastructural status. Finally, the strategy of adopting the conceptual apparatus of the Liberal tradition in the form of a rights rhetoric is problematic on the grounds that:

1 the rhetoric adds nothing of substance to the Thomist tradition and may instead distort it in serious ways;
2 alternatively, it may add something of substance to the tradition which may or may not be compatible with other elements, for example a mechanical understanding of society;
3 it may lead those who are not masters of the tradition into confusion as the dominant interpretation of the rights discourse is that of the Liberal tradition;
4 it does not fit well with an anthropology that emphasises the logic of identities-in-relation; and
5 it may ultimately end up outdated as the Genealogical tradition continues to rival the dominance of the Liberal tradition in jurisprudential thought.

8

CONCLUSION

In his assessment of *Gaudium et spes* after 30 years, Walter Kasper concluded that this document remains part of the Church's 'Magna Charta' for the Third Millennium, and, further, that we have reason to hope that the 'modern age' will be 'a new kind of *praeparatio evangelii* such as at one stage was provided by the Hellenistic civilisation of the Roman Empire'.[1] Kasper made the second of these observations after an acknowledgement that the post-Conciliar era has been characterised by a 'mis-understanding of the idea of autonomy' and 'an overadaptation to secularised bourgeois civilization or to revolutionary liberation movements'.[2] Nonetheless, he suggests that 'the secularisation of many originally Christian values created the necessary conditions for releasing the European Christian idea of humanity from the historical matrix in which it arose making it universally communicable'.[3] It is on the basis of this judgement that he draws his optimistic conclusion about the 'modern age' being a 'new kind of *praeparatio evangelii*'. The conclusion of this work, however, is that the 'secularisation of many originally Christian values' and the detachment of the Catholic faith from the historical matrix in which it took root has not made it any more 'universally communicable'. If anything, it has led to a widespread loss of faith within Europe itself and within countries like Canada, the United States and Australia, which, though not geographically lying in Europe, have fundamentally European cultures.[4] This is not to argue that, for example, African Catholics or Pacific Islander Catholics could not develop their own authentically Catholic cultures with their own local customs, but that what has actually occurred is that the culture of modernity has been treated as a new 'universal culture' replacing Greco-Latin culture, and that this culture, far from being a neutral medium for the spread of Christianity, and far from being a *praeparatio evangelii* in the manner of Classical culture, is actually a hostile medium for the flourishing of Christian practices and beliefs; and indeed, according to some scholars, it represents an 'heretical reconstruction' or 'secular parody' of the principles of an authentically Christian culture.

Moreover, it has been the conclusion of this work that those sections of *Gaudium et spes* that appear to give the Church's approval to the culture of modernity were formulated without reference to a theological framework within which the concept of culture could be 'eschatologically situated'. In the absence of any such theological framework, an endorsement of the culture of modernity, or select aspects thereof, can only be, as Rahner conceded, an act of faith. Moreover, after 35 years there is emerging from within the Thomist tradition a critique of the phenomena of government by bureaucracy, of the epistemic authority of 'experts', of the 'autonomy' of research from theological considerations, of the non-neutrality of the Liberal state and the ideological and self-centric character of its rights-based jurisprudence and of the morally impoverishing side-effects of mass culture – all of which tend against a judgement that the culture of modernity may be another *praeparatio evangelii*. Indeed, since at least the publication of Paul VI's Apostolic Exhortation, *Evangelii Nuntiandi*, which described the tragedy of our time as the 'split between the Gospel and culture', there has been a growing awareness of the non-neutrality of this particular culture and the realm of culture in general. In von Balthasar's terms, the realm of culture is the site of the 'Battle of the *Logos*'. In Schindler's terms, the choice of *logos* is between the form of love and the form of the machine. In John Paul II's terms it is a choice between a civilisation of love and a culture of death, in the language of Pickstock it is a choice between the 'polity of death' and a 'liturgical city', and in MacIntyre's conclusion it is a choice between the principles of Nietzsche and Aquinas (and the 'gods' whom each serves).

In the present work, the issue of the relationship between the Liberal and Thomist traditions has been identified as the source of an epistemic crisis for Catholic faith and practice. There is a conflict of position among Thomist scholars regarding whether the two traditions are 'complementary', or 'genetic' or 'dialectical'. Whereas Whig Thomists see the relationship between Thomism and Liberalism as complementary, and the New Natural Law theorists, though generally ambivalent about the issue, may be construed to be offering a genetic reading, the proponents of a postmodern Augustinian Thomism see it as dialectical. On their view, there are, as it were, 'irreconcilable' differences between the culture of modernity and the classical Christian world view.

In Part II of this work, arguments in favour of this 'dialectical' reading were presented. It was argued that a Christian culture-as-*Geist* requires an institutional *ethos* generated by practices open to the exercise of prudence and the reception of grace; that a Christian culture-as-*Bildung* must allow and enable virtuous participation in the transcendentals; that a Christian culture-as-*Kultur* should reflect 'the horizontal incarnation of grace' built upon a Trinitarian 'form of love'; and, further, that the Liberal tradition as embodied in the practices of the culture of modernity actually operates so as to impede the exercise of prudential judgement in favour of decision-making by reference to bureaucratic norms, subjectivises the transcendentals of the true and the good and in its bourgeois form marginalises the transcendental of beauty, fosters an anti-historical 'culture of forgetting' rather than a 'culture of celebrated recurrence' and resists the horizontal incarnation of grace by its vacuous mechanical form. In particular, it was argued in Chapter 5 that a reading of the relationship as complementary actually fosters a constructive atheism among those who continue to maintain denominational loyalties. The replacement of the priority of doxology by the priority of economic performance and 'humanist' projects (typical of the 'culture of America') was identified as the root of this constructive atheism. In Schindler's judgement, the god who flourishes within the culture of modernity is one who has not had the courage to die, but instead has become a liberal.[5] In MacIntyre's view, such a god had already been deconstructed by Feuerbach in the nineteenth century, and as a consequence the condition of the Liberal-theist is tragic:

> The moral presuppositions of liberal modernity, whether in its theory or in its social institutions, are inescapably hostile to Christianity and all attempts to adapt Christianity to liberal modernity are bound to fail.[6]

Each chapter of Part II also responded to a particular element of the 'explosive problematic' created by the treatment of culture in *Gaudium et spes*, and the conclusions of each chapter add weight to the judgement that, in the three-cornered contests between Thomists, Encyclopaedists (Liberals) and Genealogists (primarily Nietzscheans) over the question of the culture of modernity, the interests of the Thomist tradition lie with a critique and transcendence of this culture, rather than, as the popular construction of *Gaudium et spes* has presumed, in an accommodation to its practices. This places the Thomist tradition in a position of alliance with the Genealogists against the epistemological, ethical, jurisprudential and political philosophical elements of the Liberal tradition, with the consequence that the battle lines change to the front of the engagement with the Genealogical tradition and in particular the Nietzschean account of *Bildung*. In this engagement it will be imperative for the Thomist tradition to have a well-developed account of the rôle of culture in the formation of the soul. Such an account is already a central theme within the Genealogical tradition, and without it Thomists cannot adequately answer the Genealogical argument that there is no such thing as natural law, that we are all simply products of our environment, or, as the Bolshevik theorist Nikolai Bukharin put it, 'concentrated collections of social influences united in a small unit as the skin of a sausage is filled with sausage meat'.[7] Concretely, this means that there needs to be a synthesis of the natural law and virtue-ethics projects so that the tradition has a more highly developed account of how human persons can be not merely rational animals, but 'culture-transcending dependent rational animals'.

Three requirements of any satisfactory response

As was explained in the introduction, MacIntyre argues that any solution to an epistemological crisis must meet three highly exacting requirements. In relation to MacIntyre's *first* requirement – that of a radically new and conceptually enriched scheme – several conclusions were drawn. First, it was argued in Chapter 3 that attention needs to be paid to the issue of the sacramental dimension of 'practices' in ostensibly Catholic institutions. Second, although it may be possible to discuss the nature of the soul *in vacuo* as a composite of the faculties of the intellect, the memory and the will, the human person does not exist in a social vacuum, but rather has an intellect, a memory and a will that (on the Christian view) are formed though an association with other persons within institutions, such as the Church, and within relationships, such as those between the Persons of the Trinity and between the Communion of Saints. For these reasons it has been argued in Chapter 4 that there needs to be a thorough re-examination of the relations between faculties of the soul, virtues and the transcendental properties, and the effect of different cultural forms on these relations.

A third 'conceptually enriching' proposal, submitted in Chapter 5, was that a revised 'logic' such as Schindler's 'logic of identities-in-relation' should be adopted and that, as Kenneth Schmitz, William Norris Clarke, Joseph Ratzinger, John Paul II and Walter Kasper, among others, have argued, the person must be understood in terms of both relationality and substantiality. If the person is understood solely in terms of substantiality, as has been common in some Thomist accounts, then the metaphysical framework will be inadequate for the task of understanding the influence of cultures on moral formation. As John Paul II has argued, human beings are like unto God not only by reason of their spiritual nature, which accounts for their existence as persons, but also by their capacity for community with other persons. This dimension cannot be ignored in any judgement of the worth of any particular *Kultur*, institutional *ethos* or account of *Bildung*.

In Chapter 5, it was also argued, following Schindler, that every *ethos* always has a *logos* which underpins it and thus that, in any assessment of cultures from a theological perspective, the first issue should be that of an identification of the *logos* of the *Kultur*. This is a fourth conceptually enriching proposal and is certainly one of the more 'Augustinian' aspects of the proposed postmodern Augustinian Thomist synthesis.

A fifth and postmodern proposal is the adoption of MacIntyre's concept of a narrative tradition and my arguments in support of the rôle of such narrative traditions in explaining the symbiotic relationships between culture, tradition and rationality. In 'smudging the boundaries' between faith and reason and in arguing that reason can be universal but never neutral, MacIntyre steers the Thomist tradition away from the tendency in post-Enlightenment Thomism to defend Christianity in the forums of secular society by reference to Enlightenment standards of 'pure reason'. Since the critiques of Nietzsche and other members of the Genealogical tradition effectively withdrew the possibility of intellectual engagement based upon allegedly 'theologically neutral' conceptions of rationality, the Liberal tradition has been exposed to a scrutiny of its own 'mythologies'. Thomism too, must recover its self-understanding as a narrative tradition if it is to avoid such now discredited pretensions of Liberalism.

It is also significant in the context of the issue of the rival 'Anglo-American Analytical Thomist' and 'Continental Balthasarian' methodologies that it is the Continental methodology, with its openness to a consideration of the historical dimensions of issues and its tendency to give priority to an analysis of the logic of traditions, rather than to a linguistic analysis of the smallest conceptual terms of a tradition, that is better placed to undertake an examination of the 'crisis'. This preference for the Continental approach is implied in Charles Taylor's argument that the culture of modernity represents a constellation of beliefs and practices, and therefore that any analysis of this culture must take into account the relationships between the various components, rather than, as the analytical Thomists have a tendency to do, abstract concepts from their historical context and subject them to linguistic analysis. Such a methodology fosters a kind of intellectual blindness to the relationships between the various principles within any given tradition's constellation of principles, and this in turn leads to projects described by Schindler as 'synthesis by way of the addition of incompatible differences'. Moreover, this kind of methodology fits well with a mechanical metaphysic and thus the Liberal premise of the autonomy of the various provinces of culture from one another. It is not surprising therefore that analytical Thomists frequently adopt a more complementary reading of the relationship between the Thomist and Liberal traditions than do scholars in the Continental tradition.

MacIntyre's *second* requirement for any genuine solution to an epistemological crisis is that it provides a satisfactory explanation of what it was which rendered the previous tradition sterile, incoherent or both. In this work the following factors have been identified:

1   the failure of the Conciliar fathers to appreciate that modernity is a cultural formation and to clearly distinguish between pastoral strategies for the evangelisation of pre-Christian cultures where the adoption and 'baptism' of local customs may be permissible and pastoral strategies to be adopted in the dioceses of metropolitan modernity where the prevailing culture was not so much pre-Christian as post and anti-Christian;
2   the ambivalent form and language of *Gaudium et spes*;
3   the rationalist presuppositions about the translatability of language apparently held by many hierarchs and theologians;
4   the neo-scholastic extrinsicist construction of the grace–nature relationship;
5   a metaphysics of the person which focused upon substantiality and neglected the more historical dimensions of relationality;

6   a lop-sided emphasis upon the rôle of the intellectual faculty in moral judgement consistent with treating Kant as a 'secret father of the Church';

7   a concomitant neglect of a consideration of the relationship between faculties of the soul, virtues and the transcendentals;

8   a failure to distinguish between religion as an infrastructural good and religion as a superstructural good;

9   as a consequence of point 8 a failure to appreciate that secular, Protestant and Catholic cultures differ in their ranking of the goods of human flourishing; and

10   as a consequence of points 1–9, a failure to appreciate that the culture of modernity cannot be transcended by theory alone, but only by a particular kind of practice – a practice informed by a particular kind of theory rooted in that same practice.

Following Schindler, it has been argued that the kind of practice 'informed by a particular kind of theory rooted in that same practice' which has the greatest potential to transcend the culture of modernity will be of a 'liturgical' nature. This thesis is also a central argument in the works of Catherine Pickstock and may also be found, though less explicitly, in the works of Aidan Nichols and Joseph Ratzinger. The general neglect of a consideration of the place of liturgy in cultural analysis could thus be described as an eleventh property impeding a resolution of the theological crisis created by the culture of modernity.

MacIntyre's *third* requirement for any satisfactory answer to an epistemological crisis is that any new developments must be carried out in such a manner as to demonstrate a fundamental continuity within the tradition. In this work, it has been argued that the introduction of an appreciation of the cultural dimension in moral formation need not displace the natural law doctrine with its transcendental, suprahistorical aspirations. Rather, it has simply given rise to 'new' questions such as whether the goods of human flourishing are in fact incommensurable, or whether religion is a primary and or 'infrastructural good', whether a narrative tradition is a separate category necessary and preparatory to a participation in the goods and whether the adoption of the rhetoric of natural rights has been a prudent development.

Furthermore, the postmodern Augustinian Thomist project of developing a theological hermeneutic of culture by reference to an examination of the *logos* of a culture, the *ethos* of its institutions and its dominant account(s) of the principles of self-formation draws upon neglected elements of pre-Conciliar scholarship (found in the works of Przywara, Guardini, von Balthasar and Dawson, among others) – one important element of which was its understanding of the differences between Protestant and Catholic cultures. This approach is therefore in continuity with the theological tradition in a way in which many post-Conciliar accounts, enthusiastic for highly liberal and indeed neo-Lutheran plain meaning interpretations of the 'autonomy of culture' and the 'affirmation of the secular', are not.

The ongoing challenge of postmodern Augustinian Thomism

Related both to the need for an appreciation of the historical dimension in moral formation and to the difference between Protestant and Catholic cultures is the issue foreshadowed in *Fides et ratio* paragraph 72 regarding the relevance of Christianity's early inculturation in the world of Greco-Latin thought. In the post-Conciliar era, the Greco-Latin cultural patrimony of the Church was gambled on the belief that the post-war *Pax Americana* signalled the arrival of a new era analogous to that of the *Pax Romana*, in which Liberalism is the common philosophy, the rights discourse its common jurisprudential framework and a homogeneous international 'mass culture' its embodied social form. With little or no theological justification for taking such a gamble, some naively supposed that God had provided a new world order in which Christianity would flourish as an equal alongside any number of other creeds, including Enlightenment secularism, and would be usefully informed by those creeds while in turn influencing them. The division between the Whig Thomists and the proponents of a postmodern Augustinian Thomism is in part a difference over the prudence of this gamble and the value of what Leo XIII called 'Americanism'. It also represents a difference of opinion about whether the 'pedigrees' of ideas matter, whether Christianity has anything to learn from Enlightenment secularism, whether the Thomist tradition has anything to learn from the Calvinist tradition and what criteria should be used when discerning which of the 'spoils of the Egyptians' to plunder. The Augustinian Thomist position proposed in this work is very much in accord with the judgement of Origen that it is better to die in the desert than to end up in the service of the Egyptians, or, one might add, end up in a position where the 'Chosen People' start to believe that they *are Egyptians* because all cultural traces of their specific differences have been suppressed. If this 'new age in human history' (*Gaudium et spes* paragraph 54) is indeed a 'new *Kairos*' (Pontifical Council for Culture statement 1999), then the conclusion of this work is that this can only be so in the sense to which Cornelio Fabro made reference – that the truths of Revelation might begin to look like an appealing alternative to the 'holocaust-mottled dead end in which the *cogito* consumes itself'.

The work of the proponents of a postmodern Augustinian Thomism may therefore be seen as a continuation of the pre-Kantian emphasis on the symphonic harmony of the faculties of the soul, including the neglected faculty of the memory and the harmony of the community based upon an identity shaped by a narrative tradition, and an *ethos* concerned for the common good. To the extent that the culture of America requires an acceptance of the autonomy of economic and political philosophy from theology, and of each of the provinces of culture from one other and consequently a conception of religion as merely superstructural, a postmodern Augustinian Thomism requires a repudiation of 'Americanism' in favour of a retrieval of something like the Greco-Latin cultural patrimony of the Church. The precise form which such a retrieval will take is a developing theme within the corpus of postmodern Augustinian Thomist scholarship. I have argued that it rep-resents a continuation of the as yet insufficiently articulated *Ressourcement* projects of the de Lubac circle. In the context of political philosophy it also represents a project that takes it lead from St Augustine rather than from Immanuel Kant. Whereas the Conciliar generation of Catholic scholars tended to favour Kant as the most acceptable father of the Liberal tradition, members of the post-Conciliar generation are returning to St Augustine and other patristic scholars for a theological reading of the relationship between the Church and the world. In particular, it is a theological reading that rejects the Lutheran and Calvinist constructions of the secular and the sacred. Although this trend is by no means universal, it is certainly strong, and may in part be explained by the fact that the post-Conciliar generation lived through the institutional embodiment of the principles behind the at-tempted *rapprochement* with the Liberal tradition and have concluded that such strategies did nothing to convert Liberals to Christianity but certainly succeeded in causing widespread confusion among the laity, and the secu-larisation of the Church's pastoral works. Robert P. Kraynak's, *Christian Faith and Modern Democracy* provides an excellent juxtaposition of the Kantian and Augustinian alternatives, while Aidan Nichols's *Christendom Awake* similarly eschews the option of forging an alliance with the Liberal tradition, and calls instead for a 'Re-energising of the Church in Culture'.[8] Such projects are 'radical' in the true sense of the term. They require a 'root and branch' kind of renewal encapsulated by Pickstock's juxtaposition of the 'polity of death' with a 'liturgical city'.

In his essay *Zwischen Religion und Kultur*, published some 2 years before the promulgation of *Gaudium et spes*, Erich Przywara summarised the his-tory of the problematic of the relation between religion and culture in one of his many insightful analyses of 'polarities'.[9] Beginning with Justin and Tertullian, he noted that their opposition might be categorised as the either/or between religion as the ultimate strength of culture and culture as religion's opponent. Then again, he noted that the early Middle Ages are in acute contrast between Cluny and Clairvaux and the still more acute con-trast between Abelard and St Bernard – on the one side the work of culture is viewed as religious activity, on the other religion is viewed as mostly culture-less (if not hostile to culture) – *allein zu Gott*.[10] These divisions then feed into the chaos of the Reformation, when the contrast is between the culturally resplendent church of the Renaissance and later the Baroque and the icono-clastic 'imperceptible and invisible God' of the Protestants. Finally, Przywara concludes that nineteenth-century intellectual history was characterised by a division between the 'autonomy of science and culture', and, indeed, 'science and culture *as* religion', and the gradually ascendant ideals of the Catholic romantics of 'science and culture which have their immanent ideals in religion', especially in Christendom.

Przywara's summary can thus be brought up to date by adding to it the following. In post-Conciliar thought, one finds several antitheses: between the emphasis on the 'autonomy of culture', a concept endorsed in *Gaudium et spes* paragraph 59 but not defined and variously interpreted, and the idea that no realm of culture is really neutral in relation to theology or completely autonomous of any other; between an uncritical endorsement of mass culture, including the belief that the way that our buildings are constructed, the music we compose, the works of art we create, all exist in a zone outside of the ethical, and the idea that mass culture is toxic to virtue and resistant to grace; between a conception of liturgy as necessarily embodying the aesthetic and linguistic norms of the mundane and a conception of liturgy as necessarily transcending the mundane; between the promotion of Enlightenment traditions as 'magnificent achievements' and a critique of Enlightenment traditions as 'severed fragments' or 'mutations' or 'heretical reconstructions' or 'secular parodies' of the classical theistic synthesis; between those who think that doctrines can be transposed into the idioms of any culture and those who follow an expressivist theory of language according to which such transpositions are fraught with difficulty; and between those who think that beauty is an important element of faith and practice, especially worship, and Catholics who think, as Kierkegaard and other Lutherans did, that the beautiful and the ethical have no intrinsic relationship, and indeed that an attraction to the beautiful is a sure sign of spiritual retardation.

Hence, in the early twenty-first century we are still very much in the middle of the struggles that characterised the conflicting interpretations of the relationship between religion and culture from the Middle Ages up to and including the nineteenth century. Those who take a position that an attraction for the beautiful is a sure sign of spiritual retardation are the heirs of the *allein zu Gott* position, which might be construed as an extreme development of the Cistercian tendency *à la* Clairvaux, while the position of an Abelard or a St Bonaventure may be construed as the medieval antecedent for the culturally resplendent Church of the Renaissance and the Baroque and the emphasis on the transcendental of beauty which one finds in the work of the contemporary Balthasarians. Both contemporary Christians of the *allein zu Gott* variety and Christians who care about the cultural embodiment of beliefs are united against the Nietzschean and Liberal tendency to treat science and culture (both in the broadest sense of the term, but especially in the *Bildung* sense) *as* religion. However, whereas in the nineteenth century there was a certain amount of opposition to this from the Thomist camp, at present the crisis within the Thomist tradition is hampering the ability of the Thomists to offer an alternative position from that of the Nietzscheans and Liberals. Instead of seeking to critique and transcend a culture which is, on its best construction, the severed fragments of the classical theistic framework operating dysfunctionally, or, at its worst, a new heretical recon-struction of those same severed fragments, the masters of the Thomist tradi-tion have been engaged in an enterprise of détente, transposition and even in some cases of synthesis. Having been told that the Church recognises the 'legitimate autonomy of the cultural realm' they have not been particularly keen to develop a specifically Thomist account of the relationship between religion and culture.

Unfortunately, in their enthusiasm for the potentialities inherent within 'mass culture', or perhaps in seeking to avoid the errors of the Aristocratic Liberals who pursued *Bildung* and the transcendental of beauty as ends in themselves, the authors of the section on culture in *Gaudium et spes* neglected to offer an alternative account of 'religion as culture' in which beauty is not jettisoned, but 'keyed into the theological drama'. Again, it is precisely what Lercaro called the 'cultural patrimony of the Church', and what Paul VI identified as the Church's rich liturgical culture, which was historically the source of the plain person's exposure to 'high' or 'erotic' or 'aristocratic' culture and, in particular, to beauty. By depriving people of these riches through the policy of accommodating liturgical practices to the norms of 'mass culture' – a culture already identified by Guardini in the 1950s as an 'anti-culture' – the post-Conciliar Church has unwittingly undermined the ability of many of its own members to experience self-transcendence. This destruction in turn leads to a loss of 'sapiential experience' – identified by Schmitz as a necessary element of prudential judgement – and a preparation for the virtue of hope. As a consequence, plain persons fall into the pit of nihilistic despair and/or search for transcendence in the secular liturgies of the global economy, whereas the more highly educated pursue strategies of stoic withdrawal and individual self-cultivation which are destined to end in despair, and even madness, for which the secular critics of modernity – Freud and Heidegger, for example – have no viable solutions.

We should not be surprised if those who know only this culture embrace the conclusions of Nietzsche – either tacitly as broken 'Hollow Men' or self-consciously as members of an educated elite – since the 'form' of the alternative tradition is no longer visible. 'Pastoral strategies' that further blur the distinctions between the culture of modernity and a culture rooted in a specifically Trinitarian Christocentrism do nothing to restore the vis-ibility of the form and further compound the crisis. Either the Church as the Universal Sacrament of Salvation is the primary source, guardian and per-fector of culture within persons, institutions and entire societies, or culture becomes an end in itself – an ersatz religion – as in the Aristocratic Liberal and Nietzschean traditions, which in turn implodes into that anti-culture known as 'mass culture'.

NOTES

INTRODUCTION

1 R. E. Brennan, 'The Thomistic Concept of Culture', *The Thomist* 5, 1943, 111–36, at 112, referring to the authority of Augustinus Fischer-Colbrie, 'Quid Sanctus Thomas de Cultura Doceat', *Xenia Thomistica*, Rome: Polyglottis Vaticanus, 1925. Both Brennan and Fischer-Colbrie make reference to *Le Conflit de la morale et de la sociologie*, Paris: Librairie Félix Alcan, 1912, by S. Deploige, which defends the thesis that many concepts of reputed modern provenance may be found in the doctrines of Aquinas.

2 F. Kerr, *Immortal Longings: Versions of Transcending Humanity*, London: SPCK, 1997, p. 28, and Nikolaus Lobkowicz, 'What happened to Thomism? From *Aeterni Patris* to *Vaticanum Secundum*', *American Catholic Philosophical Quarterly* LXIV, 3, 1995, 397–425, at 419.

3 This is not to say that Aquinas was unaware of other cultures. As an avid reader of ancient Greek, early medieval Arab and Jewish writers in Latin translation, and an avid writer for missionaries to the Cathars and the Tartars, Aquinas was aware of cultural differences. But the problem of the influence of rival and hostile cultures upon the moral formation of Christians was not a pressing problem in the thirteenth century in the way that it was in the first five centuries or is in the twenty-first.

4 With the possible exception of the *Summa Contra Gentiles*. According to the Dominican tradition this work of St Thomas was commissioned by Raymond de Penãfort for use in the evangelisation of the Moors, although contemporary scholars argue that, for Thomas, gentiles represent 'historically, pre- or extra-Christian man, and, metaphorically, the human mind under the tutelage of nature'. See T. S. Hibbs, *Dialectic and Narrative in Aquinas: An Interpretation of the Summa Contra Gentiles*, London: University of Notre Dame Press, 1995, pp. 10–14, and M. Jordan, 'The Protreptic Structure of the *Summa Contra Gentiles*', *The Thomist* 50, 1986, 173–209.

5 Throughout this work the word 'Thomist' should be broadly construed to include not only the ideas of St Thomas but also the ideas of his Patristic antecedents which he incorporated and those of his scholastic heirs. This is consistent with the MacIntyrean usage, and is defended by the argument that St Thomas represents the pivotal point uniting the ideas of the classical and Patristic antecedents and serving as a frame of reference for post-scholastic Catholic scholarship.

6 A. MacIntyre, *Whose Justice? Which Rationality?*, London: Duckworth, 1988, p. 362.

7 H. de Lubac, *A Brief Catechesis on Nature and Grace*, R. Arnandez (trans.), San Francisco: Ignatius, 1984, p. 92.

8 See, for example, A. T. Peperzak, 'Personal–Impersonal? A Rejoinder to John Haldane', and J. Haldane, 'Holding Fast to What is Good: A Reply to Adriaan T. Peperzak', *American Catholic Philosophical Quarterly* LXXIII, 3, 1999, 497–503. It should also be noted that while the analytical school is stronger within academic institutions in England, Scotland and the United States, the influence of von Balthasar is now spreading well beyond the Continent. Aidan Nichols's introductory trilogy stands as the most prominent example of this development.

9 G. Borrador, 'Interview with Alasdair MacIntyre', *The American Philosopher*, Chicago: University of Chicago Press, 1999, p. 144 (hereafter IGB).

10 D. Schindler, 'God and the End of Intelligence: Knowledge as Relationship', *Communio* 26, Fall, 1999, 510–40, at 532 (hereafter GEI).

11 H. U. von Balthasar, *Truth is Symphonic*, San Francisco: Ignatius, 1987, and *The Theology of Karl Barth*, San Francisco: Ignatius, 1992, p. 252: 'Forms of thought do not exclude each other but, like personalities (whose expression and product they are), they are open to each other. But just as in architecture it is not a matter of merely accumulating randomly assembling stylistic elements (all you get then is a pseudo-historical pastiche that so characterises the last century) but rather of taking what remains valid in each of them and making a new creation of genius of equal rank, so too in perennial philosophy.'

12 J. Milbank, C. Pickstock and G. Ward (eds), *Radical Orthodoxy*, London: Routledge, 1999, p. 2 (hereafter RO).

13 MacIntyre personally rejects the 'Communitarian' label, and the 'virtue-ethics' label is now rather too narrow to describe what has evolved into a much broader project. See A. MacIntyre, 'I'm not a communitarian, but …'. *The Responsive Community* 1, 3, 1991, 991–2.

14 R. Cessario, 'Virtue Theory and the Present Evolution of Thomism', D. Hudson and W. Moran (eds), *The Future of Thomism*, Notre Dame, IN: University of Notre Dame Press, 1992, p. 297.

15 For accounts of the Communio ecclesiology see W. Kasper, 'The Church as "Communio"', *New Blackfriars* 74, 871, May, 1993, 232–44; H. U. von Balthasar, *The Theology of Henri de Lubac*, San Francisco: Ignatius, 1983; S. Wood, *Spiritual Exegesis and the Church in the Theology of Henri de Lubac*, Grand Rapids, MI: Eerdmans, 1998; D. Doyle, 'Henri de Lubac and the Roots of Communion Ecclesiology', *Theological Studies* 60, 1999, 209–28.

16 R. Cessario, *Moral Virtues and Theological Ethics*, Notre Dame, IN: University of Notre Dame Press, 1991, p. 88.

1 THE TREATMENT OF CULTURE IN *GAUDIUM ET SPES*

1 For example, Pius VI *Charitas* (1791) *The Papal Encyclicals 1740–1878*, New York: McGrath, 1981, pp. 177–8; Gregory XVI *Mirari Vos* (1832) *The Papal Encyclicals 1740–1878*, 235–43; Pius IX *Qui Pluribus* (1846) *The Papal Encyclicals 1740–1878*, 275–7; Leo XIII *Inscrutabili Dei Consilio* and *Quod Apostolica Muneris* (1878), *Actes de Leon XIII*, Vol. 1, Paris: Maison de la Bonne Presse, 1903, pp. 8–25, and 26–41; *Nobilissima Gallorum Gens* (1884), *Immortale Dei* (1885), *Quod Multum* (1886), *Libertas Praestantissimum* (1888), *Actes de Leon XIII*, Vol. II, Paris: Maison de la Bonne Presse, 1903, pp. 26–41, 225–41, 16–53, 81–101. The inadequacy of the Syllabus against Modernism to engage the emerging 'culture of modernity' is recognised by Peter Henrici in 'Modernity and Christianity', *Communio* 17, Summer, 1990, 141–52.

2 A. MacIntyre, 'Marxism of the Will', *Partisan Review* 36, 1969, 128–33.

3 A. Nichols, *Christendom Awake*, Edinburgh: T&T Clark, 1998, p. 1 (hereafter CA).

4 C. Taylor, 'Two Theories of Modernity', *Hastings Center Report*, March–April, 1995, 24 and 27.

5 The difference between the concepts of 'mutation', 'severance', 'heretical reconstruction' and 'secular parodies' is small. Heretical reconstruction encompasses the concept of mutation but emphasises that the new constellation is, from the perspective of credal Christianity, heresy, whereas MacIntyre's emphasis on 'severance' follows the insight of Elizabeth Anscombe that philosophers in the British analytical school of moral philosophy have had a tendency to analyse concepts that were once elements of the classical Christian synthesis *in vacuo*, that is in isolation from their original theistic context. See G. E. M. Anscombe, 'Modern Moral Philosophy', *Philosophy* XXXIII, 124, January, 1958, 1–19. Cavanaugh's notion of a secular parody is extremely close to that of heretical reconstruction and, indeed, in the context of modernity's political philosophy, he describes defences of the modern state as a 'source of an alternative soteriology to that of the Church'. See W. T. Cavanaugh, 'Beyond Secular Parodies', *Radical Orthodoxy*, London: Routledge, 1999, p. 182. A further variation from the perspective of 'cultural' critiques can be found in the thesis of Hans Blumenberg that the values and concepts of the culture of modernity are completely new concepts which fill a void created by defunct Christian concepts. See *The Legitimacy of the Modern Age*, Cambridge, MA: MIT Press, 1983. Blumenberg gives the culture of modernity a certain 'legitimacy' it lacks in the analysis of MacIntyre, Milbank, Pickstock and Cavanaugh, because it is not perceived to be either parasitic upon the values and concepts of Christendom, or a heretical reconstruction thereof. The Blumenberg thesis is however a minority position among scholars associated with cultural critiques of modernity. See Robert Pippin, 'Blumenberg and the modernity problem', *Review of Metaphysics* 40, March, 1987, 535–57.

6 K. L. Schmitz, 'Postmodernism and the Catholic Tradition', *American Catholic Philosophical Quarterly* LXXIII 2, 1969, 223–53, at 235.

7 J. O'Malley, *Tradition and Transition: Historical Perspectives on Vatican II*, Wilmington, DE: M. Glazier, 1989, p. 45.

8 Ibid., p. 67.

9 See J. A. Bonsor, *Rahner, Heidegger and Truth: Karl Rahner's Notion of Christian Truth: The Influence of Heidegger*, Lanham, MD: University Press of America, 1987; and R. Waterhouse, 'The Vacuity of Heidegger's Authenticity', *A Heidegger Critique: A Critical Evaluation of the Existential Phenomenology of Martin Heidegger*, Atlantic Highlands, NJ: Humanities Press, 1981.

10 For a particularly acute example of the significance of the concepts of 'authenticity' and 'relevance' for Rahner's theology, see *Mission and Grace*, London: Sheed & Ward, 1963, pp. 52–5, wherein Rahner argued that 'One soul apostolically won from a milieu which has already reverted to paganism is worth more than three hundred hung on to from the remnants of traditional Christianity'.

11 H. Carrier, 'The Contribution of the Council to Culture', *Vatican II: Assessments and Perspectives (1962–1987)*, René Latourelle (ed.), Mahwah, NJ: Paulist Press, 1988, pp. 442–66, at 466.

12 W. Abbott, *Documents of the Second Vatican Council*, London: Geoffrey Chapman, 1967, pp. 712–13.

13 John XXIII, *Pacem in Terrism, Acta Apostolica Sedis* 55, 1963, 257–304, at 268–9 (paragraph 50) (hereafter AAS).

14 G. Turbanti, 'The Attitude of the Church to the Modern World at and after Vatican II', *Concilium* 6, 1992, 87–97, at 92.

15 G. Weigel, *Soul of the World*, Grand Rapids, MI: Eerdmans, 1996, p. 103. The word 'Whig' comes from the Scottish 'Whiggamore' referring to west-coast Presbyterians.

16 E. E. Y. Hayles, *The Catholic Church in the Modern World: A Survey from the French Revolution to the Present*, New York: Doubleday, 1958, pp. 90–9.

17 Kenneth Schmitz argues that, although John Paul II shares the Liberal tradition's interest in the 'personal' and 'subjective' depth of human reality, his own understanding of this depth is Christocentric. *At the Center of the Human Drama: The Philosophical Anthropology of Karol Wojtyla/Pope John Paul II*, Washington, DC: Catholic University of America Press, 1993, pp. 122–3 (hereafter CHD). See also Ernest Fortin, 'Sacred and Inviolable': *Rerum Novarum* and Natural Rights', *Theological Studies* 53, 1992, 203–33 (hereafter RNNR).

18 The relationship between the Whig Thomist project and the New Natural Law project is not clearly defined. It is clear that both John Finnis and Robert George (leading proponents of New Natural Law) share Lord Acton's interpretation of St Thomas Aquinas as 'the first Whig' and thus are, in a sense, Whig Thomists. However, it remains unclear whether they would go as far in their defence of the political and economic institutions associated with the culture of America, as Michael Novak, George Weigel and Richard John Neuhaus (the leading proponents of Whig Thomism) do. There is a degree of ambivalence in the work of the New Natural Law theorists regarding whether they merely intend to adopt elements of the conceptual apparatus of the Liberal tradition for the purpose of redefining Liberal concepts by giving them a Thomist content, or whether they wish to defend some of the institutions and values based on the Liberal tradition and defend their assimilation to the Thomist tradition. This issue will be developed in Chapter 7.

19 J. A. Di Noia, 'American Catholic Theology at Century's End: Postconciliar, Postmodern and Post-Thomistic', *The Thomist* 54, 1990, 499–518, at 518.

20 See, for example, J. Borella, *The Sense of the Supernatural,* Edinburgh: T&T Clark, 1998, p. 30, and CA, pp. 9–19.

21 *Gaudium et spes* was promulgated on 7 December 1965, 1 day before the end of the Council.

22 J. Langan, 'Political Hopes and Political Tasks: A Reading of '*Gaudium et spes*' after Twenty Years', *Questions of Social Urgency: The Church in the Modern World: Two Decades after Vatican II,* J. A. Dwyer (ed.), Washington, DC: Georgetown University Press, 1986, p. 102.

 The concept of culture also appears in the following Conciliar documents, but as isolated references, not as a theme of an entire section: the *Declaration on Christian Education* (*Gravissimum Educationis*), paragraphs 6 and 8, wherein education is treated as a form of cultural development; the *Decree on the Church's Missionary Activity* (*Ad Gentes*), paragraphs 15, 16, 21 and 26, wherein it is advised that students preparing for work in the missions should study the cultures of the peoples living in the countries to which they will be sent, and Catholics, both lay and religious, are encouraged to work together with non-Catholics on cultural projects; the *Declaration on Religious Freedom* (*Dignitatis Humanae*), wherein paragraph 15 makes reference to the sociological fact that people from diverse cultures now live in close geographical proximity; and the *Decree on the Appropriate Renewal of Religious Life* (*Perfectae Caritatis*), wherein paragraph 3 makes reference to the need for the manner of 'living, praying and working' to be adapted to the requirements of a given culture, and paragraph 18 makes reference to the education of religious according to the 'prevailing manners of contemporary social life, and in its characteristic ways of feeling and thinking'.

23 See, for example, H. de Lubac, *Atheisme et science de l'homme: une double requête de Gaudium et spes*, Paris: Cerf, 1968; Walter Kasper, 'The Theological anthropology of *Gaudium et spes*', *Communio*, Spring, 1996, 129–41; and Joseph Ratzinger, 'Der

Weldienst der Kirche: Auswirkungen von Gaudium et spes im letzten Jahrzehnt', M. Seybold (ed.), *Zehn Jahre Vaticanum II*, Regensburg: Pustet, 1976.

24 W. Kasper, 'The Theological Anthropology of *Gaudium et spes*', *Communio* 23, Spring, 1996, 137.

25 C. Moeller, 'History of the Constitution', *Commentary on the Documents of Vatican II*, Vol. V, H. Vorgrimler (ed.), New York: Herder & Herder, 1969, pp. 60–1 (hereafter CDV).

26 See H. de Lubac, *A Brief Catechesis on Nature and Grace*, San Francisco: Ignatius, 1984, p. 24.

27 A. Nichols, *Catholic Thought Since the Enlightenment: A Survey*, London: Gracewing, 1998, p. 157; W. Kasper, 'The Theological Anthropology of *Gaudium et spes*', 129; E. Hamel, 'The Foundations of Human Rights in Biblical Theology: Following the Orientations of *Gaudium et spes*', *Vatican II: Assessment and Perspectives*, Vol. II, pp. 461–78.

28 F. George, *Inculturation and Ecclesial Communion: Culture and Church in the Teaching of Pope John Paul II*, Rome: Urbaniana University Press, 1990, p. 19 (hereafter IEC).

29 See, for example, the argument of David Schindler in 'The Meaning of the Human in the Technological Age', *Anthropotes* XV 1, 1999, 31–53, at 41: 'The terms "modern" and "liberal" have a genuinely analogous meaning, hence some genuine unity within their many differences, and thus they should not be interpreted nominalistically' (hereafter MHTA).

30 W. Kasper, 'The Theological Anthropology of *Gaudium et spes*', p. 133.

31 K. Rahner, 'Towards a Fundamental Theological Interpretation of Vatican II', *Theological Studies* 40, 1979, 716–28, at 726.

32 *The Wit and Wisdom of Good Pope John: Sayings and Anecdotes*, collected by Henri Fesquet, London: Harvill Press, 1964, p. 126.

33 K. Barth, *Ad Limina Apostolorum*, Edinburgh: St Andrew's Press, 1969, p. 20.

34 E. E. Y. Hayles, *Pope John and His Revolution*, London: Eyre & Spottiswood, 1985.

35 M. D'Ambrosio, '*Ressourcement* Theology, *Aggiornamento* and the Hermeneutics of Tradition', *Communio* 18, Winter, 1991, 530–55.

36 The Third Reich culture that Hitler created was essentially pagan, incorporating elements of pagan Rome and pagan Gothic tribalism and their revival in the German Romantic movement. Not a few of his elite inner circle were members of the neo-pagan society called 'Secret Germany', the objectives of which were to restore to German culture a virility that it was deemed to have lost in the ascendancy of Christian culture – a theme which was unequivocally Nietzschean. See H. Rauschning, *Gespräche mit Hitler*, New York: Europa Verlag, 1943; M. Baigant and R. Leigh, *Secret Germany*, London: Jonathan Cape, 1994; and A. K. Wiedmann, *The German Quest for Primal Origins in Art, Culture and Politics 1900–1993*, Ceredigion, UK: Mellen House, 1995.

37 T. S. Eliot, *Notes Towards the Definition of Culture*, London: Faber & Faber, 1962, pp. 21–35.

38 R. Geuss, *Morality, Culture and History*, Cambridge, UK: Cambridge University Press, 1998.

39 This idea of a 'Trinitarian form' or 'logic' is one of the leitmotifs of the work of scholars associated with the *Communio* school and will be developed in greater detail in Chapter 5.

40 J. Kleutgen, *Die Philosophie der Vorzeit*, Munich: Minerva, 1974; R. Eucken, *Die Philosophie des Thomas von Aquino und die Kultur der Neuzeit*, Hasse: C.E.M. Pfeffer, 1886. See also T. O'Meara, 'Thomas Aquinas and German Intellectuals: Neoscholasticism and Modernity in the Late 19th Century', *Gregorianum* 68, 3–4, 1987, 719–36; and *Church and Culture: German Catholic Theology (1860–1914)*, Notre Dame, IN: University of Notre Dame Press, 1991.

41 See, for example, Erich Przywara, 'Dionysisches und christliches Opfer', *Stimmen der Zeit* 65, 1934–35, 11–24; 'Um das Erbe Friedrich Nietzsches', *Ringen der Gegenwart I Gesammelte Aufsätze (1922–1927)*, Augsburg: Benno Filsner, 1929; and 'Zwischen Religion and Kultur', *'Weg zu Gott*, Einsiedeln: Johannes-Verlag, 1962 (hereafter WZG).

42 R. Guardini, 'Gedanken über das Verhaltnis von Christentum and Kultur', *Die Schildgenossen* 6, 1926, 281–315.

43 R. Guardini, *The End of the Modern World*, London Sheed & Ward, 1957, p. 68 (hereafter EWM).

44 See R. A. Krieg (ed.), *Romano Guardini: A Precursor of Vatican II*, Notre Dame, IN: University of Notre Dame Press, 1997, p. 69.

45 Erich Przywara (1889–1972) was on the staff of *Stimmen der Zeit* for 20 years and was at various times a mentor of Karl Rahner, von Balthasar and Edith Stein. In the early 1960s, von Balthasar was recovering from a period of ill health and working on the *Glory of the Lord* series while fostering the Community of St John. Romano Guardini's health was in decline throughout the period of the Council. He retired from the University of Munich in 1963 and died in 1968.

46 Aidan Nichols argues that members of Christopher Dawson's intellectual circle had already developed a 'theology of culture' well before the arrival of Vatican II. See A. Nichols, 'Christopher Dawson's Catholic Setting', *Eternity and Time*, S. Caldecott and J. Morrill (eds), Edinburgh: T&T Clark, 1997, p. 28.

47 C. M. Murphy, 'The Church and Culture since Vatican II: on the Analogy of Faith and Art', *Theological Studies*, 48, 1987, 317–33, at 322. The author is indebted to the Revd Glen Tattersall FSSP for an understanding of the importance of *Religion et Culture* in this context.

48 *Gaudium et spes* (hereafter GS) (paragraph 53) in Austin Flannery, *The Documents of Vatican II*, Dublin: Dominican Publications, 1975, p. 960. AAS 58, 1966, 1075.

49 F. M. Barnard, *Herder's Social and Political Thought*, Oxford: Clarendon, 1965.

50 Cf. GS (paragraph 54), which speaks of a 'more universal form of human culture' that will promote and express the unity of the human race while preserving 'certain features' of particular cultures.

51 John Paul II alludes to this need in *Fides et ratio*, AAS 91, 1999, 5–88, paragraphs 61 and 69: 'the study of traditional ways must go hand in hand with philosophical enquiry, an enquiry which will allow the positive traits of popular wisdom to emerge and forge the necessary link with the proclamation of the Gospel' and 'philosophical enquiry enables us to discern in different world-views and different cultures not what people think but what the objective truth is'.

52 A. C. Outler, 'After-Thoughts of a Protestant Observer of Vatican II', in *The Church and Culture since Vatican II*, J. Gremillion (ed.), Notre Dame, IN: University of Notre Dame Press, 1985, p. 153.

53 Ibid., p. 154. Recent statements of the International Theological Commission under the direction of Cardinal Ratzinger may however be construed as the start of an engagement with this problematic. See 'Faith and Inculturation', *Origins* 18, 47, 1989, 800–7.

54 Paragraph 57 (foreshadowed in paragraph 53) of GS, p. 961 of Flannery translation. AAS 58, 1966, 1077.

55 In *The Glory of the Lord*, Vol. 1, San Francisco: Ignatius, 1982, p. 90, von Balthasar makes reference to a 'great amphiboly between pantheism and Christianity' which pervaded German scholarship from Fichte to Hegel. See also W. von Humboldt: 'Über die Gesetze der Entwicklung der menschlichen Kräfte' and 'Plan einer Vergleichenden Anthropologie', *Gesammelte Werke*, A. Flitner and G. Klauss (eds), Stuttgart: Cotta, 1979.

56 'Artistocratic Liberalism' is a term coined by A. S. Kahan to describe a branch of Liberal thought which sought to foster a 'high culture' based on the freedom of artistic self-development. See A. S. Kahan, *Aristocratic Liberalism: The Social and Political Thought of Jacob Burckhardt, John Stuart Mill and Alexis de Tocqueville*, Oxford University Press, 1992 (hereafter AL).

57 J. Saward, *The Beauty of Holiness and the Holiness of Beauty*, San Francisco: Ignatius, 1996, p. 35.

58 CDV p. 332.

59 GS, Flannery translation, pp. 940–1. AAS 58, 1966, 1059.

60 Ibid., p. 941.

61 GS, Flannery translation, p. 959. AAS 58, 1966, 1075.

62 A. Dondeyne, *La foi écoute le Monde*, Paris: Cerf, 1965, p. 178.

63 GS, Flannery translation, p. 962, and W. Abbott, *The Documents of Vatican II*, London: Chapman, 1965, p. 264

64 J. Ratzinger, *A New Song for the Lord*, New York: Crossroad Publishing, 1996, p. 53 (hereafter NSL), and W. Kasper, *Faith and the Future*, London: Burns & Oates, 1985, p. 60 (hereafter FF). For an account of the subsidiarity principle, see F. H. Mueller, 'Comparative Social Philosophies: Individualism, Socialism and Solidarism', *Thought*, 60, 238, 1985, 297–309.

65 FF, p. 4.

66 Ibid., p. 4.

67 Cardinal Aloysius Ambrozic, 'Dialogue with Secularism', *Culture and Faith*, VIII–I, Civitas Vaticanum: Pontificium Consilium de Cultura, 2000, 41–46, at 44 (hereafter DS).

69 R. Lucci, 'The Proper Development of Culture', CDV, p. 251.

68 CDV, p. 267.

69 According to Lercaro's biographers, the Cardinal believed that 'the liturgical life does not consist in beautiful ceremonies but in the hearty participation of the laity'. See P. Lesoud and J.-M. Ramiz, *Giacomo Cardinal Lercaro*, Notre Dame, IN: University of Notre Dame Press, 1964, p. 25. Paul VI also believed that elements of pre-Conciliar Catholic culture were too 'rich' for 'modern people', among whom he clearly included the vast majority of Catholics. This is evident in his general audience address of 26 November 1969, which could be described as his eulogy for the Missal of 1962. Although praising the beauty of the classic Rite, referring to Latin as the 'language of the angels', and lamenting that we are 'parting with the speech of Christian centuries [and] becoming like profane intruders in the literary precincts of Sacred utterance', Paul VI nonetheless stated: 'Participation by the people is worth more – particularly by modern people, so fond of plain language which is easily understood and converted into everyday speech'. In this speech there is implied a belief that participation at Mass means oral participation, rather than contemplation, that the Catholic faithful are 'modern people, fond of plain language' and that it is possible to convert a liturgical language into the language of everyday speech. Each of these presuppositions is in itself an 'explosive problematic', the results of which to date have included the Lefebvrist schism, the qualified reinstatement of the Missal of 1962 by the Apostolic Letter *Ecclesia Dei* of 2 July 1988, the establishment of the *Ecclesia Dei Commission* to oversee the use of the privileges granted by the letter, including the formation of new 'Traditional Rite' Orders, complaints that the *Novus Ordo* is 'rationalistic' and 'Protestant' in form, and a revolutionary inorganic development imposed on the Church by a committee of liturgical 'experts' whose historical scholarship has since been subjected to academic criticism. See C. Pickstock, *After Writing*, Oxford: Blackwell, 1998, pp. 169–76 (hereafter AW); Aidan Nichols, *Looking at the Liturgy: A Critical View of its Contemporary Form*, San Francisco: Ignatius, 1996; and

J. Ratzinger, *The Spirit of the Liturgy*, San Francisco: Ignatius, 2000. In the last one, Ratzinger compared the idea of 'bringing God down to the level of the people' to the Hebrew's idolatrous worship of the golden calf, and claimed that the *Versus Populum* form of the *Novus Ordo* rite encourages a self-centricity that frequently ends in the worship of the community as a good in itself, rather than in the worship of God, and that this self-centricity is 'apostasy'. For a general discussion on 'plain language' see St Augustine, *On Christian Teaching*, R. P. H. Green (trans.), Oxford University Press, 1997, p. 33: 'But no one disputes that it is more pleasant to learn lessons presented through imagery and much more rewarding to discover meanings that are won only with difficulty'.

71 For a discussion of this issue in the work of St Thomas, see *Commentary on Aristotle's Nicomacchean Ethics*, C. I. Litzinger OP (trans.) Beloit, WI: Dumb Ox Press, 1993, pp. 7–11.

72 B. Lambert, '*Gaudium et spes* and the Travail of Today's Ecclesial Conception', *The Church and Culture since Vatican II*, J. Gremillion (ed.), Notre Dame, IN: University of Notre Dame Press, 1985, p. 36.

73 B. Lambert, '*Gaudium et spes* hier et aujourd'hui', *Nouvelle Revue Theologique* 107, 1985, 321–46, at 327.

74 B. Lambert, '*Gaudium et spes* and the Travail of Today's Ecclesial Conception', p. 38.

75 Ibid., p. 38.

76 Ibid., p. 38. It may be that in using the expression 'the ambivalence of all' Lambert was making reference to Maritain's idea that there is a double-meaning or 'ambivalence' about the world because it belongs to God by right of creation; to the devil by right of conquest because of sin; and to Christ by right of victory over the first conqueror, by His Passion. See *True Humanism*, p. 101.

77 Romano Guardini, *The End of the Modern World*, London: Sheed & Ward, 1957, pp. 68, 96 (hereafter EMW).

78 B. Lambert, '*Gaudium et spes* and the Travail of Today's Ecclesial Conception', p. 51.

79 Ibid., p. 35.

80 D. Schindler, 'Modernity, Postmodernity and Atheism', *Communio* 24, Fall, 1997, 563–79, at 578 (hereafter MPA). Cf. H. Urs von Balthasar, 'On the tasks of Catholic philosophy in our time', *Communio* 20, Spring, 1993, 147–72, at 148–9: 'Even if nature has its own regular laws and reason its own evidential character, still these laws and evidential characters can never appear as a final authority over against grace and faith' (hereafter TPT).

81 Karl Rahner, *Mission and Grace*, London: Sheed & Ward, 1963, p. 39.

82 Ibid., p. 20.

83 For the account of moral instinct see K. Rahner *Theological Investigations*, 9, New York: Crossroads, 1974, pp. 238–40. Finnis argues that Rahner seemed to equate this 'instinct' with sheer will, operating without or beyond reason. See J. Finnis, *Moral Absolutes: Tradition, Revision and Truth*, Washington DC: Catholic University of America Press, 1991, p. 100 (hereafter MATRT).

84 J. Maritain, *True Humanism*, p. xvi and pp. 162–71.

85 Ibid., p. 170.

86 Ibid., p. 170.

87 CA, p. 1.

88 J. Maritain, *The Peasant of the Garonne*, New York: Holt, Rinehart and Winston, 1968, pp. 50–63 (hereafter PG). The author is indebted to the Revd Glen Tattersall FSSP for this reference.

89 H. de Lubac, 'Nature and Grace', *The Word in History: The St Xavier Symposium*, T. Patrick Burke (ed.), London: Collins, 1968, p. 24 (hereafter WIH), and the

preface to *Atheisme et sens de l'homme: une double requête de Gaudium et spes*, Paris: Cerf, 1968.

90 K. Rahner, 'Towards a Fundamental Theological Interpretation of Vatican II', *Theological Studies* 40, 1979, 716–28, at 723.

91 Ibid., p. 723.

2 'CULTURE' WITHIN POST-CONCILIAR MAGISTERIAL THOUGHT

1 R. Fisichella, Press Conference Statement, *National Catholic Reporter*, 1, 27 March, 2002.

2 PG pp. 53–63. *Ecclesiam Suam*, AAS LVI, 1964, 609–60.

3 Paul VI, Ecclesiam Suam 48, *The Papal Encyclicals (1958–1981)*, New York: McGrath, 1981, pp. 135–60.

4 Paul VI, *Evangelii Nuntiandi*, AAS 68, 1976, 5–76.

5 W. Nicgorski, 'Response to David Schindler', *Catholicism and Secularization in America*, David Schindler (ed.), Notre Dame, IN: Communio Books, 1990, p. 15.

6 Paul VI, *Evangelii Nuntiandi*, AAS 68, 1976, 5–76 at 18 (paragraph 20).

7 While the juxtaposition of the two appears first in the papacy of John Paul II, the concept of a civilization of love can be found in the document *Justitia et Pax* of Paul VI (1971) and was adopted by John Paul II in *Dives in Misericordia* AAS 72, 1980, 1177–232.

8 See, for example, the speech of John Paul II to the scholars of Lublin University, *Christian Life in Poland*, November, 1987, 52 (hereafter SSLU).

9 GS, Flannery translation, p. 922. AAS LVIII, 1996, p. 1042.

10 D. Schindler, 'Christology and the *Imago Dei*: Interpreting *Gaudium et spes*', *Communio* 23, Spring, 1986, 156–84. See also L. Welch, '*Gaudium et spes*, the Divine Image and the Synthesis of *Veritatis Splendor*', *Communio* 24, Winter, 1997, 794–814, at 794; P. Morandé, 'The Relevance of the Message of *Gaudium et spes* today: the Church's mission in the midst of epochal changes and new challenges', *Communio* 23, Spring, 1996, 141–56, at 142, and K. Schmitz, 'The Language of Conversion and the Conversion of Language', *Communio* 21, Winter, 1994, 742–65, at 748 (hereafter LCCL).

11 D. Schindler, *Heart of the World, Center of the Church: Communio Ecclesiology, Liberalism and Liberation*, Edinburgh: T&T Clark, 1996, p. 9 (hereafter HWCC).

12 D. Schindler, 'Trinity, Creation and the Order of Intelligence in the Modern Academy', *Communio* 28, Fall, 2001, 406–29.

13 *Dominum et Vivificantem*, AAS 78, 1986, 809–900.

14 'Faith and Inculturation', paragraph 28, *Origins* 18, 47, 1989, 800–7.

15 The Pontifical Council for Culture was established by John Paul II in 1983. See AAS 74, 1983, 683–8.

16 P. Poupard, *Towards a Pastoral Approach to Culture*, Document of the Pontifical Council for Culture, 23 May 1999, Rome, p. 341 (hereafter TPAC). The questioning of the positivist presuppositions about the progress of science and technology would seem to be a 'good' in this otherwise negative list.

17 Ibid., p. 342.

18 Ibid., p. 342.

19 SSLU, p. 52.

20 TPAC, p. 342.

21 Ibid., p. 342.

22 The following elements of contemporary Liberal political and moral philosophy are criticised by John Paul II in *Evangelium Vitae*: the raising of abortion, euthanasia, contraception and reproductive technologies to the status of 'legitimate

expressions of individual freedom, to be acknowledged and protected as actual rights' (paragraph 18), the 'mentality which carries the concept of subjectivity to an extreme and recognizes as a subject of rights only the person who enjoys full or at least incipient autonomy and who emerges from a state of total dependence on others' (paragraph 19), 'the mentality which tends to equate personal dignity with the capacity for verbal and explicit, or at least perceptible, communication' (paragraph 19), and the notion of freedom which exalts the isolated individual in an absolute way' (paragraph 19). A state embracing and promoting such mentalities is described as a 'tyrant state' and any such 'democracy' 'effectively moves towards a form of totalitarianism' (paragraph 20). For criticisms of a false (Liberal) reading of the nature of freedom in *Veritatis Splendor*, see paragraphs 32, 33, 36 and 106. Paragraph 101 warns of the risk of an alliance between democracy and ethical relativism. For a criticism of pragmatism and a conception of democracy that is not grounded on unchanging values, see John Paul II, *Fides et ratio*, AAS 91, 1999, 5–18 at 75 (paragraph 89) (hereafter FR).

23 For an example of John Paul ll's attempt to adopt concepts from the Liberal tradition (in this context, liberty, equality and fraternity) and fill them with a Christian content, see his 'Allocutio' at the 1500th Anniversary Mass in celebration of the baptism of Clovis, Reims, 22 September 1996, in *Notitiae* 32, October, 1996, 716–20.

24 IEC p. 107. It should be noted that John Paul II's homilies may be written by other authors. The point that Francis George (now Cardinal Archbishop of Chicago) appears to be making in this observation is that, when John Paul II visits countries with a strong Protestant tradition, there is nothing in his statements to indicate that he has reflected upon the issue that in a country with a dominant Protestant public culture Catholics may have a tendency to be 'Catholic in theory, but Protestant in practice'.

25 C. Dawson, *Dynamics of World History*, J. J. Molloy (ed.), La Salle, IL: Sherwood Sugden & Co., 1978.

26 F. Koneczny, 'Kosciol Jako Polityczny Wychowawca Narodow', *Znak* 41, 4, 1989, 63–70; H. Strasser, and G. Schlegl, '*Gemeinschaft* or *Gesellschaft*? Two Competing Versions of Modernity in Werner Stark's and Max Weber's Sociology', *Thought* 64, 252, 1989, 51–66.

27 C. Dawson, *Dynamics of World History*, p. 203.

28 Ibid., p. 205.

29 Ibid., p. 206.

30 IEC, p. 107.

31 AAS 87, 1995, 5–42.

32 Ibid., p. 59.

33 *Veritatis Splendor*, AAS 85, 1993.

34 John Paul II, *Tertio Millennio Adveniente*, AAS 87, 1995, 5–41, at 36–7 (paragraph 52).

35 W. Kasper, 'The Theological Anthropology of *Gaudium et spes*', 137.

36 M. Lamb, 'Inculturation and Western Culture: the Dialogical Experience between Gospel and Culture', *Communio* 21, Spring, 1994, 124–41, at 133–4.

37 This usage of 'dialectical' therefore differs from the conventional Hegelian idea of antithetical theses that are capable of a higher synthesis. In this instance the word signifies a conflict which is not capable of a resolution by synthesis.

38 D. R. Finn, 'John Paul II and the Moral Ecology of Markets', *Theological Studies* 59, 1998, 662–80, at 663–4.

39 M. Vidal, 'La sospechosa cristianización del capitalismo: Judicio etico al capitalismo a partir de la enciclica Centesimus Annus', *Persona y Sociedad* 7, 1993, 115–39, at 116.

40 John Paul II, 'General Audience Homily of November 24, 1999', *L'Osservatore Romano*, 25 September 1994, 5.

41 FR (paragraph 72).

42 B. Lonergan, 'The Transition from a Classicist World-View to Historical Mindedness', *A Second Collection*, London: Darton, Longman & Todd, 1974, pp. 112 and 92. Cf. J. Finnis, *Historical Consciousness and Theological Foundations*, Toronto: Pontifical Institute of Medieval Studies, 1992.

43 DS, p. 42.

44 J. Ratzinger, 'Culture and Truth: Reflections on the Encyclical *Fides et ratio*', *Origins* 28, 36, 1999, 626–31, at 628.

45 FR, Chapters 2 and 4.

46 John XXIII, *Veterum Sapientia*, AAS 54, 1963, 129–35, at 130–1 (paragraph 6).

47 Ibid. (paragraph 9).

48 Paul VI, General Audience Address, November 26, 1969.

49 J. Ratzinger, *A New Song for the Lord: Faith in Christ and Liturgy Today*, Martha M. Matesich (trans.), New York: Crossroad Herder, 1996; and *The Spirit of the Liturgy*, San Francisco: Ignatius, 2000.

50 CA, p. 31.

51 H. J. Burbach, 'Sacro-Pop', *Internationale katholische Zeitschrift Communio* 3, 1974, 91–4.

52 C. Pickstock, 'A Short Essay on the Reform of the Liturgy', *New Blackfriars*, February, 1997, 64.

53 G. Olsen, 'Christian Faith in a Neo-Pagan Society', P. Williams (ed.), *Historicism and Faith*, Scranton, PA: FCS Publications, 1981, pp. 16–34, at 28.

54 D. Torevell, *Ritual, Modernity and Liturgical Reform*, Edinburgh: T&T Clark, 2000.

55 G. Motzkin, *Time and Transcendence: Secular History, the Catholic Reaction and the Rediscovery of the Future*, Dordrecht: Kluwer, 1992, p. 198.

56 *Catholic World* news report, *AD 2000*, 15, 3, 2002, 5.

3 THE EPISTEMIC AUTHORITY OF 'EXPERTS' AND THE *ETHOS* OF MODERN INSTITUTIONS

1 A. MacIntyre, *After Virtue: A Study in Moral Theory*, London: Duckworth, 1981, pp. 11 and 18 (hereafter AV).

2 A. MacIntyre, 'Interview with Dmitri Nikulin', *Deutsche Zeitschrift für Philosophie*, 44, 1996, 671–83, at 674. For excerpts in English translation see T. Rowland, 'The Reflections of a Romantic Thomist: Alasdair MacIntyre's Interview with Dmitri Nikulin of *Voprosy Filosofi*', *Political Theory Newsletter* 9, 1, 1998, 47–55.

3 Ibid., p. 674.

4 A. MacIntyre, 'Social Science Methodology as the Ideology of Bureaucratic Authority', *Through the Looking Glass: Epistemology and the Conflict of Enquiry*, M. W. Falco (ed.), Washington, DC: University Press of America, 1979, p. 50.

5 A. MacIntyre, AV p. 66. Cf. J. Borella, *The Sense of the Supernatural*, Edinburgh: T&T Clark, 1998, p. 1: 'Ideology is the occasion of a reversal of the moral relationship between theory and practices'.

6 A. MacIntyre, AV, p. 30.

7 Ibid., p. 66.

8 Ibid., p. 30.

9 Ibid., p. 28. MacIntyre defines 'character traits' as the 'incarnation of a rôle' not a 'mere assemblage of psychological traits'. See A. MacIntyre, 'Marxism of the Will: A Review Essay', *Partisan Review* 36, 1969, 128–33, at 129.

10 Ibid., p. 28.

11 A. MacIntyre, 'Corporate Modernity and Moral Judgment: Are They Mutually Exclusive?' *Ethics and Problems of the 21st Century*, K. E. Goodpaster and K. M. Sayre, Notre Dame, IN: University of Notre Dame Press, 1979, pp. 122–35, at 124 and 126.
12 Ibid., p. 125.
13 Ibid., p. 126.
14 V. Havel, 'Politics and Conscience', *Salisbury Review*, January, 1985, 34.
15 V. Belohradsky, 'Bureaucracy, Ideology and Evil', *Salisbury Review* 2, 1, 1983, 11–12.
16 A. MacIntyre, 'Corporate Modernity and Moral Judgment: Are they Mutually Exclusive?', op. cit., p. 132.
17 Ibid., p. 132.
18 Ibid., p. 132.
19 For example, 'Post-Aristotelian Political Philosophy and Modernity', *Aufstieg und Niedergang der Römischen Welt*, W. Haase and H. Temporini (eds), Berlin: Walter de Gruyter, 1994; and 'Post-Aristotelian Philosophy and Political Theory', *Cithara* III, November, 1963, 56–80.
20 M. Hadas, *The Stoic Philosophy of Seneca: Essays and Letters*, New York: Norton, 1958, p. 20.
21 J. V. Schall, 'Post-Aristotelian Political Philosophy and Modernity', op. cit., p. 4910.
22 Ibid., pp. 4909–10. In a more contemporary context, James V. Schall has also made reference to the tendency he has observed among Rhodes scholarship applicants to eschew any association with any particular religious or philosophical tradition, and to present this indifference as a desirable property or 'virtue' in a Rhodes candidate.
23 C. Taylor, *Sources of the Modern Self: The Making of the Modern Identity*, Cambridge, UK: Cambridge University Press, 1989, p. 21. For an account of such behaviour as an example of 'inauthenticity' see K. Wojtyla, *The Acting Person*, A. Potocki (trans.), Dordrecht: D. Reidell, 1979, pp. 288–91.
24 For a discussion of the issue of tragic choice and stoic withdrawal from a more deeply theological perspective, see A. Nichols *No Bloodless Myth: A Guide Through Balthasar's Dramatics*, Edinburgh: T&T Clark, 1999, p. 38. Nichols summarises the Balthasarian argument as 'Christian theology alone can prevent the nullification of the tragic dimension because it combines an account of God's redemptive initiative in his free creation's favour with an affirmation of the unmerited quality of his self-gift'. This means that the 'wounds of the tragic hero in his self-destruction are not healed if they are merely subsumed into a stoic passionlessness'.
25 A. MacIntyre, 'Social Science Methodology as the Ideology of Bureaucratic Authority', op. cit., pp. 57–8.
26 Ibid., p. 50.
27 For a development of this argument see A. Fisher, 'Is there a distinctive rôle for the Catholic hospital in a pluralist society?', *Issues for a Catholic Bioethics*, Luke Gormally (ed.), London: The Linacre Centre, 1999, pp. 200–29. In the context of health care practices, Fisher observes that there is unavoidable rivalry between patients, health professionals, health managers, policy-makers, governments, taxpayers and insurers over resources, power, influence and ideology. In such circumstances the notion of bureaucratic neutrality is a nonsense. See 'An Ethical View on Resource Allocation in Health Care', *Ethics and Resource Allocation in Health Care*, Norm Ford (ed.), Melbourne: Chisholm Centre, 1996, pp. 22–8, at 28.

28 Congregation for Catholic Education, 'The Catholic School on the Threshold of the Third Millennium', Vatican City, 28 December, 1997.

29 John Paul II, *Fides et ratio*, AAS 91, 1999, 5–88, at 53 (paragraph 61).

30 R. Hittinger, 'Christopher Dawson: A View from the Social Sciences', *The Catholic Writer: The Proceedings of the Wethersfield Institute* 2, 1989, 31–47.

31 A. MacIntyre, 'Natural Law as Subversive: the Case of Thomas Aquinas', *Journal of Medieval and Early Modern Studies* 26, 1, 1996, 69.
  When MacIntyre uses the term 'plain persons' he is making reference to those who have not had any academic training in philosophy. It is not a comment upon their social status.

32 A. MacIntyre, 'Review of Aquinas's Theory of Natural Law: An Analytic Reconstruction by Anthony Lisska', *International Philosophical Quarterly* XXXVII, 145, 1997, 98.

33 Ibid., p. 98.

34 Ibid., p. 98.

35 Ibid., p. 98.

36 Ibid., p. 5–7.

37 M. Polanyi, *The Tacit Dimension*, London: Routledge, 1967. A similar position has been developed by Hans George-Gadamer. MacIntyre acknowledges that 'Gadamer has developed a line of thought which has affinities to the line of thought which I have developed, but we differ at crucial points. That in Gadamer which I reject is that which he takes from Heidegger'. See T. Pearson, 'An Interview with Alasdair MacIntyre', *Kinesis* 23, 1, 1996, 40–50, at 49 (hereafter ITDP).

38 A. Louth, *Discerning the Mystery: An Essay on the Nature of Theology*, Oxford: Clarendon Press, 1983, pp. 61–2.

39 A. MacIntyre, 'Plain Persons and Moral Philosophy: Rules, Virtues and Goods', *American Catholic Philosophical Quarterly* LXVI, 1, 1992, 3–19, at 12.

40 Ibid., p. 11.

41 A. MacIntyre, *Three Rival Versions of Moral Enquiry: Encyclopaedia, Genealogy, Tradition*, London: Duckworth, 1990, p. 63.

42 The sociological phenomenon of converts from chronically dysfunctional non-Catholic families is an example of this kind of reasoning process. Instead of concluding that all families are dysfunctional and seeking some kind of 'therapeutic' solution by recourse to professional 'counsellors', some conclude that the cause of the dysfunctionality is the flawed conception(s) of marriage and family life operative in modern and postmodern intellectual traditions, and that only the Catholic tradition offers a model of normality free from internal contradictions and tragic moral options.

43 A. MacIntyre, 'The Theses on Feuerbach: A Road Not Taken', *Artifacts, Representations and Social Practice*, C. C. Gould and R. S. Cohen (eds), Amsterdam: Kluwer, 1994, pp. 277–90 (hereafter TTF).

44 A. MacIntyre, TTF, pp. 277–90.

45 Ibid., p. 279.

46 Ibid., p. 280.

47 Ibid., p. 280.

48 Ibid., p. 280.

49 For similar arguments in Schiller, see *On the Aesthetic Education of Mankind*, Oxford: Clarendon, 1967, especially the 'Sixth Letter'; and W. von Humboldt, *The Limits of State Action*, J. W. Burrow (ed.), Cambridge, UK: Cambridge University Press, 1969. For a comparison of Marx and Schiller see P. J. Kain, *Schiller, Marx and Hegel: State, Society and the Aesthetic Ideal of Ancient Greece*, Montreal: Queens' University Press, 1982. For a comparison of Aristotle and Schiller see C. Cordner, 'The

Aristotelian Character of Schiller's Ethical ideal', *International Studies in Philosophy*, 22, 1, 1990, 21–36. For an account of the latently Aristotelian elements in Marx which concurs with MacIntyre's judgement, see George McCarthy, *Romancing Antiquity: German Critique of the Enlightenment from Weber to Habermas*, Oxford: Rowman & Littlefield, 1997.

50 A. MacIntyre, TTF, p. 280.

51 Ibid., p. 281.

52 A. MacIntyre, 'Interview with Dmitri Nikulin', op. cit., p. 674.

53 T. Pearson, ITDP, p. 45.

54 A. MacIntyre, 'Interview with Dmitri Nikulin', op. cit., p. 674.

55 Karl Polanyi was principally an economic historian and critic of capitalism. Michael Polanyi, his brother, was a natural and a social scientist who taught sociology at Manchester University with MacIntyre. John Polanyi, the Nobel Prize-winning chemist, is the son of Michael Polanyi. John Polanyi also has a son called Michael, who is a political scientist. MacIntyre makes explicit reference to the work of Karl Polanyi, and MacIntyre's notion of tradition-constituted rationality shares themes in common with the work of Michael Polanyi, the grandfather of the contemporary political scientist. See K. Polanyi, *The Great Transformation: The Political and Economic Origins of Our Times*, Boston: Beacon Press, 1944.

56 MacIntyre's critique of capitalist practices does not however place him within the orbit of the schools of liberation theology. He does not take any principles from the Marxist tradition which deal with issues in philosophical anthropology and he is not in any sense influenced by its tendency to immanentise the *eschaton*, or to develop a Christology based upon a Marxist hermeneutic.

57 This is not to suggest that the Aristotelian Marxist label should generally be adopted, for plain persons are unlikely to make sense of the expression at all. John Paul II's term 'Solidarity' or 'Solidarism' would appear to be the better option, because it differentiates the body of Catholic social justice thought from all secular socialist alternatives.

58 Gregory Baum notes that although earlier encyclicals lamented the exploitation of labour through inadequate and unjust wages, through harsh and dangerous conditions of work and through lack of security at times of illness, accident and old age, they did not consider what Marx identified as the problem of alienation. See 'The Impact of Marxism on the Thought of John Paul II', *Thought* 62, March, 1987, 26–38, at 27.

59 John Paul II, *Laborem Exercens*, AAS 73, 1981, 577–644, at 589–94 (paragraphs 6 and 7).

60 Ibid. (paragraph 15.2).

61 John Paul II, *Centesimus Annus*, AAS 83, 1991, 793–867, at 852–4 (paragraph 48).

62 John Paul II, *Redemptor Hominis*, AAS 72, 1979, 257–324, at 289–95 (paragraph 16).

63 Paul VI, *Populorum Progressio*, AAS 59, 1967, 257–99, at 270 (paragraph 26).

64 John Paul II, 'The Constitution of Culture through Human Praxis', *Person and Community: Selected Essays*, Theresa Sandok (trans.), New York: Peter Lang, 1993, pp. 263–79.

65 Ibid., p. 271.

66 Ibid., p. 271.

67 Ibid., p. 271.

68 D. Maugenest, 'The Encyclical *Laborem Exercens*: Its Context and Originality' *Lumen Vitae*, XLI, 4, 1986, 226–32.

69 Ibid., p. 230. The 'Slavophiles' were intellectuals in the nineteenth century who eschewed the liberal model of economic development and the emphasis on the rights of the individual over and above the interests of the common good. See A.

Walicki, *The Controversy over Capitalism: Studies in the Social Philosophy of the Russian Popularists*, Oxford: Clarendon, 1969.

70 J. Milbank, *Theology and Social Theory: Beyond Secular Reason*, Oxford: Basil Blackwell, 1990, p. 34.

71 Ibid., pp. 177, 191 and 193.

72 Ibid., p. 178.

73 Ibid., p. 187.

74 See, for example, A. MacIntyre, *Marxism: An Introduction*, London: SCM Press, 1953, p. 9. Cf. D. L. Schindler (ed.), 'Grace and the Form of Nature and Culture', *Catholicism and Secularization in America*, Notre Dame, IN: Communio Books, 1990 (hereafter GFN).

75 A. MacIntyre, 'Marxists and Christians', *The Twentieth Century*, Autumn, 1961, 28–37, at 33.

76 A. O. Rorty, 'Social and Political Sources of *Akrasia*', *Ethics* 107, July, 1997, 644–57, at 654.

77 MacIntyre states that 'what a person manifesting *akrasia* lacks is full *epistémé* operative on this particular occasion and the full disposition of character that could sustain and embody that operation', and by contrast in 'any modern prescriptivist account of morality, not only can there be no place for, indeed no conception of the relevant species of *epistémé*, but there can be no logical possibility of the kind of gap between knowledge and action which *akrasia* exemplifies. See A. MacIntyre, 'The relationship of philosophy to its past', *Philosophy in History: Essays on the Historiography of Philosophy*, R. Rorty, J. B. Schneewind and Q. Skinner (eds), Cambridge, UK: Cambridge University Press, 1984, pp. 31–49, at 37.

78 A. MacIntyre, *Three Rival Versions of Moral Enquiry*, op. cit., p. 193.

79 A. MacIntyre, 'Corporate Modernity and Moral Judgement', op. cit., p. 129.

80 A. MacIntyre, 'Social Structures and their Threats to Moral Agency', *Philosophy* 74, 1999, 311–29, at 317: 'To have integrity is to refuse to be, to have educated oneself so that one is no longer able to be, one kind of person in one social context, while quite another in other contexts. It is to have set inflexible limits to one's adaptability to the rôle that one may be called upon to play'.

81 These strategies of 'social survival' are not only apparent within secular institutions but can also be observed within the bureaucratic agencies of the Church herself.

4 'MASS CULTURE' AND THE 'RIGHT TO CULTURE'

1 Stephen Lukes, 'The Meanings of Individualism', *Journal of the History of Ideas*, January–March, 1971, 54.

2 H. G. Gadamer, *Truth and Method*, New York: Crossroads, 1992, p. 11.

3 H. G. Schenk, *The Mind of the European Romantics: An Essay in Cultural History*, London: Constable, 1966, p. 96.

4 Shaftesbury, *Characteristics of Men, Manners, Opinions and Times*, P. Eyres (ed.), Oxford: Clarendon, 1999.

5 E. Cassirer, *The Platonic Renaissance in England*, Austin: University of Texas, 1953, p. 197; C. Elson, *Wieland and Shaftesbury*, New York: Columbia University Press, 1913.

6 L. Elders, *The Metaphysics of Being of St Thomas Aquinas*, Leiden: E. J Brill, 1993, p. 50: 'By the end of the seventeenth century the transcendentals no longer signify something characteristic of all things, they are now an answer of the human subject, moulding the neutral facts it perceives into its own a priori categories'.

7 F. C. Beiser, '*Bildung* in Early German Romanticism', *Philosophies in Education: New Historical Perspectives*, Amélie Oskenberg Rorty (ed.), London: Routledge, 1998, p. 292.

8 *Kant's Political Writings*, H. Reiss (ed.), Cambridge, UK: Cambridge University Press, 1970. Cf. E. Cantore, 'Scientific Humanism for the Third Millennium', *Seminarium* 23, 1985: 203–26, at 210–11.

9 W. von Humboldt, *The Limits of State Action*, J. W. Burrow (ed.), Cambridge, UK: Cambridge University Press, 1969, p. 46.

10 Ibid., p. 45.

11 Schiller's *Werke*, letter dated 18 February, 1793, cited in P. Guyer, *Kant and the Experience of Freedom*, Cambridge, UK: Cambridge University Press, 1993, p. 119.

12 In his autobiography, Mill acknowledges his debt to the works of continental scholars, especially their conceptions of individuality, and makes specific reference to Goethe and von Humboldt, and to the Italian educationalist Pestalozzi. J. S. Mill, *Autobiography*, New York: Columbia University Press, 1944, p. 178.

13 J. S. Mill, *Essays on Politics and Culture*, G. Himmelfarb (ed.), New York: Doubleday, 1962. Cf. A. J. Harris, 'John Stuart Mill's Theory of Progress', *Ethics* 66, April, 1956, 157–75, at 163.

14 J. W. Burrow, *Introduction to The Limits of State Action*, Cambridge, UK: Cambridge University Press, 1969, p. xxxv.

15 R. E. Norton, *The Beautiful Soul*, Ithaca, NY: Cornell University Press, 1995, p. 251.

16 J. W. Burrow, *Introduction to The Limits of State Action*, p. xxx.

17 EMW, p. 78. Cf. H. de Lubac, *Three Jesuits*, San Francisco, Ignatius, p. 55: 'There is nothing more demanding than the taste for mediocrity. Beneath its ever moderate appearance there is nothing intemperate; nothing surer in its instinct; nothing more pitiless in its refusals. It suffers no greatness, shows beauty no mercy'.

18 *Veritatis Splendor* (paragraph 57), AAS 85, 1993, 1133–228.

19 See E. B. F. Midgely, *The Ideology of Max Weber: A Thomist Critique*, Aldershot: Gower, 1983, p. 56: 'According to [Nietzsche's] evolutionary ideology of continuous human transformation, no condition of man contains human nature as such; every condition of man is, at once, sub-human in comparison with some other condition of man and also super-human in comparison with yet another condition of man'.

20 Erich Przywara suggests that the major distinction between von Humboldt and Nietzsche is that the von Humboldt project represents the humanism of an idealised humanity, whereas Nietzsche is only interested in 'heroic humanity' – that is, the humanism of those few who have the capacity to live beyond good and evil. See *Humanitas: Der Mensch Gestern und Morgen*, Nürnberg: Glock und Lutz, 1952, p. 745. In von Balthasar's analysis, Nietzsche not only turns the transcendentals against one another, as in the proposition that 'truth is ugly', but also seeks to demonstrate that the transcendentals are inwardly contradictory. See *Theo-Logik: Wahrheit der Welt*, Vol. 1, Einsiedeln: Johannes Verlag, 1985.

21 J. Golomb, *In Search of Authenticity: From Kierkegaard to Camus*, London: Routledge, 1995, p. 12.

22 Ibid., p. 83.

23 Ibid., p. 83.

24 F. Nietzsche, *Gesammelte Werke*, Vol. 16, Munich: Musarion Verlag, 1920–29, p. 60, and *The Gay Science*, Walter Kaufmann (trans.), New York: Vintage, 1994, p. 203.

25 F. Nietzsche, *Untimely Meditations*, R. J. Hollingdale (trans.), Cambridge, UK: Cambridge University Press, 1983, pp. 62–3. Related to this anti-memory orientation is Nietzsche's doctrine of the eternal recurrence which has as its purpose the subsuming of past and future into a perpetual present. See Keith Ansell-Pearson, *Introduction to Nietzsche as a Political Thinker*, Cambridge, UK: Cambridge University Press, 1994. For an excellent exposition of the general hopelessness of the Nietzschean accounts of the self, see M. A. Casey, *Meaninglessness*, Melbourne: Freedom Publishing, 2000.

26 F. Nietzsche, *Untimely Meditations*, p. 63.

27 Paul de Man, 'Literary History and Literary Modernity', *Daedalus* 99, 1970, 384–404, at 388.

28 Alasdair MacIntyre, 'Corporate Modernity and Moral Judgement: Are they Mutually Exclusive?', *Ethics and Problems of the 21st Century*, K. M. Sayre and K. E. Goodpaster, Notre Dame, IN: Notre Dame University Press, 1979, p. 133 (hereafter CMMJ).

29 P. Connerton, *How Societies Remember*, Cambridge, UK: Cambridge University Press, 1989, p. 64. Where De Man uses the expression 'cultures of deliberate forgetting', Connerton speaks of cultures of 'forced forgetting'. The major difference between the two is that one is coercive and the other is self-inflicted.

30 R. Hittinger, 'Theology and Natural Law Theory', *Communio* 17, Fall, 1990, 402–9, at 403.

31 Jacques Le Goff argues that Pierre de la Ramée (Ramus) demanded in his *Scholae in Liberales Artes* (1569) that the ancient techniques of memorisation be replaced with his own method, which has continued to inspire an 'anti-memory' current of thought. See *History and Memory*, New York: Columbia University Press, 1992. Catherine Pickstock argues that the effect of the Ramist and Cartesian reduction of memory to a mental action for the retrieval of objects destroys the rôle of memory as the link between knowledge, tradition and the transcendent. See AW, pp. 54–71.

32 St Augustine, *The Confessions*, R. S. Pine-Coffin (ed.), London: Penguin, 1961, p. 215 and pp. 218–19.

33 St Bonaventure, *The Journey of the Mind to God*, P. Boehner (trans.), Cambridge, UK: Hackett, 1993, p. 21.

34 Albertus Magnus, *De Bono, Tractatus* IV, *Quaestio* II De *Partibus Prudentiae*. Translation from Appendix B of Mary Carruthers, *The Book of Memory: A Study of Memory in Medieval Culture*, Cambridge, UK: Cambridge University Press, 1990.

35 St Thomas Aquinas, *De Veritate*, R. W. Mulligan (trans.) Chicago: H. Regnery, 1954.

36 Pamela Hall, *Narrative and the Natural Law: An Interpretation of Thomistic Ethics*, Notre Dame, IN: University of Notre Dame Press, 1994, p. 40.

37 Romanus Cessario, *Moral Virtues and Theological Ethics*, Notre Dame, IN: University of Notre Dame Press, 1991, p. 88.

38 S. Pinckaers 'Christ, Moral Absolutes and the Good: Recent Moral Theology', *The Thomist* 55, 1991, 117–40, at 139.

39 Ibid., pp. 77–9.

40 K. Schmitz, 'St Thomas and the Appeal to Experience', *CTSA Proceedings* 47, 1992, 1–20, at 3 (hereafter TAE).

41 W. Gerhard, 'The Intellectual Virtue of Prudence', *The Thomist* VIII, October, 1945, 413–56, at 413: 'Knowledge is the end of the intellect but knowledge is a great antiphony: to understand it we must constantly refer to now this member, now that, between which there is a constant interplay of activity constituting knowledge'.

42 In the Thomist framework, the transcendentals express modes of being. This differs from the Kantian sense of transcendental, which refers to knowledge that does not derive from experience but is given a priori by the human subject. Angelo Scola emphasises that von Balthasar's understanding of the transcendentals does not follow Kant, and that this was a major difference and cause of conflict between him and Rahner. See A. Scola, *Hans Urs von Balthasar: A Theological Style*, Edinburgh: T&T Clark, 1991, p. 27. There is also a difference of opinion over whether Aquinas recognised beauty as a theoretically separable

transcendental from the good. Both John of La Rochelle and Bonaventure clearly identified beauty as a transcendental in its own right, and it is this position that is followed by von Balthasar, Benedict Groeschel and John Paul II, among others. Scholars, however, remain divided over the issue of whether Aquinas was in agreement with this position. See C. Fabro, 'Il Transcendentale tomistico', *Angelicum* 60 1983, 534–58; and M. Jordan, 'The Grammar of *esse*: re-reading Thomas on the transcendentals', *The Thomist* 44, 1980, 1–26, and 'The Evidence of the transcendentals and the place of beauty in Thomas Aquinas', *International Philosophical Quarterly* 29, December, 1989, 394–407. Armaud Maurer suggests that in 'downplaying beauty relative to truth and goodness, St Thomas reveals his basic Aristotelianism and his lukewarmness to Platonism'. See A. A. Maurer, *About Beauty: A Thomistic Interpretation*, Houston: Center for Thomistic Studies, 1983, pp. 2–3.

43 H. U. von Balthasar, *The Glory of the Lord*, Vol. IV, *The Realm of Metaphysics in Antiquity*, Edinburgh: T&T Clark, 1989, pp. 28–9.

44 The relationships between intellect and faith, will and love, and memory and hope forms the framework of the spirituality of St John of the Cross. In his dissertation published in English translation as *Faith According to St John of the Cross*, San Francisco: Ignatius, 1981, p. 54, Karol Wojtyla states that this threefold division of the spiritual faculties and theological virtues seems to have been adapted from John Baconthorpe, an English Carmelite.

45 *The Collected Works of St John of the Cross*, Washington, DC: ICS Publications, 1991, p. 400.

46 TAE, p. 6, and St Thomas Aquinas, *Summa Theologica* I–II, 40, 5 and 6.

47 The Franciscan scholar Benedict Groeschel has developed a thesis that different personality types, and their spiritual strengths and weaknesses, are related to the degree to which individuals are attracted to and participate in each of the transcendentals. See *Spiritual Passages: The Psychology of Spiritual Development*, New York: Crossroad, 1989.

48 Norris Clarke's argument that the human person needs to be understood in terms of both relationality and substantiality has been adopted by David Schindler and Kenneth Schmitz, among others. In an early article, Schindler alluded to this need, and also to the argument that in any account of prudential judgement the memory is a very important faculty of the soul, with his statement that 'objectivity cannot be dealt with in exclusively cognitional terms – that is, in terms of the intellect alone'. See 'History, Objectivity and Moral Conversion', *The Thomist* XXXVII, July, 1973, 569–88, at 581.

49 John Paul II, *Dominum et Vivificantem* (paragraph 55), AAS 78, 1986, 809–900.

50 M. Regnier, 'L'Homme, nature ou histoire?', *Etudes* 329, 1968, 447–50.

51 John Paul II, *Dominum et Vivificantem* (paragraph 56).

52 The work of E. Michael Jones on the effect of architecture and modern music on moral formation provides concrete examples of how the technocratic marginalisation of beauty can lead to a loss of hope and a narrowing of the moral imagination. See E. Michael Jones, *Living Machines*, San Francisco: Ignatius, 1995, and *Dionysos Rising*, San Francisco: Ignatius, 1994. Earlier twentieth-century work by the French authors Paul Claudel and Charles Péguy also addressed related themes.

53 EMW, pp. 88–9.

54 H. U. von Balthasar, *The Glory of the Lord*, Vol. I, p. 25.

55 John Paul II, *Ecclesia in America*, AAS 91, 1999, 737–815.

56 H. U. von Balthasar, *A Theology of History*, San Francisco: Ignatius, 1994, p. 125.

57 C. Taylor, *The Ethics of Authenticity*, Harvard University Press, 1991, 'Die immanente Gegenaufklärung', *Aufklärung heute,* Stuttgart: Klett-Cotta, 1997 and *A Catholic Modernity?*, James L. Heft (ed.), Oxford University Press, 1991 (hereafter ACM).

58 Charles Taylor, *Sources of the Self: The Making of the Modern Identity*, Cambridge, UK: Cambridge University Press, 1989, p. 495 (hereafter SSMMI).

59 Ibid., p. 317.

60 Alasdair MacIntyre, 'Critical Remarks on the *Sources of the Self* by Charles Taylor', *Philosophy and Phenomenological Research* LIV, 1, 1994, 188.

61 ACM, p. 16.

62 Cf. *Lumen Gentium,* Chapters IV and V.

63 ACM, p. 22.

64 SSMMI, pp. 14 and 23.

65 ACM, pp. 22–3.

66 CHD, pp. 132–42, at 131 and 136. In his analysis of the Lutheran revolution, Maritain also argued that Luther concentrated on an interiority freed from being and that it was this severance which rendered the Lutheran self vulnerable to political manipulation. See *Three Reformers* London: Sheed & Ward, 1950.

67 C. Taylor, 'Die immanente Gegenaufklärung', pp. 54–5.

68 Ibid., p. 60.

69 Ibid., pp. 60–1.

70 Ibid., p. 61.

71 Ibid., p. 63.

72 Ibid., p. 62.

73 Alasdair MacIntyre, *Three Rival Versions of Moral Enquiry: Encyclopaedia, Genealogy, Tradition,* London: Duckworth, 1990, p. 165 (hereafter TRV).

74 K. Schmitz, 'The First Principle of Personal Becoming', *Review of Metaphysics* 47, June, 1994, 765.

75 When asked in an interview whether he was a Catholic in a 'traditional and orthodox sense', MacIntyre replied: 'There is no other sense'. See *Kinesis* 23, Summer, 1996, 47.

76 Daniel Westberg has identified four patterns of interpretation of Thomist prudence: (a) those associated with conscience, (b) directive of human action, (c) reformulated conscience and (d) affective orientation. He argues that the proper relationship between intellect and will has thus become the crux of the problem in understanding the nature of *prudentia* in Aquinas. See D. Westberg, *Practical Reason: Aristotle, Action, Prudence in Aquinas*, Oxford: Clarendon, 1994, p. 39. The proposal outlined above also acknowledges the need for a Thomist psychology of action, but adds to Westberg's reference to the intellect and will an emphasis upon the faculty of memory.

77 EMW, p. 107.

5 THE *LOGOS* OF THE *KULTUR* OF MODERNITY

1 Implicit within these positions is a reliance upon elements of the theology of Origen, according to which every created reality is a composite of a superior (spiritual) and inferior (material) level of existence. Accordingly, 'when the human mind contemplates some material thing, it has the power to discern the deeper intelligible principles or forms which give the matter meaning (*logos*) within the cosmic system'. See J. Kobler, *Vatican II, Theophany and the Phenomenon of Man*, New York: Peter Lang, 1991, p. 61, and W. Kasper, 'The *Logos* character of reality', *Communio* 15, Fall, 1988, 274–84.

2 D. Schindler, GFN, p. 170.

3   D. Schindler, 'Towards a Eucharistic Evangelization', *Communio* 19, Winter, 1992, 549–75, at 558 (hereafter TEE). Cf. W. Kasper, *Transcending All Understanding: The Meaning of Christian Faith Today*, San Francisco: Ignatius, 1989, p. 81 (hereafter TAU).

4   H. U. von Balthasar, 'Der Begriff der Natur in der Theologie', *Zeitschrift für katholische Theologie* 75, 1953, 452–61.

5   GFN, p. 30. See also Hans Urs von Balthasar, *A Short Primer for Unsettled Laymen*, San Francisco: Ignatius, 1985, p. 61.

6   MacIntyre's most extensive analysis of the prospects of reason without revelation is found in *AV*, pp. 36–62. He argues that once revelation was set aside as a source of moral norms, the philosophers of the Enlightenment needed to found morality on some other source and 'zigzagged' between possible alternatives. Thus Kant reacted to Hume's account to found an ethical system upon the passions by emphasising the rôle of the faculty of reason; and Kierkegaard reacted to the problems posed by Kant by positing the idea that one must choose between a fundamental ethical or aesthetic orientation.

7   A. MacIntyre, *Marxism: An Introduction*, London: SCM Press, 1953, p. 9.

8   A. MacIntyre, *Marxism and Christianity*, Notre Dame, IN: University of Notre Dame Press, 1984, p. 142. Reprint of 1968 edition (hereafter MC).

9   Ibid., p. 142.

10 Ibid., pp. 142–3.

11 Maurice Blondel, *The Letter on Apologetics and History and Dogma*, Alexander Dru and Illtyd Trethowan (trans.), New York: Rinehart & Winston, 1964, pp. 278–87 (hereafter LAHD).

12 L. Dupré, *Passage to Modernity: An Essay in the Hermeneutics of Nature and Culture*, New Haven, CT: Yale University Press, 1993, p. 171 (hereafter PM).

13 Cf. G. Chantraine, 'Beyond Modernity and Postmodernity: The Thought of Henri de Lubac', *Communio* 17, Summer, 1990, 207–19, at 209.

14 PM, p. 54.

15 This shift, however, was not universally accepted, and indeed Joseph Komonchak has suggested that one way to understand the divisions at Vatican II is to divide the Fathers and their *periti* into three schools on the basis of their understanding of the grace–nature relationship: the Neo-Thomists, proponents of Nouvelle Théologie and Transcendental Thomists. See 'Interpreting the Second Vatican Council', *Landas: Journal of Loyola School of Theology*, 1, 1987, 81–90.

16 D. Schindler, 'Faith and the Logic of Intelligence', *Catholicism and Secularization in America*, Notre Dame, IN: Communio Books, 1990, p. 171 (hereafter FLI).

17 For a summary account of the principles of Schindler's philosophical anthropology see 'Which Ontology is Necessary for an Adequate Anthropology?', *Anthropotes*, 15/2, 1999, 423–6.

18 FLI, p. 172–3.

19 Ibid., p. 179.

20 W. Norris Clarke, *Person and Being*, Milwaukee, WI: Marquette University Press, 1993, p. 14.

21 FLI, p. 15.

22 J. Ratzinger, 'Concerning the Notion of Person in Theology', *Communio* 17, 1990, 438–54; and TAU, p. 98.

23 FLI, p. 173.

24 Ibid., p. 173.

25 Ibid., p. 174.

26 Ibid., p. 174.

27 Ibid., p. 177.

28 Ibid., p. 177. See also RO, p. 4.

29 T. Chappell, 'Thomism and the Future of Catholic Philosophy', *New Blackfriars* 80, April, 1999, 172–5, at 174.
30 Ibid., p. 174. This statement overlooks the fact that there was not just one Enlightenment project, or indeed one Enlightenment, but several projects associated with the German, French and British (predominately Scottish) Enlightenments. Further, MacIntyre's criticism of the various projects is much more complex than the argument that they lacked a *telos*, and, indeed, MacIntyre's account of the rise of the culture of modernity does not begin with the various Enlightenments. Instead, he has an 'economic wave' building from the twelfth century, a 'theological wave' building from Duns Scotus (*c.* 1265–1308), a 'political wave' building from the fifteenth century and a 'moral wave' developing from the eighteenth century. In this his assessment is in accord with Louis Dupré, who has argued that 'the very heterogeneity of the originating principles forces us to look for a more primitive historical cultural layer, than the scientific conceptions of the seventeenth century'. See PM, pp. 2–3.
31 Ibid., p. 173.
32 FLI, p. 175.
33 A. MacIntyre, 'A Crisis in Moral Philosophy: Why is the Search for the Foundations of Ethics so Frustrating', *Knowing and Valuing: The Search for Common Roots*, H. Engelhardt and D. Callahan (eds), New York: The Hastings Center, 1980, pp. 19–35, at 28.
34 GFN, p. 19.
35 CHD, pp. 134–5.
36 GFN, pp. 19–20.
37 An excellent example of this 'mechanical' reading is found in Kasper's statement, to which reference was made in Chapter 1, that the fundamental concept of the modern age is that secular matters are to be decided in a secular fashion, political matters in a political fashion, and economic matters in an economic fashion.
38 CA, pp. 16–17.
39 A. MacIntyre, 'The American Idea', D. N. Doyle and O. D. Edwards (eds), *America and Ireland 1776–1976*, Westport, CT: Greenwood, 1980, pp. 61–2.
40 M. Gauchet, *The Disenchantment of the World: A Political History of Religion*, Princeton, NJ: Princeton University Press, 1997.
41 Ibid., p. 164.
42 CA, p. 13.
43 WIH, pp. 32–3.
44 Ibid., p. 35.
45 Ibid., p. 33.
46 D. Schindler, 'The Religious Sense and American Culture', *Communio* 25, Winter, 1998, 679–99, at 681.
47 Ibid., p. 683.
48 L. Dupré, 'Secularism and the Crisis of our Culture: A Hermeneutic Perspective', *Thought* 51, 202, September, 1976, 271–82, at 281 (hereafter SCC).
49 K. Schmitz, 'Catholicism in America', *Communio* 19, Fall, 1992, 474–8, at 475.
50 M. Novak, 'Wealth and Virtue: The Development of Christian Economic Teaching', *The Capitalist Spirit: Toward a Religious Ethic of Wealth Creation*, Peter Berger (ed.), San Francisco: Ignatius, 1990, p. 51.
51 M. Novak, *The Spirit of Democratic Capitalism*, New York: Simon & Schuster, 1982, pp. 29 and 69.
52 D. Schindler, 'Christological aesthetics and *Evangelium Vitae*: Toward a definition of liberalism', *Communio* 22, Summer, 1995, 193–224, at 197 (hereafter CAEV). The expression 'structure of sin' is used by John Paul II. It emphasises the fact

that, although only persons can sin, institutional structures and hence whole cultures can be so constituted as to foster vice rather than virtue.

53 Ibid., pp. 200–1.
54 Ibid., p. 209.
55 Ibid., p. 209.
56 Ibid., p. 209. Cf. M. J. Schuck, 'John Courtney Murray's Problematic Interpretation of Leo XIII and the American Founders', *The Thomist* 55, 4, 1991, 595–613.
57 CAEV, p. 211.
58 HWCC, p. 103.
59 For an overview of the intellectual history of the construction of the relationship between action and contemplation, see H. U. von Balthasar, *Word and Redemption*, New York: Herder & Herder, 1964, pp. 109–25. Von Balthasar argues that for Aquinas the two dispositions form part of a deeper unity but contemplation takes priority in a causal sense, and, further, that St Thérèse of Lisieux offers a more developed account of the relationship in her spiritual writings than that offered by classical Thomism. See also von Balthasar, *Thérèse of Lisieux: The Story of a Mission*, Donald Nicholl (trans.), London: Sheed & Ward, 1953, pp. 138–40.
60 P. Henrici, 'Modernity and Christianity', 151. Cf. Lawrence Welch, '*Gaudium et spes*, the Divine Image, and the Synthesis of *Veritatis Splendor*', 808: 'Christ teaches us [in the parable of the Rich Young Man] that fulfilment of the Law comes to us only as a gift'.
61 Leo XIII, *Testem benevolentiae*, January 22, 1899, ASS 31, 1898–9.
62 D. Schindler, 'Reorienting the Church on the Eve of the Millennium', 734. Cf. Catherine Pickstock's thesis on the 'rival sacrality of the polity of death' in AW, pp. 135–40. Cf. Boniface Luykx, 'An Eastern Catholic View', in *Catholicism and Secularization in America*, 211–14, at 212: 'Much more attention should be given to worship as the generator of grace, of culture and of the eschatological dimension in life'.
63 J. Ratzinger, 'Truth and Freedom', *Communio* 23, Spring, 1996, 16–35; and *In the Beginning ... A Catholic Understanding of the Story of Creation and the Fall*, Grand Rapids, MI: Eerdmans, 1986, p. 32.
64 J. Ratzinger, *The Spirit of the Liturgy*, op. cit., pp. 15–16.
65 J. Ratzinger, *In the Beginning*, op. cit., p. 32.
66 C. Pickstock, 'Liturgy and Modernity', *Telos* 113, Fall, 1998, 19–41, at 24.
67 HWCC, p. 109.
68 E. Michael Jones, *Living Machines*, op. cit., p. 42.
69 TEE, p. 549–75, at 575.
70 MHTA, p. 21.
71 For a historiography of different conceptions of the relationship between history and tradition, see C. Dahlhaus, 'Historicism and Tradition', *Foundations of Music History*, Cambridge, UK: Cambridge University Press, 1983, pp. 53–71.
72 H. de Lubac, *Catholicisme*, Paris: Cerf, 1938, p. 264. This is the principle of GS (paragraph 22).
73 GFN, p. 14.
74 MHTA, p. 13.
75 O. O'Donovan, *The Desire of the Nations: Recovering the Roots of Political Philosophy*, Cambridge, UK: Cambridge University Press, 1996, p. 247.
76 W. T. Cavanaugh, 'The City: Beyond Secular Parodies', *Radical Orthodoxy*, London: Routledge, 1999, pp. 182–201.
77 MHTA, p. 19.
78 GFN, p. 151.
79 MHTA, p. 41.
80 Ibid., p. 41.

81 H. U. von Balthasar, *Love Alone*, London: Burns & Oates, 1963, p. 29.
82 John Paul II, *Christifideles Laici* (paragraph 59), AAS 81, 1989, 393–522.
83 SCC, p. 281.

6 CULTURE AND THE RATIONALITY OF THE TRADITION

1 TRV, pp. 59–60.
2 E. Gilson, *Letters to Henri de Lubac*, San Francisco: Ignatius, 1986, p. 24.
3 Y. Simon, *Maritain's Philosophy of the Sciences*, New York: Sheed & Ward, 1943, p. 159.
4 R. G. Collingwood, *The Idea of History*, Oxford: Clarendon Press, 1946.
5 A. MacIntyre, 'Interview with Cogito', 69.
6 A. MacIntyre, 'Précis *of* Whose Justice? Which Rationality?', *Philosophy and Phenomenological Research* 51, 1, 1991, 150.
7 A. MacIntyre, 'Aquinas's Critique of Education', *Philosophers on Education: New Historical Perspectives*, A. O. Rorty (ed.), London: Routledge, 1998, p. 96.
8 Alasdair MacIntyre, 'Natural Law as Subversive: The Case of Aquinas', *Journal of Medieval and Early Modern Studies*, 26, 1, 1995, 61–83 (hereafter NLS).
9 W. Stark, *The Sociology of Knowledge: Toward a Deeper Understanding of the History of Ideas*, London: Transaction Publishers, 1991, *The Social Bond*, Vols I–IV, New York: Fordham, 1978–1987, *The Ideal Foundations of Economic Thought*, London: Routledge and Kegan Paul, 1944.
10 A. Nichols has also drawn attention to the significance of historical factors for de Lubac's understanding of the development of doctrine against the 'logicist' positions of the neo-Thomists. See *From Newman to Congar: The Idea of the Development of Doctrine from the Victorians to the Second Vatican Council*, Edinburgh: T&T Clark, 1990, pp. 195–213.
11 J. Ratzinger, 'Culture and Truth: Reflections on the Encyclical *Fides et ratio*', 627. Cf. FR (paragraph 87).
12 Alasdair MacIntyre, Whose Justice? Which Rationality? London: Duckworth, 1988, p. 7 (hereafter WJWR).
13 Ibid., p. 355.
14 Cf. K. Schmitz, *The Gift: Creation*, Milwaukee, WI: Marquette University Press, 1982, p. 55: 'A tradition is a chain of actual benefactions. It is not parentage in general that gives life, or technical insight that invents a tool; rather it is *this* giver and *that* receiver'.
15 WJWR, pp. 8, 353–4, 362. Cf. J. H. Newman, *The Development of Christian Doctrine*, London: Sheed & Ward, 1960, p. 264: 'Doctrine is percolated, as it were, through different minds, beginning with writers of inferior authority in the Church, and issuing at length in the enunciation of her Doctors'.
16 LAHD, p. 215
17 Ibid., p. 287.
18 A. MacIntyre, 'Some Enlightenment Projects Reconsidered', *Questioning Ethics: Contemporary Debates in Philosophy*, R. Kearney, and M. Dooley (eds), London: Routledge, 1998, pp. 245–58, at 250.
19 Ibid., p. 250.
20 Ibid., p. 250.
21 Ibid., p. 252.
22 International Theological Commission: 'Memory and Reconciliation: the Church and the Faults of the Past', *The Pope Speaks* 45, 4, 2000, 208–49, at 224.
23 This issue was also a problem at the time of the First Vatican Council. In a letter to Ambrose Phillipps de Lisle, John Henry Newman wrote: 'Theological language,

like legal, is scientific and cannot be understood without the knowledge of long precedent and tradition, nor without the comments of theologians'. See *Letters and Diaries XXVII*, 153, as cited by Fergus Kerr in 'Did Newman Answer Gladstone?', *John Henry Newman: Reason, Rhetoric and Romanticism*, David Nicholls and Fergus Kerr (eds), Bristol: The Bristol Press, 1991, p. 136.

24 M. S. Massa, *Catholics and American Culture*, New York: Crossroad, 1999, p. 159.

25 John XXIII, 'Opening Address to the Council', AAS 54, 1962, 792. Cf. GS, p. 62.

26 CA, p. 59.

27 IEC, p. 88.

28 See *Adoremus Bulletin* VIII, 9, December–January, 2002, 4. Cf. Mark S. Massa, *Catholics and American Culture*, op. cit., p. 159: 'For those who cherished the fortress-like peace provided by Catholicism on the battle-scarred plains of modernity, the 'new Mass' was perceived as the Trojan horse through which the secure, medieval walls of Holy Mother Church would be breached; for those who sought a closer engagement of the Church with the intellectual and social problems of contemporary civilization, the new liturgy represented the best opportunity in 400 years to 'modernise' the Church by providing (almost literally) a 'new experience of God'. In the event, both groups were arguably more prescient than liturgists and bishops who believed that worship could be 'updated' while retaining the older theology and ecclesial self-identity largely unchanged'.

29 MacIntyre became interested in the issue of the translatability of languages in the early 1940s, when George Thomson, a Professor of Greek, was engaged in a project of translating Platonic dialogues into Irish. See IGB, p. 141.

30 Ibid., p. 47.

31 F. Kerr, *Theology after Wittgenstein*, Oxford: Basil Blackwell, 1986, p. 11.

32 K. Wojtyla, 'The Human Person and Natural Law', *Person and Community: Selected Essays* (trans. Theresa Sandok OSM), New York: Peter Lang, 1993, p. 183.

33 John Paul II, 'Society Doesn't Understand What the Church is Saying, John Paul II Warns', press release, *Zenit News Agency*, Vatican City, 18 January 2002, Number ZE020118. See also J. Ratzinger, 'The Ecclesiology of Vatican II', Pastoral Congress of the Diocese of Aversa, *L'Osservatore Romano*, 4–23 January 2002, 6–8.

34 Ibid.

35 MacIntyre tends to use the expression 'masters' rather than 'scholar-saints', but the latter expression has been chosen to emphasise the idea, common to MacIntyre and Schindler and von Balthasar, that 'mastering a tradition' is as much an exercise of the will and memory as of the intellect. In other words, to master the Thomist tradition one needs to be holy, not just intellectually gifted.

36 MPMT, p. 292.

37 A significant issue that has not been directly addressed by MacIntyre is the relationship between the magisterial authority within the Catholic tradition and that of scholar-saints in the resolution of crises within the tradition. An oblique reference to the issue is found in TRV, p. 125: 'Except for the finality of scripture and dogmatic tradition, there is and can be no finality [to a tradition]'. Implied here is the idea that there is a core to the tradition which cannot be changed and for which there is no possibility of development since the core is derived directly from Revelation, which ended with the death of the last of the Apostles. Since MacIntyre is a self-described 'orthodox Catholic' it may be presumed that he regards the magisterium as the final tribunal in questions of faith and morals above that of the scholar-saints in a juridical sense, although in all probability, in the resolution of any 'crisis' within the tradition, the magisterium will call upon the scholarship and judgement of the scholar-saints.

38 H. U. von Balthasar, *The Theology of Henri de Lubac*, San Francisco: Ignatius, 1991, p. 76, fn. 52. Cf. LCCL at 763: 'I distinguish between the accumulation of detailed

scholarly knowledge brought about by historical research, including the use of the historical–critical method, and the effective memory carried forward by a concrete living tradition'.

39 TRV, pp. 200–1.

40 Ibid., p. 201.

41 A. MacIntyre, *Difficulties in Christian Belief*, London: SCM Press, 1959, pp. 107–8.

42 D. Hudson, *The Future of Thomism*, p. 21.

43 Alasdair MacIntyre, 'Interview with Dmitri Nikulin', *Voprosy filosofii* 1, 1996, 91–100; and in German translation in *Deutsche Z. Philosophie* 444, 1996, 671–83, at 677 (hereafter IDN).

44 A. MacIntyre, 'What has Christianity to say to the Moral Philosopher?', John Coffin Memorial Lecture, University of London, 21 May 1998, p. 21.

45 IDN, p. 677.

46 A. Nichols, *The Shape of Catholic Theology*, Collegeville, MN: The Liturgical Press, 1991, pp. 48–9.

47 HWCC, pp. 301–2.

48 D. Schindler relates the arguments of John Paul II to the Thomist maxim that 'all things naturally tend to God implicitly'. See *De Veritate* (Q. 22 a.2) and GEI, p. 511–40, at 520.

49 FR (paragraph 14).

50 L. Strauss, *Spinoza's Critique of Religion*, Chicago: University of Chicago Press, 1965, p. 30.

51 Alasdair MacIntyre, *Dependent Rational Animals*, La Salle, IL: Open Court, 1999, pp. 156–7.

52 A. Nichols, *No Bloodless Myth*, Edinburgh: T&T Clark, 2000, p. 4.

53 This criticism of *Fides et ratio* can also be found in A. Kenny, 'The Pope as philosopher', *The Tablet*, 26 June 1999, 874–6, at 875.

54 FR (paragraph 73).

55 TRV, p. 101.

56 Ibid., pp. 138–9.

57 This is not to suggest that MacIntyre and Milbank are in complete agreement. Milbank criticises MacIntyre for making an argument against nihilism by reference to the relationship between virtue, dialectics and the notion of tradition in general and instead Milbank wishes to completely 'detach virtue from dialectics'. John Milbank, *Theology & Social Theory: Beyond Secular Reason*, Oxford: Blackwell, 1990, pp. 326–77 (hereafter BSR).

58 TRV pp. 140–1. To this statement could be added that included within the Augustinian account of virtue is the idea that some practices that would be classified as 'virtuous' by Aristotelian standards, may not be by the 'higher' Augustinian standards, which include judgement of the subjective dimension of actions, that is the intentions and motivations behind the performance of the apparently virtuous act. For a discussion of the difference between Aristotelian and Augustinian virtue, see G. Scott Davis, 'The Structure and Function of the Virtues in the Moral Theology of St Augustine', *Congresso internazionale su S. Agostino nel xvii centenario della sua conversione*, Vol. III, Rome: Institutum Patristicum Augustinianum, 1987, pp. 9–18.

59 This list was selected from almost two pages of names of scholarly converts in M. Sheehan, *Apologetics and Catholic Doctrine*, P. Joseph (ed.), London: St Austin Press, 2001, pp. 171–2.

60 BSR, p. 347.

61 H. U. von Balthasar, *A Theology of History*, San Francisco: Ignatius, 1994, p. 110, and FR (paragraph 33).

62 F. Wilhelmsen, *Hilaire Belloc: No Alienated Man*, London: Sheed & Ward, 1954, p. 69: 'Bellocian history depends for success on a vital tradition acting like a road the historian can travel down and back again at will – the Bellocian concept of history might well be called Anselmian: historical understanding follows faith'.

63 C. Fabro, *God in Exile*, Toronto: Newman, 1964, p. 69.

64 A. MacIntyre, *First Principles, Final Ends and Contemporary Moral Issues*, Milwaukee, WI: Marquette University Press, 1990, p. 2.

65 To hold otherwise would be to concede the inverse of Nietzsche's claim that 'it is our preference that decides against Christianity – not arguments'; in other words, that it is our preference which decides in favour of our Christianity – not our arguments. For a discussion of this issue, see H. de Lubac, *The Drama of Atheist Humanism*, San Francisco: Ignatius, 1995, p. 49.

66 A. Louth, *Discerning the Mystery*, pp. 73–96.

7 NATURAL LAW AND THE CULTURE OF THE TRADITION

1 On this point MacIntyre and Finnis are in agreement. See John Finnis, *Natural Law and Natural Rights*, Oxford: Clarendon Press, 1980, p. 398 (henceforth NLNR).

2 TRV, p. 133. Cf. K. Reames, 'Metaphysics, History, and Moral Philosophy: the Centrality of the 1990 Aquinas Lecture for MacIntyre's Argument for Thomism', *The Thomist* 62, 1998, 410–13.

3 J. Finnis, 'Natural Inclinations and Natural Right: Deriving "Ought" from "Is" according to Aquinas', *Lex et Libertas: Freedom and Natural Law According to St Thomas*, L. J. Elders and K. Hedwig (eds), Vatican City: Libreria Editrice, 1987.

4 A. MacIntyre, AV, p. 57.

5 A. MacIntyre, 'How Moral Agents Became Ghosts', *Synthese* 53, November, 1982, 295–312, at 305.

6 Thomas Pearson, Thomas Pearson, 'An Interview with Alasdair MacIntyre', *Kinesis* 23, 1, 1996, 43.

7 Ibid., p. 43.

8 TRV, p. 134.

9 A. MacIntyre, 'Bernstein's Distorting Mirrors: A Rejoinder', *Soundings* 67/1, 1984, 38–9.

10 MATRT, pp. 45–6.

11 This fact is emphasised in C. J. Thompson, 'Benedict, Thomas or Augustine? The Character of MacIntyre's Narrative' *The Thomist* 59, 3, July, 1995, 379–409, at 401.

12 NLNR, pp. 89–90, 98 and 410.

13 One example of where Finnis does acknowledge the significance of culture on moral formation, although he does not relate the insight to the New Natural Law framework, is in *Fundamentals of Ethics*, Oxford: Clarendon, 1983, p. 126: 'In all cultures, the promptings of feelings and of prior projects and commitments will present themselves to the endlessly intellectualising mind as moral intuitions'.

14 NLNR, p. v.

15 J. Finnis, 'The Catholic Church and Public Policy Debates in Western Liberal Societies: the Basis and Limits of Intellectual Engagement', *Issues for a Catholic Bioethic*, L. Gormally (ed.), London: Linacre Centre, 1999, p. 261. See also 'On the Critical Legal Studies Movement', *American Journal of Jurisprudence* 30, 1985, 21–42, at 21, where Finnis states that the term 'liberalism' has no place in a critical theory of jurisprudence.

16 J. Finnis, 'The Catholic Church and Public Policy Debates', ibid., p. 261.

17 MacIntyre argues that St Thomas was the target of a mocking ballad, *La discorde de l'université et des Jacobins*, by the jongleur Rutebeuf. See NLS, p. 74.

18 NLS, p. 66.

19 Ibid., p. 66.

20 TRV, p. 77.

21 N. Biggar, "Karl Barth and German Grisez on the Human Good: An Ecumenical Rapprochement', *The Revival of Natural Law: Philosophical, theological and ethical responses to the Finnis-Grisez School*, N. Biggar and R. Black (eds), Aldershot: Ashgate, 2000, p. 178.

22 E. Fortin, 'The New Rights Theory and Natural Law', *Review of Politics*, 44, 1982, 590–612, at 605. Cf. Germain Grisez, *The Way of the Lord Jesus*, Vol. I, Chicago: Franciscan Herald Press, 1983, p. 127: 'As Nietzsche argued, it [a good life] must have room for self-realization and creativity'. This statement was made without any reference to the critiques of the Nietzschean account of authenticity and creativity found in, for example, de Lubac, Przywara and von Balthasar.

23 C. Covell, *The Defence of Natural Law*, London: St Martin's Press, 1992, p. 234.

24 ACM, p. 36.

25 J. Boyle, 'Natural Law and the Ethics of Traditions', R. P. George (ed.) *Natural Law Theory: Contemporary Essays*, Oxford: Clarendon Press, 1992, p. 4.

26 Ibid., pp. 4 and 11.

27 CMMJ, p. 131.

28 The tendency of the New Natural Law school to neglect the significance of the relations between faculties of the soul was acknowledged by Robert George in 'A Defence of the New Natural Law Theory', *American Journal of Jurisprudence* 41, 1996, 47–61, at 50, wherein he stated that 'Neither Finnis nor his collaborators, have been concerned with the question of motivation apart from the prescriptivity of practical reasons'.

29 Anthony Matteo, 'In Defence of Moral Realism', *Telos* 106, Winter, 1996, 64–77, at 75–6.

30 A. MacIntyre, 'How Can We Learn what *Veritatis Splendor* has to Teach?', *The Thomist* LVI, 2, 171–95, at 188.

31 N. Biggar, 'Karl Barth and Germain Grisez on the Human Good: An Ecumenical Rapprochement', *The Revival of Natural Law: Philosophical, Theological and Ethical Responses to the Finnis-Grisez School*, Aldershot: Ashgate, p. 177.

32 Ibid., p. 177.

33 R. Black, 'Is the New Natural Law Theory Christian', *The Revival of Natural Law: Philosophical, Theological and Ethical Responses to the Finnis-Grisez School*, Aldershot: Ashgate, 2000, p. 158.

34 J. Schall, 'The Intellectual Context of Natural Law', *American Journal of Jurisprudence* 38, 1993, 85–108, at 102.

35 R. Hittinger, *A Critique of the New Natural Law Theories*, Notre Dame, IN: University of Notre Dame Press, 1987, pp. 195–6.

36 I. Markham, *Truth and the Reality of God: An Essay in Natural Theology*, Edinburgh: T&T Clark, 1998, p. 115.

37 E. Fortin, 'The New Rights Theory and Natural Law', op. cit., pp. 608–9.

38 TRV, p. 141.

39 This would only be true of the narrative tradition of Thomism. In both Aristocratic Liberalism and the thought of Nietzsche, an experience of the good of religion is viewed as preparatory to 'higher' stages of development, at which point it may be discarded.

40 J. Boyle, 'The Place of Religion in the Practical Reasoning of Individuals and Groups', *American Journal of Jurisprudence* 43, 1999, 1–24, at 13.

41 Ibid., p. 20. The expression 'reflexive goods' refers to a distinction made by Germain Grisez between goods which are necessary both for their own sake and the sake of other goods (the 'reflexive goods') and goods that are 'existential' or not directly related to each other.

42 G. Grisez, 'The Natural End of Man', *The New Catholic Encyclopaedia*, Vol. IX, Washington, DC: Catholic University of America, 1967, pp. 132–9.

43 G. Grisez, *The Way of the Lord Jesus*, Vol. I, pp. 127–8. Cf. J. Finnis, 'Practical Reasoning, Human Goods and the End of Man', *New Blackfriars* 66, October, 1985, 438–51, at 445.

44 A. Scola, 'Following Christ: on John Paul II's encyclical *Veritatis Splendor*', *Communio* 20, Winter, 1993, 724–7, at 724.

45 Ibid., pp. 724–5.

46 A. Scola, 'Christologie et morale', *Nouvelle Revue Théologie* 109, 1987, 382–410, at 409–10. Cf. Servais Pinckaers, 'Christ, Moral Absolutes and the Good: Recent Moral Theology', op. cit., p. 136: 'Faith has been separated too much from morality. If St Thomas places faith at the head of the virtues, this means that with hope and charity it enlightens and inspires all of a Christian's activity from within'.

47 D. Schindler, 'Response to Lowery', *Communio* 18, Fall, 1991, 461.

48 GFN, p. 23.

49 TEE, p. 564.

50 P. Hall, *Narrative and the Natural Law*, op. cit., p. 32.

51 NLNR p. 93, and G. Grisez (ed.), *Beyond the New Morality*, Notre Dame, IN: Notre Dame University Press, 1980, pp. 73–5. Benedict Ashley suggests that those goods described by Grisez as 'existential' should be construed as both the means to and the fruit of contemplation. See 'What is the End of the Human Person/The Vision of God and Integral Human Fulfilment', L. Gormally (ed.), *Moral Truth and Moral Tradition: Essays in Honour of Peter Geach and Elizabeth Anscombe*, Dublin: Four Courts, 1994, pp. 69–86, at 86.

52 NLNR, p. 221.

53 A. MacIntyre, 'Community, Law, and the Idiom and Rhetoric of Rights', *Listening* XXVI, 2, 1991, 96–110, at 96–7 (hereafter CLIRR).

54 Ibid., p. 108. Speaking of his own jurisprudential framework, MacIntyre claims that 'in scope of subject matter, as well as in universality, it will have to have the structure of the precepts and arguments of the natural law, whose justification can ultimately only be spelled out, as Aquinas spelled it out, in theological terms'. MacIntyre emphasises the explicitly theological character of his conception of justice by stating that those who uphold such a conception will not only 'resist the acknowledgment of what a variety of groups in contemporary society suppose to be their rights, but they will be seen to do so for theological reasons, reasons carrying no weight for those who aspire to claim such rights'. See pp. 108–9.

55 Ibid., p. 76. For a sympathetic discussion of Maritain's attempt to synthesise natural law with natural rights, which nonetheless concurs with MacIntyre's assessment that Maritain was too optimistic about the interpretations which would be given to the endorsed list of rights, see J. Schall, *Maritain: The Philosopher in Society*, Oxford: Rowman and Littlefield, 1998, pp. 79–98 (hereafter JMPS).

56 A. MacIntyre, 'Politics, Philosophy and the Common Good', *The MacIntyre Reader*, Kelvin Knight (ed.) Cambridge: Polity Press, 1998, pp. 235–55, at 236.

57 WJWR, p. 379.

58 Ibid., p. 384–5.

59 JMPS, p. 95.

60 LCCL, p. 761. In an earlier work, Schmitz acknowledged that the terminology of natural rights has 'disconcerted some Catholics' and that 'no doubt an

indiscriminate and imprecise, unreflective and uncritical use might well contribute to undermining Catholic doctrine by inserting an excessive and irresponsible individualism into its teaching about the constitution of the human person'. See CHD, p. 123.

61 J. Langan, 'Human Rights in Roman Catholicism', *Journal of Ecumenical Studies* xix, Summer, 1982, 25–39, at 38.

62 R. P. Kraynak, *Christian Faith and Modern Democracy: God and Politics in the Fallen World*, Notre Dame, IN: University of Notre Dame Press, 2001, pp. 177–8.

63 JMPS, p. 95.

64 Cf. K. Schmitz, 'Enriching the Cupola', *Review of Metaphysics* 27, March, 1974, 492–512, at 499.

65 CLIRR, 109.

66 Ibid., p. 109.

67 See also Aloysius Cardinal Ambrozic, *Our Yesterday and our Today*, Pastoral Letter, Advent 1999.

68 J. Finnis, *Aquinas*, Oxford: Oxford University Press, 1998, p. 136.

69 Ibid., p. 133. Finnis's position resembles that of the nineteenth-century Italian 'Kantian Thomist' Antonio Rosmini-Serbati, who argued that '[Rational right] arises from the protection which Ethics, or the moral law, affords to the useful good, or more generally, to all the eudaemonologic goods which man can enjoy'. See *The Philosophical System of Antonio Rosmini-Serbati*, Thomas Davidson (trans. and ed.), London: Kegal Paul, 1882, p. 371. Bernard Brady argues that Thomas used *ius* primarily in an objective sense, that is in terms of what is right or just, and that he also used it in a subjective sense as referring to personal moral claims; however, the latter use was dependent on a prior understanding of 'that which is right'. See 'An Analysis of the Use of Rights Language in Pre-Modern Catholic Social Thought', *The Thomist* 57, January, 1993, 97–121. Cf. Ernest Fortin, 'On the Presumed Medieval Origin of Individual Rights', *Communio* 26, Spring, 1999, 55–79; and 'Natural Law and Social Science', *American Journal of Jurisprudence* 30, 1985, 16: 'I, for one, am not aware of a single text in which Thomas speaks of universal and inalienable right'. For MacIntyre's own genealogy, see CLIRR, pp. 102–3, where he locates what Finnis calls the 'watershed' between Aquinas and Suarez in the arguments of a series of Franciscan scholars, most notably Duns Scotus, and their adoption by John XXII in the bull *Quia vir reprobus*. MacIntyre acknowledges his debt to the work of Richard Tuck, *Natural Rights: Their Origin and Development*, Cambridge, UK: Cambridge University Press, 1979, wherein Tuck argued that rights theories are a product of the very late Middle Ages, and particularly of the anti-Thomist writers such as Ockham and Gerson; they fell out of use in the Renaissance, but were recovered in a pure form by the seventeenth-century authors from Grotius onwards. In his later book, *The Rights of War and Peace: Political Order from Grotius to Kant*, Oxford: Oxford University Press, 1999, Tuck modifies his account of the significance of the Renaissance; nonetheless, his account of the earliest origins of the rights doctrine in anti-Thomistic writers stands. Brian Tierney in *Rights, Laws and Infallibility in Medieval Thought*, Aldershot: Variorum, 1997, p. 618, argues: 'In Aristotle or Gaius or Aquinas we can find a vague notion of rights, though the concept remains peripheral and unelucidated in their thought. The main point for us is that they have no idea of subjective rights as human or natural rights, rights inherent in the person as such'. H. R. Rommen in 'The Genealogy of Natural Rights', *Thought* 29, 114, 1954, 403–25, traces the natural right concept to William of Occam, according to whom the rational creature was mostly distinguished by its liberty, which is the principle of its will.

70 TRV, p. 76. Cf. RNNR p. 221: 'If the texts cited by Tuck, Tierney and Villey prove anything, it is that rights as the Middle Ages understood them were subordinated to an antecedent law that circumscribes and relativizes them'.

71 M. Conti, Statement at the Opening of the Sister's of the Gospel of Life Crosshill Centre, as reported by F. McDermott, 'The Ball and the Cross', *St Austin Review*, April, 2002, 47.

72 NLNR, pp. 206–7.

73 Ibid., p. 210.

74 J. L. O'Donovan, 'Historical Prôlegomena to a Theological View of Human Rights', *Studies in Christian Ethics* 9, 2, 1996: 52–66, at 54 (hereafter HPTV).

75 GFN, p. 17.

76 GFN, p. 18. Cf. John Paul II, *Veritatis Splendor* (paragraph 37) on the subject of the 'erro,neous concept of autonomy'.

77 J. L. O'Donovan, HPTV, p. 64.

78 R. P. Kraynak, *Christian Faith and Modern Democracy*, op. cit., p. 112.

79 Charles Taylor argues for the existence of such a connection. See SSMMI, p. 12.

80 GFN, p. 18.

81 J. Finnis, 'Catholic Social Teaching since *Populorum Progressio*', *Liberation Theology*, James Schall (ed.), San Francisco: Ignatius, 1982, pp. 304–21, at 314.

82 Ibid., p. 315.

83 TPT, pp. 155–6.

84 Fortin argues that the reason why Catholic intellectuals began to adopt the rights rhetoric in the late nineteenth century is that Catholic intellectual life had been impoverished by the closure of educational institutions during the French Revolution and the Napoleonic Wars, that proponents of Thomism were divided between Suarezian and anti-Suarezian factions and that they were desperately searching for intellectual tools with which to deal with socialism. See RNNR, p. 231.

85 Ibid., p. 158.

86 J. Finnis, 'Catholic Social Teaching since *Populorum Progressio*', op. cit., p. 316.

87 Cf. HPTV, p. 55.

88 John Paul II, *Evangelium Vitae* 18. In a speech to the Vatican Diplomatic Corps in January 1989 John Paul II also acknowledged that 'the 1948 Declaration does not contain the anthropological and moral basis for the human rights that it proclaims'. Cited in Mary Ann Glendon, 'Foundations of Human Rights: the Unfinished Business', *American Journal of Jurisprudence* 44, 1999, 1–14.

89 TPT, p. 170.

8 CONCLUSION

1 W. Kasper, 'The theological anthropology of *Gaudium et spes*', 129, and FF, p. 91.

2 FF p. 90.

3 Ibid., p. 91.

4 This is not to deny the existence of non-European indigenous cultures, but the dominant culture in each case is definitely European.

5 GFN p. 24.

6 A. MacIntyre, 'Interview with Cogito', 67.

7 N. Bukharin, *Historical Materialism*, London: George Allen & Unwin, 1926, p. 98.

8 CA, p. 1.

9 WZG, p. 502.

10 Ibid., p. 502.

ABBREVIATIONS

AAS   *Acta Apostolica Sedis.*

ACM   Charles Taylor, 'A Catholic Modernity?', *A Catholic Modernity?*, J. L. Heft (ed.), Oxford: Oxford University Press, 1999.

AL   A. S. Kahan, *Aristocratic Liberalism: The Social and Political Thought Jacob Burckhardt, John Stuart Mill and Alexis de Tocqueville*, Oxford: Oxford University Press, 1992.

AV   Alasdair MacIntyre, *After Virtue: A Study in Moral Theory*, London: Duckworth, 1981.

BSR   John Milbank, *Theology & Social Theory: Beyond Secular Reason*, Oxford: Basil Blackwell, 1990.

CA   Aidan Nichols, *Christendom Awake,* Edinburgh: T&T Clark, 1999.

CAEV   David L. Schindler, 'Christological Aesthetics and Evangelium Vitae: Towards a Definition of Liberalism', *Communio* 22, Summer, 1995, 193–225.

CDV   Herbert Vorgrimler (ed.) *Commentary on the Documents of the Second Vatican Council*, London: Burns and Oates, 1967.

CHD   Kenneth L. Schmitz, *At the Center of the Human Drama: The Philosophical Anthropology of Karol Wojtyla/Pope John Paul II*, Washington, DC: Catholic University of America Press, 1993.

CLIRR   Alasdair MacIntyre, 'Community, Law and the Idiom and Rhetoric of Rights', *Listening* XXVI, 2, 1991, 96–110.

CMMJ   Alasdair MacIntyre, 'Corporate Modernity and Moral Judgement: Are they Mutually Exclusive?' *Ethics and Problems of the 21st Century*, K. M. Sayre and K. E. Goodpaster (eds), Notre Dame, IN: Notre Dame University Press, 1979.

DS   Aloysius Ambrozic, 'Dialogue with Secularism', *Culture and Faith, VIII–I*, Vatican City: Pontificium Consilium de Cultura, 2000, 41–6.

EMW   Romano Guardini, *The End of the Modern World*, London: Sheed & Ward, 1957.

FLI   David L. Schindler, 'Faith and the Logic of Intelligence', *Catholicism and Secularization in America*, David Schindler (ed.), Notre Dame, IN: Communio Books, 1990.

ABBREVIATIONS

FF   Walter Kasper, *Faith and the Future*, London: Burns & Oates, 1985.
FR   John Paul II, *Fides et ratio*, Sydney: St Paul's, 1998.
GEI   David L. Schindler, 'God and the End of Intelligence: Knowledge as Relationship', *Communio* 26, Fall, 1999, 510–40, at 532.
GFN   David Schindler, 'Grace and the Form of Nature and Culture', *Catholicism and Secularization in America*, D. L. Schindler (ed.), Notre Dame, IN: Communio Books, 1990.
GS   *Gaudium et spes.*
HPTV   L. O'Donovan, 'Historical Prôlegomena to a Theological View of Human Rights', *Studies in Christian Ethics* 9, 2, 1996, 52–66.
HWCC   David L. Schindler, *Heart of the World, Center of the Church: Communion, Ecclesiology, Liberalism and Liberation*, Edinburgh: T&T Clark, 1996.
IDN   Alasdair MacIntyre, 'Interview with Dmitri Nikulin', *Deutsche Z. Philosophie* 444, 1996, 671–83.
IEC   Francis George, *Inculturation and Ecclesial Communion: Culture and Church in the Teaching of Pope John Paul II*, Rome: Urbaniana University Press, 1990.
IGB   Giovanna Borradori, 'Interview with Alasdair MacIntyre', *The American Philosopher*, Chicago: University of Chicago Press, 1994.
ITDP   Thomas Pearson, 'An Interview with Alasdair MacIntyre', *Kinesis* 23, 1, 1996, 40–50.
JMPS   James Schall, *Jacques Maritain: The Philosopher in Society*, Lanham, MD: Rowman and Littlefield, 1998.
LAHD   Maurice Blondel, *The Letter on Apologetics and History and Dogma*, Alexander Dru and Illtyd Trethowan (trans.), New York: Rinehart & Winston, 1964.
LCCL   Kenneth L. Schmitz, 'The Language of Conversion and the Conversion of Language', *Communio* 21, Winter, 1994, 742–5.
MATRT   *John Finnis, Moral Absolutes: Tradition, Revision and Truth*, Washington, DC: Catholic University of America Press, 1991.
MHTA   David L. Schindler, 'The Meaning of the Human in the Technological Age', *Anthropotes* XV, 1, 1999, 31–53.
PG   J. Maritain, *The Peasant of the Garonne*, New York: Holt, Rinehart and Winston, 1968.
MPMT   Thomas S. Hibbs, 'MacIntyre's Post Modern Thomism: Reflections on Three Rival Versions of Moral Enquiry', *The Thomist* 57, April, 1993, 277–99.
NLNR   John Finnis, *Natural Law and Natural Rights*, Oxford: Clarendon Press, 1980.
NLS   Alasdair MacIntyre, 'Natural Law as Subversive: The Case of Aquinas', *Journal of Medieval and Early Modern Studies* 26, 1, 1995, 61–83.
PM   Louis Dupré, *Passage to Modernity: An Essay in the Hermeneutics of Nature and Culture*, New Haven, CT: Yale University Press, 1993.

RNNR   Ernest Fortin, 'Sacred and Inviolable': Rerum Novarum and Natural Rights, *Theological Studies* 53, 1992, 203–33.

RO   John Milbank, Graham Ward and Catherine Pickstock (eds), *Radical Orthodoxy*, London: Routledge, 1999.

SCC   Louis Dupré, 'Secularism and the Crisis of our Culture: A Hermeneutic Perspective', *Thought* 51, 202, 1976, 271–82.

SSLU   John Paul II, Speech to scholars of Lublin University, *Christian Life in Poland,* November, 1987.

SSMMI   Charles Taylor, *Sources of the Self: The Making of the Modern Identity*, Cambridge, UK: Cambridge University Press, 1989.

TAE   Kenneth L. Schmitz, 'St. Thomas and the Appeal to Experience', *Catholic Theological Society of America Proceedings*, 47, 1992, 1–20.

TAU   Walter Kasper, *Transcending all Understanding: The Meaning of Christian Faith Today*, San Francisco: Ignatius, 1989.

TEE   David L. Schindler, 'Towards a Eucharistic Evangelizaiton', *Communio* 19, Winter, 1992, 549–75.

TPAC   The Pontifical Council for Culture, 'Towards a Pastoral Approach to Culture', *The Pope Speaks*, 23 May 1999, pp. 334–67.

TPT   Hans Urs von Balthasar, 'On the Tasks of Catholic Philosophy in our Time', *Communio* 20, Spring, 1993, 147–72.

TRV   Alasdair MacIntyre, *Three Rival Versions of Moral Enquiry: Encyclopaedia, Genealogy, Tradition*, London: Duckworth, 1990.

TTF   Alasdair MacIntyre, 'The Theses on Feuerbach: A Road Not Taken',*Artifacts, Representations and Social Practice,* Dordrecht: Kluwer Academic Publishers: 277–90.

WIH   Henri de Lubac, 'Nature and Grace', *The Word in History: The St Xavier Symposium*, T. Patrick Burke (ed.), London: Collins, 1968.

WJWR   *Alasdair MacIntyre, Whose Justice? Which Rationality?* London: Duckworth, 1988.

WZG   Erich Przywara, 'Zwischen Religion und Kultur', *Weg Zu Gott*, Einsiedeln: Johannes Verlag, 1962.

BIBLIOGRAPHY

David L. Schindler

'History, Objectivity and Moral Conversion', *The Thomist* 38, July, 1973, 569–88.

'Theology and the Historical–Critical Claims of Modernity', *Communio* VI, Spring, 1979, 73–94.

'Metaphysics and the Problem of Historicism in Contemporary Theology', *Historicism and Faith*, P. L. Williams (ed.), Scranton, PA: Northeast Books, 1980, 87–101.

'Is America Bourgeois?', *Communio* 14, Fall, 1987, 262–90.

'Catholicism, Public Theology and Postmodernity: On Richard John Neuhaus's Catholic Moment', *The Thomist* 53, January, 1989, 107–43.

'On Meaning and the Death of God in the Academy', *Communio* 17, Summer, 1990, 192–206.

'Grace and the Form of Nature and Culture', *Catholicism and Secularization in America*, David Schindler (ed.), Notre Dame, IN: Communio Books, 1990.

'Towards a Eucharistic Evangelization', *Communio* 19, Winter, 1992, 549–75.

'Christology and the Church's 'Worldly' Mission: Response to Michael Novak', *Communio* 19, Spring, 1992, 164–78.

'The Church's 'Worldly' Mission: Neoconservatism and American Culture', *Communio* 18, Fall, 1992, 365–97.

'Christology, Public Theology and Thomism: Balthasar, de Lubac and Murray', *The Future of Thomism*, D. W. Hudson (ed.), Notre Dame, IN: University of Notre Dame Press, 1992.

'Norris Clark on Person, Being and St Thomas', *Communio* 20, Fall, 1993, 580–92.

'Religious Freedom, Truth and American Liberalism: Another Look at John Courtney Murray', *Communio* 21, Winter, 1994, 696–741.

'Economics and the Civilization of Love', *The Chesterton Review* 20, May–August, 1994, 189–211.

'The Person: Philosophy, Theology and Receptivity', *Communio* 21, Spring, 1994, 172–90.

'Christological Aesthetics and *Evangelium Vitae:* Toward a Definition of Liberalism', *Communio* 22, Summer, 1995, 193–225.

'Christology and the *Imago Dei:* Interpreting *Gaudium et spes*', *Communio* 23, Spring, 1996, 129–41.

Heart of the World, Center of the Church: Communio Ecclesiology, Liberalism and Liberation, Edinburgh: T&T Clark, 1996.

'Reorienting the Church on the Eve of the Millennium: John Paul II's New Evangelization', *Communio* 24, Winter, 1997, 728–80.

'Modernity, Postmodernity and the Problem of Atheism', *Communio* 24, Fall, 1997, 563–80.

'Institution and Charism: The Missions of the Son and the Spirit in Church and World', *Communio* 25, Summer, 1998, 253–74.

'Luigi Giussani on the 'Religious Senses' and the Cultural Situation of Our Time', *Communio* 25, Spring, 1998, 141–51.

'Once Again: George Weigel, Catholicism and American Culture', *Communio* 15, Spring, 1998, 92–121.

'The 'Religious Sense' and American Culture', *Communio* 25, Winter, 1998, 679–99.

'Which Ontology is Necessary for an Adequate Anthropology', *Anthropotes* 15/2, 1999, 423–6.

'God and the End of Intelligence: Knowledge as Relationship', *Communio* 26, Fall, 1999, 510–40.

'Trinity, Creation and the Order of Intelligence in the Modern Academy', *Communio* 28, Fall, 2001, 406–29.

Alasdair MacIntyre

Marxism: An Interpretation, London: SCM Press, 1953.

Difficulties in Christian Belief, London: SCM Press, 1959.

'Marxists and Christians', *The Twentieth Century* CLXX, Autumn, 1961, 28–37.

'Marx', *Western Political Philosophers*, M. Cranston (ed.), London: Bodley Head, 1964.

'Against Utilitarianism' *Aims in Education*, T. H. B. Hollins (ed.), Manchester: Manchester University Press, 1964.

A Short History of Ethics, New York: Macmillan, 1966.

Secularization and Moral Change, Oxford University Press, 1967.

'The Idea of a Social Science', *Aristotelian Society Supplement* XLI, 1967, reprinted in Bryan R. Wilson, *Rationality*, Oxford: Basil Blackwell, 1970, pp. 112–30.

The Religious Significance of Atheism, with Paul Ricoeur, New York: Columbia University Press, 1969.

'Marxism of the Will: A Review Essay', *Partisan Review*, 36, 1969, 128–33.

'Existentialism', *Sartre: A Collection of Critical Essays*, Mary Warnock (ed.), New York: Anchor Books, 1971, pp. 1–59.

'Ideology, Social Science and Revolution', *Comparative Politics* V, April, 1973, 321–42.

'Epistemology Crises, Dramatic Narrative and the Philosophy of Science', *The Monist* 60, 4, October, 1977, 453–73.

Against the Self-Images of the Age: Essays on Ideology and Philosophy, London: Duckworth, 1978.

'Corporate Modernity and Moral Judgement: Are They Mutually Exclusive?', *Ethics and Problems of the 21st Century*, K. M. Sayre and K. E. Goodpaster (eds), Notre Dame, IN: Notre Dame University Press, 1979, pp. 122–35.

'Social Science Methodology as the Ideology of Bureaucratic Authority', *Through the Looking Glass: Epistemology and the Conduct of Enquiry*, M. W. Falco (ed.), Washington, DC: University Press of America, 1979, pp. 42–58.

'Contexts of Interpretation: Reflections on Hans-George Gadamer's Truth and Method', *Boston University Journal* XXVI, 3, 1980, 173–9.

'A Crisis in Moral Philosophy: Why the Search for the Foundations of Ethics is so Frustrating', *Knowing and Valuing: The Search for Common Roots*, H. T. Engelhardt and D. Callahan (eds), New York: The Hastings Center, 1980, pp. 18–36.

'The American Idea', *America and Ireland 1776–1976*, D. N. Doyle and O. D. Edwards (eds), Westport, CT: Greenwood Press, 1980.

After Virtue: A Study in Moral Theory, London: Duckworth, 1981.

'How Moral Agents Became Ghosts', *Synthese* 53, November, 1982, 295–312.

'Philosophy and its History', *Analyse und Kritik* VII, 1982, 234–48.

'Rights, Practices and Marxism: Reply to Six Critics', *Analyse und Kritik* VII, 1982, 234–48.

'Intelligibility, Goods and Rules', *Journal of Philosophy* 79, November, 1982, 653–63.

'Moral Arguments and Social Contexts', *The Journal of Philosophy*, LXXX, 10, 1983, 590–1.

'The Magic in the Pronoun "My"', *Ethics* XCIV, 1 October, 1983, 113–25.

'Moral Rationality, Tradition and Aristotle: A Reply to Onora O'Neill, Raymond Gaita and Stephen R. I. Clarke', *Inquiry* XXVI, 4, 1984, 447–66.

'After Virtue and Marxism', *Inquiry* XXVII, 2, 1984, 251–4.

'The Relationship of Philosophy to its Past', *Philosophy in History: Essays on the Historiography of Philosophy*, R. Rorty, J. B. Schneewind and Q. Skinner (eds), Cambridge, UK: Cambridge University Press, 1984, 31–48.

'The Virtues, the Unity of a Human Life and the Concept of a Tradition', *Liberalism and its Critics*, M. Sandel (ed.), Oxford: Basil Blackwell, 1984, 125–48.

'Bernstein's Distorting Mirrors: A Rejoinder', *Soundings* XVII, 1, 1984, 31–41.

'Which God Ought we to Obey and Why?', *Faith and Philosophy* III, 4, 1986, 359–71.

'Practical Rationalities as Forms of Social Structure', *Irish Philosophical Journal* IV, 1–2, 1987, 3–19.

Whose Justice? Which Rationality? London: Duckworth, 1988.

First Principles, Final Ends and Contemporary Philosophical Issues, Milwaukee, WI: Marquette University Press, 1990.

Three Rival Versions of Moral Enquiry: Encyclopaedia, Genealogy, Tradition, London: Duckworth, 1990.

'The Return to Virtue Ethics', *The Twenty-fifth Anniversary of Vatican II*, Russell E. Smith (ed.), Braintree: The Pope John Center, 1990, 239–49.

'The Form of the Good, Tradition and Enquiry', *Value and Understanding: Essays for Peter Winch*, Raymond Gaita (ed.), Routledge: London, 1990, pp. 242–62.

'Precis of *Whose Justice? Which Rationality?*', *Philosophy and Phenomenological Research*, LI, 1, 1991, 149–52.

'Community, Law and the Idiom and Rhetoric of Rights', *Listening* XXVI, 2, 1991, 96–110.

'I'm not a communitarian, but ...', *The Responsive Community* 1, 3, 1991, 91–2.

'How to Seem Virtuous without actually Being So', Occasional Paper Series I, Lancaster: Center for the Study of Cultural Values, 1991.

'An Interview with Alasdair MacIntyre', *Cogito* V, 2, 1991, 67–73.

'Plain Persons and Moral Philosophy: Rules, Virtues and Goods', *American Catholic Philosophical Quarterly* LXVI, 1, 1992, 3–19.

'Review of John Finnis', *Moral Absolutes: Tradition, Revision and Truth*', *Ethics* CIII, 4, 1993, 811–12.

'The Theses on Feuerbach: A Road Not Taken', *Artifacts, Representations and Social Practice*, R. E. Cohen and C. C. Gould (eds), Dordrecht: Kluwer Academic Publishers, 1994, pp. 277–90.

'Moral Relativism, Truth and Justification', *Moral Truth and Moral Tradition: Essays in Honour of Peter Geach and Elizabeth Anscombe*, L. Gormally, (ed.), Dublin: Four Courts Press, 1994, pp. 6–24.

'Interview with Dmitri Nikulin in *Voprosy filosfi*, 1, 1996, 91–100.

'Interview with Thomas D. Pearson', *Kinesis* 23, 1, 1996, 40–50.

'Natural Law as Subversive: the Case of Aquinas', *Journal of Medieval and Early Modern Studies*, 26, 1, 1996, 61–83.

'Review of Anthony Lisska's *Aquinas's Theory of Natural Law*', *International Philosophical Quarterly* XXXVII 91, 145, 1997, 95–9.

'Aquinas's Critique of Education: Against his own Age, Against ours', *Philosophers on Education*, R. O. Rorty (ed.), London: Routledge, 1998, pp. 95–108.

'Aquinas and Moral Disagreement', The John Ziegler Memorial Lecture, Xavier University, Chicago, December 2, 1998.

'What has Christianity to say to the Moral Philosopher?' John Coffin Memorial Lecture, University of London, May 21, 1998.

'Some Enlightenment Projects Reconsidered', *Questioning Ethics: Contemporary Debates in Philosophy*, P. Kearney and M. Dooley (eds), London: Routledge, 1998.

'Social Structures and their Threats to Moral Agency', *Philosophy* 74, 1999, 311–29.

Dependent Rational Animals, Chicago: Open Court, 1999.

General references

Ackerman, B. *Social Justice and the Liberal State*, New Haven, CT: Yale University Press, 1980.

Ambrozic, A. 'Dialogue with Secularism', *Culture and Faith* VIII–I, Vatican City: Pontificium Consilium de Cultura, 2000, 41–6.

Anscombe, G. E. M. 'Modern Moral Philosophy', *Philosophy* XXXIII, 124, 1958, 1–19.

Ashley, B. 'What is the End of the Human Person/ The Vision of God and Integral Human Fulfilment', *Moral Truth and Moral Tradition: Essays in Honour of Peter Geach and Elizabeth Anscombe*, L. Gormally (ed.), Dublin: Four Courts, 1994, 69–86.

Ayres, L. and Jones, G. *Christian Origins: Theology, Rhetoric and Community*, London: Routledge, 1998.

Augustine, St *The Confessions*, R. S. Pine-Coffin (ed.), London: Penguin, 1961.

Augustine, St *On Christian Teaching*, R. P. H. Green (trans. and ed.), Oxford: Oxford University Press, 1997.

von Balthasar, H. U. 'Der Begriff der Natur in der Theologie', *Zeitschrift für katholische Theologie*, 75, 1953, 452–61.

—— *Thérése of Lisieux: The Story of a Mission*, Donald Nicholl (trans.) London: Sheed & Ward, 1953.

—— *Love Alone*, London: Burns & Oates, 1963.

—— *Word and Redemption*, New York: Herder & Herder, 1964.

—— *The Theology of Henri de Lubac*, San Francisco: Ignatius, 1983.

—— *A Short Primer for Unsettled Laymen*, San Francisco: Ignatius, 1985.

—— *Truth is Symphonic*, San Francisco: Ignatius, 1987.

—— *The Theology of Karl Barth*, San Francisco: Ignatius, 1991.

—— 'On the Tasks of Catholic Philosophy in our Time', *Communio* 20, Spring, 1993, 147–72.

—— *A Theology of History*, San Francisco: Ignatius, 1994.

—— *Tragedy Under Grace: Reinhold Schneider on the Experience of the West*, San Francisco: Ignatius, 1997.

Barnard, F. M. *Herder's Social and Political Thought*, Oxford: Clarendon, 1965.

Barth, K. *Ad Limina Apostolorum*, Edinburgh: St Andrew's Press, 1969.

Beck, L. W. 'Five Concepts of Freedom in Kant', *Philosophical Analysis and Reconstruction: A Festschrift to Stephen Korner*, J. T. J. Srzednicki (ed.), Dordrecht: Martinus Nijhoff, 1987.

Beiser, F. C. *Enlightenment, Revolution and Romanticism: The Genesis of Modern German Political Thought 1790–1800*, Cambridge, MA: Harvard University Press, 1992.

Belohradsky, V. 'Bureaucracy, Ideology and Evil', *Salisbury Review* 2, 1, 1983, 11–12.

Berger, P. (ed.) *The Capitalist Spirit: Toward a Religious Ethic of Wealth Creation*, San Francisco: Ignatius, 1990.

Biggar, N. *The Revival of Natural Law: Philosophical, Theological and Ethical Responses to the Finnis-Grisez School*, Ashgate: Aldershot, 2000.

Black, R. *Christian Moral Realism: Natural Law, Virtue and the Gospel*, Oxford: Oxford University Press, 2001.

Blondel, M. *The Letter on Apologetics and History and Dogma*, Alexandre Dru and Illtyd Trethowan (trans.), New York: Hold, Reinhart and Winston, 1964.

Bonaventure, St. *The Journey of the Mind to God*, P. Boehner (trans.), Cambridge: Hackett, 1993.

Bonsor, J. A. *Rahner, Heidegger and Truth; Karl Rahner's Notion of Christian Truth: The Influence of Heidegger*, Washington, DC: University Press of America, 1987.

Borella, J. *The Sense of the Supernatural*, Edinburgh: T&T Clark, 1998.

Boyle, J. 'The Place of Religion in the Practical Reasoning of Individuals and Groups', *American Journal of Jurisprudence* 43, 1999, 1–24.

Brennan, R. E. 'The Thomistic Concept of Culture', *The Thomist*, 5, 1943, 112–23.

Bruford, W. *The German Tradition of Self-Cultivation: 'Bildung' from Humboldt to Thomas Mann*, Cambridge, UK: Cambridge University Press, 1975.

Buckley, J. J. 'A Return to the Subject: The Theological Significance of Charles Taylor's Sources of the Self', *The Thomist* 55, 3, 1991, 497–511.

Caldecott, S. and Morrill, J. (eds) *Eternity and Time*, Edinburgh: T&T Clark, 1997.

Cantore, E. 'Scientific Humanism for the Third Millennium', *Seminarium*, 23, 1985, 203–26.

Carrier, H. 'The Contribution of the Council to Culture', *Vatican II: Assessments and Perspectives*, 1962–1987, Rene Latourelle (ed.), Mahwah, NJ: Paulist Press, 1988, pp. 442–66.

Cassirer, E. *The Platonic Renaissance in England*, Austin: University of Texas, 1953.

Cessario, R. *Moral Virtues and Theological Ethics*, Notre Dame, IN: University of Notre Dame Press, 1991.

Cessario, R. *Christian Faith and the Theological Life*, Washington, DC: Catholic University of America Press, 1996.

Chantraine, G. 'Beyond Modernity and Postmodernity: the Thought of Henri de Lubac', *Communio* 17, Summer, 1990, 207–19.

Chappell, T. 'Thomism and the Future of Catholic Philosophy', *New Blackfriars* 80, 938, April, 1999, 172–5.

Ciapolo, R. T. (ed.) *Postmodernism and Christian Philosophy*, Notre Dame, IN: University of Notre Dame Press, 1997.

Colby, M. 'Moral Traditions, MacIntyre and Historicist Practical Reason', *Philosophy and Social Criticism* 21, 3, 1995, 53–78.

Collingwood, R. G. *The Idea of History*, Oxford: Clarendon Press, 1946.

Connerton, P. *How Societies Remember*, Cambridge, UK: Cambridge University Press, 1989.

Covell, C. *The Defence of Natural Law*, London: St Martin's Press, 1992.

D'Agostini, F. 'Analitici, Continentali, Tomisti: la filosofia e il sense dell "essere"', *Divus Thomas* 24, 3, 1999, 53–79.

Dahlhaus, C. 'Historicism and Tradition', *Foundations of Music History*, Cambridge, UK: Cambridge University Press, 1983, 53–71.

D'Ambrosio, M. '*Ressourcement* Theology, *Aggiornamento* and the Hermeneutics of Tradition', *Communi* 18, Winter, 1991, 530–55.

Dawson, C. *Religion and Culture*, London: Sheed & Ward, 1948.

Dawson, C. *Dynamics of World History*, J. J. Molloy, (ed.), La Salle, IL: Sherwood Sugden & Co, 1978.

Deferrari, R. J. *The Sources of Catholic Doctrine*, translated from the Thirtieth Edition of Henry Denzinger's *Enchiridion Symbolorum*, London: B. Herder, 1955.

Deploige, S. *Le Conflit de la Morale et de la Sociologie*, Paris: Librairie Félix Alcan, 1912.

Di Noia, J. A. 'American Catholic Theology at Century's End: Postconciliar, Postmodern and Post Thomistic', *The Thomist* 54, 1990, 499–519.

Di Noia, J. A. and Cessario, R. (eds) *Veritatis Splendor and the Renewal of Moral Theology*, Princeton, NJ: Sceptor Publishers, 1999.

Dondeyne, A. *La foi ecoute le Monde*, Paris: Cerf, 1965.

Doyle, D. 'Henri de Lubac and the Roots of Communion Ecclesiology', *Theological Studies* 60, 1999, 209–28.

Dupré, L. 'Secularism and the Crisis of our Culture', *Thought* 51, 202, 1976, 271–82.

—— *Marx's Social Critique of Culture*, New Haven, CT: Yale University Press, 1983.

—— 'The Glory of the Lord: Hans Urs von Balthasar's Theological Aesthetic', *Hans Urs von Balthasar: His Life and Work*, Schindler, D. L. (ed.), San Francisco: Ignatius, 1991.

—— *Passage to Modernity: An Essay in the Hermeneutics of Nature and Culture*, New Haven, CT: Yale University Press, 1993.

—— *Metaphysics and Culture*, Milwaukee, WI: Marquette University, 1994.

Egan, J. M. 'Notes on the Relation of Reason and Culture in the Philosophy of St Thomas', *Angelicum* 15, 1938.

Elders, L. J. *The Metaphysics of Being of St Thomas Aquinas in Historical Perspective*, Leiden: E. J. Brill, 1993.

Eliot, T. S. *Notes Towards the Definition of Culture*, London: Faber & Faber, 1962.

Elson, C. *Wieland and Shaftesbury*, New York: Columbia, 1913.

Eucken, R. *Die Philosophie des Thomas von Aquino und die Kultur der Neuzeit*, Hasse: C. E. M. Pfeffer, 1886.

Fabro, C. *God in Exile: Modern Atheism*, Arthur Gibson (trans.), New York: Newman Press, 1968.

Ferry, L. *Rights: The New Quarrel between the Ancients and Moderns*, Chicago: Chicago University Press, 1990.

Fesquet, H. *The Wit and Wisdom of Good Pope John*, London: Harvill Press, 1964.

Finn, D. R. 'John Paul II and the "Moral Ecology of Markets"', *Theological Studies* 59, 1998, 662–80.

Finnis, J. *Natural Law and Natural Rights*, Oxford: Clarendon, 1980.

—— 'Catholic Social Teaching since *Populorum Progressio*', *Liberation Theology*, James V. Schall (ed.), San Francisco: Ignatius, 1982.

—— *Fundamentals of Ethics*, Oxford: Clarendon, 1983.

—— *Moral Absolutes: Tradition, Revision and Truth*, Washington, DC: Catholic University of America Press, 1991.

—— *'Historical Consciousness' and Theological Foundations*, Toronto: Pontifical Institute of Medieval Studies, 1992.

—— *Aquinas*, Oxford: Oxford University Press, 1998.

—— 'The Catholic Church and Public Policy Debates in Western Liberal Societies: the Basis and Limits of Intellectual Engagement', *Issues for a Catholic Bioethic*, L. Gormally (ed.), London: Linacre Centre, 1999.

Fischer-Colbrie, A. 'Quid Sanctus Thomas de Cultura Doceat', *Xenia Thomistica*, Rome: Polyglottis Vaticanis, 1925.

Fisher, A. 'An Ethical View on Resource Allocation in Health Care', N. Ford (ed.), *Ethics and Resource Allocation in Health Care*, Melbourne: Chisholm Centre, 1996, 22–8.

—— 'Is There a Distinctive Rôle for the Catholic Hospital in a Pluralist Society?', *Issues for a Catholic Bioethic*, L. Gormally, (ed.), London: The Linacre Centre, 1999.

Fortin, E. 'The New Rights Theory and Natural Law', *Review of Politics* 44, 1982, 485–95.

—— 'From *Rerum Novarum* to *Centesimus Annus:* Continuity or Discontinuity?', *Faith and Reason* XVII, Winter, 1991.

—— 'Sacred and Inviolable: *Rerum Novarum* and Natural Rights', *Theological Studies* 53, 1992, 203–33.

Gadamer, H. G. 'Culture and Words – from the Point of View of Philosophy', *Universitas* 24, 1982, 179–88.

—— *Truth and Method*, New York: Crossroads, 1992.

Galston, W. *Liberal Purposes: Goods, Virtues and Diversity in the Liberal State*, Cambridge, UK: Cambridge University Press, 1991.

Gardner, L., Moss, D., Quash, B. and Ward, G. *Balthasar: At the End of Modernity*, Edinburgh: T&T Clark, 1999.

Garrigou-Lagrange, R. 'La nouvelle théologie ou va-t-elle', *Angelicum* 23, 1946, 126–45.

Gauchet, M. *The Disenchantment of the World: A Political History of Religion*, Princeton, NJ: Princeton University Press, 1997.

George, F. *Inculturation and Ecclesial Communion: Culture and Church in the Teaching of Pope John Paul II*, Rome: Urbaniana University Press, 1990.

George, R. P. (ed.) *Natural Law Theory: Contemporary Essays*, Oxford: Clarendon, 1992.

—— (ed.) *Natural Law, Liberalism and Morality: Contemporary Essays*, Oxford: Clarendon, 1996.

—— 'Natural Law and Liberal Public Reason', *American Journal of Jurisprudence* 42, 1997, 31–49.

—— (ed.) *Natural Law and Moral Inquiry: Ethics, Metaphysics and Politics in the work of Germain Grisez*, Washington, DC: Georgetown University Press, 1998.

—— *In Defence of Natural Law*, Oxford: Clarendon, 1999.

Gerhard, W. A. 'The Intellectual Virtue of Prudence', *The Thomist* 8, 1945, 413–56.

Geuss, R. *Morality, Culture and History*, Cambridge, UK: Cambridge University Press, 1998.

Gilson, E. *Letters to Henri de Lubac*, San Francisco: Ignatius, 1986.

Le Goff, J. *History and Memory*, New York: Columbia University Press, 1992.

Golomb, J. *In Search of Authenticity: From Kierkegaard to Camus*, London: Routledge, 1995.

Grisez, G. 'The Natural End of Man', *The New Catholic Encyclopaedia*, Volume IX, Washington, DC: Catholic University of America, 1967, pp. 132–9.

—— *The Way of the Lord Jesus*, Vol. I, Chicago: Franciscan Heral Press, 1983.

Grisez, G. and Shaw, R. *Beyond the New Morality: the Responsibilities of Freedom*, Notre Dame, IN: University of Notre Dame Press, 1974.

Guardini, R. 'Gedanken über das Verhältnis von Christentum und Kultur', *Die Schildgenossen* 6, 1926, 281–315.

—— *The End of the Modern World*, London: Sheed & Ward, 1957.

Hadas, M. *The Stoic Philosophy of Seneca: Essays and Letters*, New York: Norton, 1958.

Haldane, J. 'Holding Fast to What is Good: A Reply to Adriaan T. Peperzak', *American Catholic Philosophical Quarterly*, LXIII, 3, 1999, 497–503.

Hall, P. *Narrative and the Natural Law: An Interpretation of Thomistic Ethics*, Notre Dame, IN: University of Notre Dame Press, 1994.

Hamel, E. 'The Foundations of Human Rights in Biblical Theology: Following the Orientations of *Gaudium et spes*', *Vatican II: Assessment and Perspectives*, Vol. II, René Latourelle (ed.), Mahwah, NJ: Paulist Press, 1988, 461–78.

Hayles, E. E. Y. *The Catholic Church in the Modern World: A Survey from the French Revolution to the Present*, New York: Doubleday, 1958.

—— *Pope John and His Revolution*, London: Eyre & Spottiswood, 1965.

Henrici, P. 'Modernity and Christianity', *Communio* 17, Summer, 1990, 140–51.

Hering, P. H. 'De iure subiective sumpto apud Sanctum Thoman', *Angelicum* 16, April, 1939, 296–98.

Hibbs, T. S. *Dialectic and Narrative in Aquinas: An Interpretation of the Summa Contra Gentiles*, London: Notre Dame, IN: University of Notre Dame Press, 1995.

Hibbs, T. S. 'MacIntyre's Postmodern Thomism: Reflections on *Three Rival Versions of Moral Enquiry*', *The Thomist* 57, April, 1993, 277–99.

Hittinger, R. *A Critique of the New Natural Law Theories*, Notre Dame, IN: University of Notre Dame Press, 1987.

—— 'After MacIntyre: Natural Law Theory, Virtue Ethics and Eudaimonia', *International Philosophy Quarterly*, December, 1989, 449–61.

—— 'Theology and Natural Law Theory', *Communio* 17, Fall, 1990, 402–8.

—— 'Veritatis Splendor and the Theology of the Natural Law', *Veritatis Splendor and the Renewal of Moral Theology*, J. A. Di Noia and Romanus Cessario (eds), Chicago: Midwest Theological Forum, 1994.

Hudson, D. and Moran, D. W. (eds) *The Future of Thomism*, Notre Dame, IN: University of Notre Dame Press, 1992.

Humboldt, von W. *The Limits of State Action*, J. W. Burrow (trans. and ed.), Cambridge, UK: Cambridge University Press, 1969.

Jordan, M. 'The Protreptic Structure of the *Summa Contra Gentiles*', *The Thomist* 50, 1986, 173–209.

Kahan, A. S. *Aristocratic Liberalism: The Social and Political Thought of Jacob Burckhardt, John Stuart Mill and Alexis de Tocqueville,* Oxford: Oxford University Press, 1992.

Kasper, W. *Faith and the Future,* London: Burns & Oates, 1985.

—— 'The *Logos* character of reality', *Communio* 15, Fall, 1988, 274–84.

—— *Transcending All Understanding: The Meaning of Christian Faith Today,* San Francisco: Ignatius, 1989.

—— 'The Church as "Communio"', *New Blackfriars* 74, 871, May, 1993, 232–44.

—— 'The Theological anthropology of *Gaudium et spes*', *Communio* 23, Spring, 1996, 129–41.

Kelly, G. A. *Idealism, Politics and History: Sources of Hegelian Thought,* Cambridge, UK: Cambridge University Press, 1969.

Kenny, A. 'The Pope as Philosopher', *The Tablet,* 26 June, 1999, 874–6.

Kerr, F. *Theology after Wittgenstein,* Oxford: Basil Blackwell, 1986.

—— 'Did Newman Answer Gladstone?', *John Henry Newman: Reason, Rhetoric and Romanticism,* David Nicholls and Fergus Kerr (eds), Bristol: The Bristol Press, 1991.

—— *Immortal Longings: Versions of Transcending Humanity,* London: SPCK, 1997.

Knasas, J. F. X, (ed.) *Jacques Maritain: The Man and His Metaphysics,* Notre Dame, IN: American Maritain Association, 1988.

Kobler, J. F. *Vatican II, Theophany and the Phenomenon of Man,* New York: Peter Lang, 1991.

Koneczny, F. 'Kosciol Jako Polityczny Wychowawca Narodow', *Znak* 4, 1989, 63–70.

Kraynak, R. P. *Christian Faith and Modern Democracy: God and Politics in a Fallen World,* Notre Dame, IN: University of Notre Dame Press, 2001.

Kreyche, R. J. 'Virtue and Law in Aquinas: Some Modern Implications', *Southwestern Journal of Philosophy* 5, 1974, 111–41.

Krieg, R. A. (ed.) *Romano Guardini: A Precursor of Vatican II,* Notre Dame, IN: University of Notre Dame Press, 1997.

Lamb, M. 'Modernism and Americanism revisited dialectically: A Challenge for Evangelisation', *Communio* 21, Winter, 1994, 631–62.

—— 'Inculturation and Western culture: The Dialogical Experience between Gospel and Culture', *Communio* 21, Spring, 1994, 124–42.

Lambert, B. '*Gaudium et spes* and the Trevail of Today's Ecclesial Conception', *The Church and Culture since Vatican II,* J. Gremillion, (ed.), Notre Dame, IN: University of Notre Dame Press, 1985.

—— '*Gaudium et spes* hier et aujourd'hui', *Nouvelle Revue Theologique* 107, 1985, 321–46.

Langan, J. 'Political Hopes and Political Tasks: A Reading of "Gaudium et spes" after Twenty Years', *Questions of Social Urgency: The Church in the Modern World: Two Decades After Vatican II,* J. A. Dwyer, (ed.), Washington, DC: Georgetown University Press, 1986.

Larmore, C. *Patterns of Moral Complexity,* Cambridge, UK: Cambridge University Press, 1987.

Lesourd, P. and Ramiz, J.-M. *Giacomo Cardinal Lercaro,* Notre Dame, IN: University of Notre Dame Press, 1964.

Lilla, M. (ed.) *New French Thought,* Princeton, NJ: Princeton University Press, 1994.

Lobkowicz, N. 'What Happened to Thomism? From *Aeterni Patris* to *Vaticanum Secundum*', *American Catholic Philosophical Quarterly* LXIV, 3, 1995, 397–425.

Louth, A. *Discerning the Mystery: An Essay on the Nature of Theology*, Oxford: Clarendon Press, 1983.

de Lubac, H. *Athéisme et science de l'homme: une double requéte de Gaudium et spes*, Paris: Cerf, 1968.

—— 'Nature and Grace', *The Word in History: The St Xavier Symposium*, T. P. Burke, (ed.), London: Collins, 1968.

—— *The Eternal Feminine: A Study on the Text of Teilhard de Chardin*, New York: Harper & Row, 1972.

—— H. A. *Brief Catechesis on Nature and Grace*, R. Arnandez (trans.), San Francisco: Ignatius, 1984.

Luke, S. 'The Meanings of Individualism', *Journal of the History of Ideas*, January–March, 1971, 45–67.

Lyotard, J. F. *The Post-Modern Condition: A Report on Knowledge*, G. Bennington (trans.), manchester: Manchester University Press, 1984.

McCarthy, G. E. *Romancing Antiquity: German Critique of the Enlightenment from Weber to Habermas*, London: Roman & Littlefield, 1997.

Maritain, J. *True Humanism*, London: Geoffrey Bles, 1938.

—— *Art and Scholasticism*, London: Sheed & Ward, 1939.

—— *The Peasant of the Garonne*, New York: Holt, Rinehart and Winston, 1968.

Markham, I. *Truth and the Reality of God: An Essay in Natural Theology*, Edinburgh: T&T Clark, 1998.

Maurer, A. A. *About Beauty: A Thomistic Interpretation*, Houston: Center for Thomistic Studies, 1983.

May, W. E. *An Introduction to Moral Theology*, Huntington, IN: Our Sunday Visitor, 1991.

Milbank, J. *Theology and Social Theory: Beyond Secular Reason*, Oxford: Basil Blackwell, 1990.

—— 'The Politics of Time: Community, Gift and Liturgy', *Telos* 113, Fall, 1998, 41–69.

Milbank, J. Ward, G. and Pickstock, C. (eds), *Radical Orthodoxy*, London: Routledge, 1999.

Moeller, C. 'History of the Constitution', *Commentary on the Documents of Vatican II*, H. Vorgrimler (ed.), New York: Herder and Herder, 1969.

Momonchak, J. 'Interpreting the Second Vatican Council', *Landas: Journal of Loyola School of Theology* 1, 1987, 81–90.

Morandé, P. 'The Relevance of the Message of *Gaudium et spes* Today: The Church's Mission in the Midst of Epochal Changes and New Challenges', *Communio* 23, Spring, 1996, 141–56.

Murphy, C. M. 'The Church and Culture since Vatican II: on the Analogy of Faith and Art', *Theological Studies*, 48, 1987, 317–33.

Nichols, A. *From Newman to Congar: The Idea of Doctrinal Development from the Victorians to the Second Vatican Council*, Edinburgh: T&T Clark, 1990.

—— *The Shape of Catholic Theology: An Introduction to its Sources*, Collegeville, MN: The Liturgical Press, 1991.

—— *Looking at the Liturgy: A Critical View of its Contemporary Form*, San Francisco: Ignatius, 1996.

—— 'Christopher Dawson's Catholic Setting', *Eternity and Time*, S. Caldecott and J. Morill (eds), Edinburgh: T&T Clark, 1997.

211

—— *The Word Has Been Abroad,* Edinburgh: T&T Clark, 1998.

Olsen, G. 'Cultural Dynamics: Secularization and Sacralization', *Christianity and Western Civilization,* San Francisco: Ignatius, 1995.

—— 'America as an Enlightenment Culture', *Actas del IV Congreso 'Cultura Europea'* Pamplona, 1998, 121–8.

O'Malley, J. W. *Tradition and Transition: Historical Perspectives on Vatican II,* Wilmington, DE: M. Glazier, 1989.

O'Meara, T. 'Thomas Aquinas and German Intellectuals: Neoscholasticism and Modernity in the Late 19th Century', *Gregorianum* 68, 3–4, 1987, 719–36.

—— *Church and Culture: German Catholic Theology,* 1860–1914, Notre Dame, IN: University of Notre Dame Press, 1991.

Outler, A. C. 'After-Thoughts of a Protestant Observer at Vatican II', *Church and Culture since Vatican II,* J. Gremillion (ed.), Notre Dame, IN: University of Notre Dame Press, 1985, pp. 153–5.

Peperzak, A. T. 'Personal–Impersonal? A Rejoinder to John Haldane', *American Catholic Philosophical Quarterly* LXXIII, 3, 1999, 503–4.

Pickstock, C. *After Writing: On the Liturgical Consummation of Philosophy,* Oxford: Basil Blackwell, 1998.

—— 'Liturgy and Modernity', *Telos* 113, Fall, 1998, 19–41.

Pinckaers, S. 'Christ, Moral Absolutes and the Good: Recent Moral Theology', *The Thomist* 55, 1, 1991, 117–40.

—— *The Sources of Christian Ethics,* Washington, DC: Catholic University of America Press, 1995.

Poupard, P. 'Towards a Pastoral Approach to Culture', Document of the Pontifical Council for Culture, *The Pope Speaks,* May, 23, 1999, 334–67.

Przywara, E. 'Um das Erbe Friedrich Nietzsches', *Ringen der Gegenwart I. Gesammelte Aufsätze (1922–1927),* Augsburg: Benno Filsner, 1929.

—— 'Dionysisches und christliches Opfer', *Stimmen der Zeit* 65, 1934–35: 11–24.

—— *Humanitas: Der Mensch Gestern und Morgen,* Nürnberg: Glock und Lutz, 1952.

—— *Weg zu Gott,* Einsiedeln: Johannes-Verlag, 1962.

Rahner, K. *Mission and Grace: Essays in Pastoral Theology,* London: Sheed & Ward, 1963.

—— *Theological Investigations,* Vol. 9, New York: Crossroads, 1974.

—— 'Towards a Fundamental Theological Interpretation of Vatican II', *Theological Studies* 40, 1979, 716–28.

Ratzinger, J. 'Der Weltdienst der Kirche: Auswirkungen *von Gaudium et spes* im letzten Jahrzehnt', M. Seybold (ed.), *Zehn Jahre Vaticanum II,* Regensburg: Pustet, 1976.

—— 'Concerning the Notion of Person in Theology', *Communio* 17, 1990, 438–54.

—— *A New Song for the Lord,* New York: Crossroad Publishing, 1996.

—— 'Culture and Truth: Reflections on the Encyclical *Fides et ratio*', *Origins,* 28, 36, 1999.

—— *The Spirit of the Liturgy,* San Francisco: Ignatius, 2001.

Ratzinger, J., Schürmann, H. and von Balthasar, H. U. *Principles of Christian Morality,* San Francisco: Ignatius, 1975.

Rawls, J. *A Theory of Justice,* Cambridge, MA: Harvard University Press, 1971.

—— *Political Liberalism,* New York: Columbia University Press, 1993.

Reames, K. 'Metaphysics, History and Moral Philosophy: The Centrality of the 1990 Aquinas Lecture to MacIntyre's Argument for Thomism', *The Thomist* 62, 1998, 419–45.

Roehr, S. *A Primer on German Enlightenment,* Columbia, MO: University of Missouri Press, 1995.

Rorty, A. O. 'Social and Political Sources of *Akrasia*', *Ethics* 107, July, 1997, 644–57.

Sandel, M. *Liberalism and the Limits of Justice,* Cambridge, UK: Cambridge University Press, 1982.

Schall, J. V. 'Some Philosophical Aspects of Culture and Religion', *New Scholasticism* 31, April, 1957, 209–36.

—— 'Luther and Political Philosophy: the Rise of Autonomous Man', *Faith and Reason* 8, 2, 1982, 7–31.

—— *Reason, Revelation and the Foundations of Political Philosophy,* Baton Rouge, LA: Louisiana State University Press, 1987.

—— 'On Being Dissatisfied with Compromises: Natural Law and Human Rights', *Loyola Law Review* XXXVIII, 2, 1992, 289–309.

—— 'The Intellectual Context of Natural Law', *The American Journal of Jurisprudence,* 38, 1993, 85–108.

—— 'Post-Aristotelian Political Philosophy and Modernity', *Aufstieg und niedergang Der Römischen Welt,* W. Haase and H. Temporini (eds), Berlin: Walter de Gruyter, 1994.

—— *At the Limits of Political Philosophy,* Washington, DC: Catholic University of America Press, 1996.

—— *Maritain: The Philosopher in Society,* Oxford: Rowman and Littlefield, 1998.

—— 'The Natural Restoration of Fallen Angels in the Depths of Evil: Concerning the Obscure Origins of Absolute human Autonomy in Political Philosophy', Paper presented to the American Maritain Association Meeting, University of Notre Dame, October 20, 2000.

Schenk, H. G. *The Mind of the European Romantics: An Essay in Cultural History,* London: Constable, 1966.

Schmitz, K. L. 'Enriching the Cupola', *Review of Metaphysics* 27, March, 1974, 492–512.

—— *The Gift: Creation,* Milwaukee, WI: Marquette University Press, 1982.

—— 'Neither with nor without Foundations', *Review of Metaphysics,* 42, September 1988, 3–36.

—— 'From Anarchy to Principles: Deconstruction and the Resources of Christian Philosophy', *Communio* 16, Spring, 1989, 69–89.

—— 'Postmodern or modern-plus?', *Communio* 17, Summer, 1990, 152–66.

—— 'St. Thomas and the Appeal to Experience', *Catholic Theological Society of America Proceedings,* 47, 1992, 1–20.

—— *At the Center of the Human Drama: The Philosophical Anthropology of Karol Wojtyla/Pope John Paul II,* Washington, DC: Catholic University of America Press, 1993.

—— 'The First Principle of Personal Becoming', *Review of Metaphysics* 47, June, 1994, 757–74.

—— 'Liberal Liberty and Human Freedom', 20 *Chesterton Review,* May–August, 1994, 213–27.

—— 'The Language of Conversion and the Conversion of Language', *Communio* 21, Winter, 1994, 742–65.

—— 'Created Receptivity and the Philosophy of the Concrete', *The Thomist* 61, 3, 1997, 339–73.

—— 'Postmodernism and the Catholic Tradition', *American Catholic Philosophical Quarterly* LXXIII 2, 1999, 233–53.

—— 'From Convertibility to Convergence: the Absoluteness of Truth and the Realization of the Person in God's Plan', *Anthropotes* 15/2, 1999, 369–73.

Schuck, M. J. 'John Courtney Murray's Problematic Interpretations of Leo XIII and the American Founders', *The Thomist* 55, 4, 1991.

Scola, A. 'Christologie et morale', *Nouvelle Revue Theologie* 109, 1987, 382–410.

—— *Hans Urs von Balthasar: A Theological Style,* Edinburgh: T&T Clark, 1991.

—— 'Following Christ: On John Paul II's encyclical *Veritatis Splendor*', *Communio*, Winter, 1993, 233–53.

Scott Davis, G. 'The Structure and Function of the Virtues in the Moral Theology of St Augustine', *Congresso internazionale su s. Agostino nel Xvi centenario della conversione,* Vol. III, Rome: Institutum Patristicum Augustinianum, 1987, 9–18.

Sheehan, M. *Apologetics and Catholic Doctrine,* P. Joseph (ed.), London: St Austin Press, 2001.

Slade, F. 'Was ist Aufklärung? Notes on Maritain, Rorty and Bloom: With Thanks but no Apologies to Immanuel Kant', *The Common Things: Essays on Thomism and Education,* D. McInerny (ed.) London: University of Notre Dame Press, 1999.

Sweetman, B. (ed.) *The Future of Modernism: The Cartesian Legacy and Contemporary Pluralism,* Notre Dame, IN: University of Notre Dame Press, 1999.

Taylor, C. *Sources of the Self: The Making of Modern Identity,* Cambridge, UK: Cambridge University Press, 1989.

—— *The Ethics of Authenticity,* Cambridge, MA: Harvard University Press, 1991.

—— 'Inwardness and the Culture of Modernity', *Philosophical Interventions in the Unfinished Project of Enlightenment,* A. Honneth, T. McCarthy and C. Offe (eds), Boston: MIT Press, 1992.

—— 'Two Theories of Modernity', *Hastings Center Report,* March–April, 1995, 24–33.

—— 'Die immanente Gegenaufklärung', *Aufklärung heute,* Stuttgart: Klett-Cotta, 1997.

—— 'A Catholic Modernity?', *A Catholic Modernity?* J. L. Heft (ed.), Oxford: Oxford University Press, 1999, 13–39.

Thiele, L. P. *Friedrich Nietzsche and the Politics of the Soul: A Study in Heroic Individualism,* Princeton, 1990.

Thompson, C. J. 'Benedict, Thomas or Augustine? The Character of MacIntyre's Narrative', *The Thomist,* 59, July, 1995, 379–409.

Tierney, B. *Rights, Laws and Infallibility in Medieval Thought,* Aldershot: Variorum, 1997.

Torevell, D. *Losing the Sacred: Ritual, Modernity and Liturgical Reform,* Edinburgh: T&T Clark, 2000.

Tuck, R. *Natural Rights: Their Origin and Development,* Cambridge, UK: Cambridge University Press, 1979.

—— *The Rights of War and Peace: Political Order from Grotius to Kant,* Oxford: Oxford University Press, 1999.

Turbanti, G. 'The Attitude of the Church to the Modern World at and after Vatican II', *Concilium* 6, 1992, 87–97.

Vidal, M. 'La sospechosa cristianización del capitlismo: Judicio etico al capitalismo a partir de la enciclica Centesimus Annus', *Persona y Sociedad* 7, 1993, 115–39.

Waldron, J. *Liberal Rights: Collected Papers (1981–1997)*,Cambridge, UK: Cambridge University Press, 1993.

Watkin, E. I. *A. Philosophy of Form*, London: Sheed & Ward, 1950.

Weigel, G. *Soul of the World*, Grand Rapids, MI: Eerdmans, 1996.

Weigel, G. and Royal, R. (eds) *Building the Free Society: Democracy, Capitalism and Catholic Social Teaching*, Grand Rapids, MI: Eerdmans, 1993.

Welch, L. J. *'Gaudium et spes*, the Divine Image and the Synthesis of *Veritatis Splendor'*, *Communio* 24, Winter, 1997, 794–814.

Wetzel, J. *Augustine and the Limits of Virtue*, Cambridge, UK: Cambridge University Press, 1992.

Wiedmann, A. *The German Quest for Primal Origins in Art, Culture and Politics 1900–1933*, Ceredigion: Mellon House, 1995.

Wilhelmsen, F. 'The Aesthetic Object and the Act of Being', *The Modern Schoolman* 29, 1950, 277–91.

Wippel, J. F. *Mediaeval Reactions to the Encounter between Faith and Reason*, Milwaukee, WI: Marquette University Press, 1995.

Wojtyla, K. *Faith According to Saint John of the Cross*, J. Aumann (trans.), San Francisco: Ignatius, 1981.

Wood, S. *Spiritual Exegesis and the Church in the Theology of Henri de Lubac*, Grand Rapids, MI: Eerdmans, 1998.

INDEX

Laborem Exercens 66, 67
Lamb, Matthew 43, 100, 104, 178 n37
Lambert, Bernard 29, 30, 44, 72, 90, 92
Langan, John 17, 151
language: disassociation from tradition
    149; instrumentalist account of 49;
    linguistic analysis 163; and problems
    of ideology 149; problems with
    linguistic transposition 8, 123, 151,
    167; theories of (expressivist and
    instrumental) 121, 122, 156
Latin, in the Catholic tradition 47, 48,
    49
leitourgia 58, 59
Leo XIII 11, 16, 106, 165
Lercaro, Cardinal 27, 28, 29, 38, 45, 168;
    and culture 28; and the Liturgy 175
    n70
Liberal economic philosophy 40, 68
Liberal jurisprudence 63, 136, 156, 158,
    160
Liberal moral tradition (ethical theory)
    40, 42, 62, 78
Liberal political philosophy 40, 64, 68
Liberal tradition xiii, xiv, 2, 3, 15, 16,
    17, 20, 31, 32, 40, 41, 42, 45, 49,
    50, 53, 67, 82, 86, 163, 167, 168;
    claim of theological neutrality 17;
    compartmentalisation of self 77;
    confrontation with Genealogical
    tradition 2; Finnis on Liberalism
    139; and health care 58, 59; on
    human nature 86; inadequacies
    of xiii, 71; and institutions 58;
    internal contradictions 16; Liberal
    rationalism 2, 68; MacIntyre on
    Liberalism 104, 140; modern Liberal
    state 109, 160; and natural rights
    153; problem of using Liberal
    idioms 151; problem of modern
    Liberal tradition 153; and problem
    with rights 148; and relationship
    with Protestant tradition 40, 41;
    and relationship with Thomist
    tradition 11, 43, 49, 157, 160;
    and transcendentals 75, 160;
    transformation of 75; separation of
    sacred and secular 68
liberty 74, 76
Liturgy 48, 49,106, 107, 121, 167, 168;
    reform of 48, 49, 175 n71, 176 n71,
    192 n28
Lobkowicz, Nikolaus 1

Locke, John 17, 150
logos 3, 21, 38, 92, 164; explanation of
    3, 21; infrastructural *logos* of culture
    147; religion as *logos* 147
Lonergan, Bernard 45, 72
Louis IX 117
Louth, Andrew 62, 133
Lubac, Henri de 4, 18, 33, 34, 35, 36, 50,
    92, 93, 94, 95, 108, 145, 158, 184 n17;
    correspondence with Gilson 115; on
    culture 4, 50; de Lubac circle 166;
    full self-knowledge 131; on *Gaudium
    et spes* 18; secularism 102; theology of
    grace 94
Lukes, Steven 73
Luther, Martin 89, 187 n66
Lutheran tradition 86, 87, 88, 91, 166
Luykx, Boniface, 190 n62

Machiavelli, Nicolo 89
machine, form of (mechanistic logic) xiv,
    29, 97, 109, 110, 160, 161, 163
MacIntyre, Alasdair xiv, 2, 3, 4, 5, 6, 7,
    12, 15, 16, 17, 31, 41, 43, 50, 53, 54,
    66, 67, 69, 73, 84, 85, 86, 88, 89, 92,
    93, 94, 96, 116, 132, 146, 160, 181
    n37, 183 n77, 183 n80, 187 n75, 192
    n29, 192 n35, 192 n37; approaches
    to the truth 130; on Aquinas 117,
    136, 137, 139, 152; acquisition of
    the goods of human flourishing
    (knowledge of the natural law)
    61, 62; Aristotelian Marxist 65;
    Aristotelian–Marxist–Thomist
    critique 54, 71; Aristotelian–Thomist
    tradition 57; on autonomy 55; belief
    (the embodiment of) 119; bifurcation
    of the person 55; breakdown of
    traditions 57–8; bureaucratic
    ideology 58; civilisation of love
    151; classification of 5, 170 n13;
    conception of justice 196 n54; crisis
    of epistemology (or epistemological
    crisis) 2, 3, 4, 53, 88, 89, 162, 163;
    culture of America 101; culture of
    death 151; definition of the human
    person 142; difference from Charles
    Taylor 152; on the difference
    between Thomism and Liberalism
    43; differences with New Natural
    Law school 141; embodiment of
    the moral and metaphysical 55,
    124; emotivism 54, 55, 57, 142;